THE WAR IN BOSNIA

BOSNIA

HOW TO SUCCEED AT GENOCIDE

Translation from Bosnian

THE WAR IN BOSNIA

BOSNIA

HOW TO SUCCEED
AT GENOCIDE

Translation from Bosnian

MUHAMED BOROGOVAC

COPYRIGHT © 2017 BY MUHAMED BOROGOVAC.

LIBRARY OF CONGRESS CONTROL NUMBER:		2016919126
ISBN:	HARDCOVER	978-1-5245-6011-9
	SOFTCOVER	978-1-5245-6010-2
	EBOOK	978-1-5245-6009-6

Print information available on the last page.

Rev. date: 10/30/2019

To order additional copies of this book, contact:
Xlibris
1-888-795-4274
www.Xlibris.com
Orders@Xlibris.com
751236

CONTENTS

Abbreviations...xiii
Important Names and Concepts xv
Preface xxiii
Introduction to the English Edition xxv
Introduction to the First Issue...xxvii

PART I

1. Ethnic Structure of Bosnia-Herzegovina 3
   1.1. The Serbs 3
   1.2. The Croats...7
   1.3. The Bosniaks 9

2. Bosnia and Herzegovina within Yugoslavia 15
   2.1. Bosnia-Herzegovina before the Agrokomerc Affair...........15
   2.2. The Serbian Academy Fights for Izetbegović's Freedom 20
   2.3. The Agrokomerc Affair...21
   2.4. Izetbegović's Party of Democratic Action—SDA.............23
   2.5. The First Congress of the SDA.....................................25

3. Yugoslavia Ceased to Exist by Legal Dissolution.....................27
   3.1 The Yugoslav Fédération 27
   3.2 The Yugoslav People's Army and the Territorial Defense...................28
   3.3 The Assembly, Presidency, and the Government of Yugoslavia.........30

4. The War...35
   4.1 The War in Slovenia 35
   4.2 The War in Croatia...36
   4.3 What Tuđman Considers "Logical" Borders 37

5. The New World Order 39

6. The War in the Tuzla Region..41
   6.1 The Patriotic League in Tuzla.......................................41

6.2 The Attack on the SDA Headquarters in Tuzla.................................. 44
6.3. Tuzla before the Serbian Attack 48
6.4. The Liberation of Tuzla 49
6.5. First Negotiations about Territories.................................... 51

7.   The SDA Cadre Politics during the War 55
7.1. The Influx of New Members in SDA 55
7.2. Izetbegović's Envoy Armin Pohara Arrives in Tuzla 57

8.   The Negotiations.. 60
8.1. The Second Conversation with Izetbegović 60
8.2 The International Law or the Negotiations............................. 64
8.3. The Decision to Negotiate 66
8.4. The Decision to Accept Karadžić to be a Partner in the Negotiations 67
8.5. Consenting to Negotiate the Constitution of the Republic
     Bosnian and Herzegovina.. 69

9.   The Consequences of Negotiations on the Bosnian Constitution 70
9.1. Questioning the Recognition of Bosnia-Herzegovina.................. 70
9.2. Destroying the Motivation for the Struggle........................... 72
9.3. The Demilitarization of Sarajevo—Betrayal of Goražde 74

10. Controversies over Some of Izetbegović's Statements.......................... 77

11. The Bosnian Congress.. 84
11.1. Balog's and Sendijarević's Correspondence with Izetbegović 84
11.2. The Accusation by Bosnian Congress against Izetbegović
      for High Treason.. 90
11.3. Who Are Indeed the "Young Muslims"—Izetbegović and Šaćirbey.... 94
11.4. Why the American Arms Embargo to Bosnia Was Never Lifted 97
11.5. The Activities of the Bosnian Congress................................ 102

12. The End of the War.. 103
12.1. The Betrayal of Bihać... 103
12.2. The Fall of Srebrenica 104
12.3. The Betrayal of Žepa 106
12.4. Political Consequences of the Fall of Srebrenica and Žepa 106
12.5. The Serbs Are Defeated on the Battlefield 108
12.6. The Methodology of Deceit... 109
12.7. Army and Politics 111

PART II

Appendix

13. The Dayton Agreement 117

14. The USA's Role in the Partition of Bosnia 135
    14.1 Clinton's Bosnian Storm... 135
    14.2 Requiem for a Nation 138

15. Post-Dayton Elections.. 140
    15.1 Petition against Elections in Bosnia 140
    15.2 The Correspondence between European Authorities (OSCE)
         and Bosnian Refugees 141

16. His Holiness, the Pope in Bosnia 151

17. Legal Suit against Dayton Agreement 154

18. Legal Suit against Yugoslavia for Genocide 160

19. Bosnian Declaration of Independence.. 164

20. The Declaration of the Republic of Bosnia-Herzegovina 167

To the heroic army of the Republic of Bosnia and Herzegovina

We are going all the way to Drina River.

—Captain Hajro Mešić,
Commander, Defenses of Teočak and Zvornik

(Referring to pushing the Serbian aggressors back to the traditional border between Bosnia and Serbia.)

The war will end when Lilies fly over Banja Luka and Grude.

—Sefer Halilović,
Ex–Supreme Commander, Bosnian Army

(Referring to the Bosnian flag flying over the territories currently occupied by the Chetniks and HVO.)

Bosnia doesn't need peace, Bosnia needs freedom.

—Zaim Imamović
Commander, Goražde

The safe heavens are those where the
Bosnian Army is in control.

—Atif Dudaković
Commander, Fifth Core

We (Bosnian Army) are going to have a parade in Banja Luka.

—Mehmed Alagić
Commander, Seventh Core

(Referring to the final liberation of the occupied territories.)

Abbreviations

AVNOJ. Anti-fašističko Vijeće Narodnog Oslobođenja Jugoslavije – Antifascist Council of the People's Liberation of Yugoslavia.

   (Refers to the historic meeting in 1943 of anti-fascists of all ethnic backgrounds on the territory of the future Yugoslav federation, when Yugoslav Federation was established and historic borders of the republics that joined federation were confirmed.)

B&H. Bosnia and Herzegovina, Bosnia-Herzegovina.

EU. European Union.

EC. European Community.

HDZ. Hrvatska Demokratska Zejednica - Croats party under control of Franjo Tuđman.

HVO. Hrvatsko Vijeće Odbrane - Rebel Croat units in B&H.

JNA. Jugoslovenska Narodna Armija -Yugoslav Peoples' Army.

KOS. Kontra Obavještajna Služba - JNA counterintelligence service.

PL. Patriotic League, Bosniaks' volonitiers' units.

RS. Republika Srpska - The Serbian Republic in Bosnia constituted in Dayton.

R B&H. Republic of Bosnia and Herzegovina.

SDA. Stranka Demokrateske Akcije - Party of Democratic Action (Muslim party founded by Alija Izetbegović)

SDS. Srpska Demokratska Stranka - Serbian Democratic Party.

SKJ. Savez Komunista Jugoslavije - League of Communists of Yugoslavia.

TO. Teritorijalna Odbrana - Territorial Defense Force.

UDBA. Unutrašnja Državna Bezbjednost - Yugoslav secret police, Yugoslav version of KGB.

UN. United Nations.

UNPROFOR. United Nations Protection Force.

ZAVNOBIH. Zasjedanje Antifašističkog Vijeća Narodnog Oslobođenja BIH - An assembly of Bosnian antifascists established during the World War II. They made the decision to recreate Bosna and Herzegovina (which was divided between Serbs and Croats in 1939) as a state in its historic borders, recognized by European countries in the 1912 Berlin Congress. Later, in AVNOJ 1943, they made the decision to join Yugoslav federation as a member state.

Important Names and Concepts

Abdić, Fikret. A member of the Bosnian presidency who rebelled against BH in order to keep power in his municipality, Velika Kladusa.

Akashi, Yasushi. Senior UN envoy in the Bosnian peace negotiations. He was fired by Izetbegović after the fall of Srebrenica. However, Akashi was "fired only so that the fault for the fall of Srebrenica falls on only one person, and thus Izetbegović has the excuse to retain UNPROFOR. By removing Akashi, Izetbegović released the UN from any culpability related to the loss of "safe havens," and this kept the UNPROFOR in BH, even though the UN no longer brought food to or protected the Bosnians. Izetbegović needed the UN to stay in Bosnia; otherwise, if they left, the American arms embargo against Bosnia would have been lifted. The American condition to arm Bosnians was the departure of UNPROFOR from Bosnia, see Chapter 11.4 for details.

Andrić, Ivo. A very important man for understanding the Serbian people. Ivo Andrić was a famous in the area as a Serbian writer whose historic novels spread hatred against Bosnian Muslims. He described Bosnian medieval heroes as either stupid, homosexuals, or maniacs who mistreated the Serbs. He described Bosniaks as an evil people. His "historical" novels were exploited in the Yugoslav school system, starting from as early as Elementary school, in order to destroy any dignity of Bosniak students. The students were never taught the truth about events described in his novels, and so his twisted anti-"Turks" imagination became a historic truth in the Yugoslav school system. Ivo Andrić won the Nobel Prize for Literature in 1960. His novels were both literature and politics, but unlike Solzhenitsyn, he did not target a political regime but the Bosnian people. He was the man who signed the alliance between the Serbs and Nazi-Germany in 1941. It seems that awarding him the Nobel Prize was purely a political act.

Anti-Bureaucratic Revolution. The movement of Serbian crowds in Yugoslavia during 1988-1989 who illegally, under the pressure of demonstrations, removed uncooperative leaders of non-Serb ethnic groups from power.

Badinter, Robert. A French Constitutional judge, chairman of the EC Arbitration Committee on Yugoslavia (1991). That committee concluded that according to Yugoslav Constitution, Bosnia-Herzegovina has a legal right to declare independence if 50 percent plus one citizen voted for freedom on the referendum of all citizens of the Republic of Bosnia-Herzegovina. The referendum took place on March 1, 1992, and 64 percent of all citizens voted for independence. Then the European Union, the USA, and the UN recognized Bosnia as a sovereign nation, member of UN, c.f. UN Res. 755, dated May 20, 1992.

Bajramović, Sejdo. Illegally appointed Kosovo representative instead of Rizza Sapunxhiu to the Yugoslav presidency in 1991—loyal to Milošević instead of to Kosovo Albanians. It was possible to be done during the Milošević's dictatorship. Such Milošević's (Serbian) behavior triggered requests for independence in Slovenia, Croatia, Bosnia, Macedonia, and, later, Kosovo—and finally Montenegro.

Bijedić Džemal. Bosnian patriot, a supporter of the Yugoslav Constitution of 1974 that decentralized Yugoslavia. Allegedly killed by JNA generals in an airplane "accident" in 1977 when he was president of the Yugoslav government.

Boban, Mate. Rebel Bosnian Croat leader. Declared separate Croat state in Bosnia, the so-called Herceg-Bosna. It was later proven that he was an agent of the secret Yugoslav police (which was dominated by Serbs) during the Yugoslavia rule.

Boutros Ghali. UN Secretary General, the man whose duty was to implement the UN Charter. Americans vetoed his reelection for the UN Secretary General in 1996 because of many violations of the UN Charter. Many of his violations of the UN Charter were against Bosnia-Herzegovina. He was strongly sided with the Serbs.

Bosniaks. The official name of the most numerous ethnic group in Bosnia-Herzegovina since September 28, 1993, when an assembly of the Bosniak people returned their historic name. Before September 1993, the official name was "Bosnian Muslims." Hence, "Bosnian Muslim" is a name of the ethnic group rather than the religious group. Bosniaks were not recognized as a separate ethnic group, and their historic name "Bosniak" was forbidden during Yugoslav (Serbian) rule over Bosnia for the purpose of assimilation of Bosniaks into Serbs. Many Bosniaks were assimilated into Serbs, including Alija Izetbegović, who declared himself as a Serb until the census in 1971. His affiliation with Serbs explains many strange decisions that helped the Serbs during the war while Izetbegović was Bosnian president.

brotherhood and unity. A way of living, promoted by Tito, based on tolerance among various ethnic groups in the diverse Yugoslav society.

Cetniks or Chetniks. Name used by Serb nationalists for their soldiers, who committed genocide against Bosniaks in WW II and in the Bosnian War of 1992–1995.

Christopher, Warren. US Secretary of State from 1992 to 1997.

Delimustafić, Alija. Bosnian Minister of the Interior (1991–92) and a proven Serbian agent.

Dizdarević, Raif. Bosnia's representative in the Yugoslav presidency. Even though he was of Bosniak background, he was known as a Serbian supporter and the man who introduced the unconstitutional Serbian dictatorship in the Kosovo province on February 28, 1989. At that time, he was president of the Yugoslav Presidency.

Doko, Jerko. Croat, Bosnian Defense Minister (1991). A supporter of the unified Bosnia. Removed by Izetbegović on the request of rebel Croats.

Drnovšek, Janez. Slovenia's representative in the Yugoslav presidency before the dissolution of the Yugoslavia.

Duraković, Nijaz. Bosnia's Socialist Party leader, and later a member of Bosnia's presidency. He was a supporter of the 1974 Bosnian Constitution.

Eagleburger, Lawrence. Acting US Secretary of State in 1992.

Festić, Ibrahim. Professor of the constitutional law and a Bosnian patriot. He was in the Constitutional Commission that created the 1974 Constitution of the Republic of Bosnia Herzegovina. He was one of the patriots who stopped the division of Bosnia called the Union of three Bosnian Republics. That plan adopted by Izetbegović, Milošević, and Tuđman was rejected by the Bosniak Assembly in 1993, an ad hoc assembly established by Izetbegović to backstab the legitimate Parliament of the Republic Bosnia-Herzegovina. Bosnian patriots used this assembly to return the historic name of the Bosniak people.

Filipović, Muhamed. Representative in several Bosnian negotiating teams.

Ganić, Ejub. Yugoslav representative to the Bosnian presidency. He was a citizen of Serbia and educated in Serbia. Before the war, he came to Bosnia to replace the retired commander of JNA Institute of the Technology, Colonel Obradović. It is well known that only the people of the highest clearance among the Serbs could work in that type of position. Before the war, he was the founder of the pro-Serbian "Yugoslav" Party among the Bosniaks. When that party collapsed, Dr. Ganić was accepted for a leading position in SDA, to be handy to Izetbegović.

Gligorov, Kiro. The Communist veteran who guided Macedonia to independence as its president since 1991.

Halilović Sefer. First commander of the Bosnian Army, the supporter of the Bosnian Constitution 1974. He was removed by Izetbegović after he confronted Izetbegović for accepting a division of Bosnia during the peace process. He was the mastermind of the action of Bosnian Army that defeated HVO in the southern Bosnia and eased the siege of Sarajevo.

Holbrooke, Richard. Assistant US Secretary of State, mediator in Dayton.

Izetbegović, Alija. Bosnian president of the Presidency during the war in Bosnia.

Karadžić, Radovan. Rebel Serb, negotiator with Izetbegović, accused of war crimes by George H. Bush's administration in December 1992, indicted as a war criminal in 1995. As a war criminal, he was the main burden to the recognition of his creation, Republika Srpska—a Serbian state constituted on 49 percent of Bosnia in Dayton. Bosnians call his indictment "laundry of his masterpiece, the graveyard state Republika Srpska."

Kljuić, Stjepan. Croat member of the Bosnian presidency. He advocated for unified Bosnia. He was illegally removed by Izetbegović in 1992 on the request of Mate Boban, the leader of Bosnian Croats established by the influence of the Croatian president Franjo Tuđman among B&H Croats. Kljujic was reinstated 1994 upon the request of the Bosnian Parliament.

Koljević, Nikola. Serbian member of the Bosnian presidency before the war.

Komšić, Ivo. Croat member of the Bosnian presidency. He was a supporter of the unified Bosnia-Herzegovina.

Krajišnik Momčilo. The closest of Karadžić's partner. He was a member of the first post–Dayton Bosnian trilateral presidency, even though he was alleged, and later convicted, as a war criminal by the International Criminal Court in the Hague.

Krunić, Boško. Vojvodina representative in the Yugoslav presidency, ousted in the Anti-Bureaucratic Revolution in 1988.

Kučan, Milan. Slovene Communist Party leader who became the first president of the independent Slovenia.

Kukanjac, Milutin. General of the JNA; commander of Sarajevo.

Lagumdžija, Zlatko. Bosnian Communist leader. Together with Izetbegović, he was captured by the Serbs at the Sarajevo airport on May 2, 1992, and released on May 3, 1992.

McKenzie, Lewis. Canadian General, UN Commander in BH in 1992.

Mahmutčehajić, Rusmir. SDA leader and member of the Bosnian government in 1993. He miraculously succeeded in organizing the production of ammunition in the completely surrounded Bosnia during the war against both Serbs and Croats. He was removed from power by Izetbegović without any explanation.

Manolić, Josip. Croat patriot who insisted that Bosnia-Herzegovina should be supported instead of attacked by Croatia. Because of his willingness to fight against the Serbs for the liberation of Bosnia and Croatia, instead of fighting for the Serbs in Bosnia, he was removed from power by Tuđman.

Mesić, Stipe. Croatia's representative in the Yugoslav presidency. He was removed from power by Tuđman for the same reason as Manolić.

Mikulić, Branko. High-ranking Croat politician in the prewar Bosnian government. A supporter of the Constitution of the Republic of Bosnia and Herzegovina adopted in 1974. (That constitution guaranteed the independence of the R B&H in the case of the dissolution of Yugoslavia.)

Milošević, Slobodan. President of Serbia, responsible for the genocide in Bosnia.

Mladić, Ratko. General of the JNA. He was commander of the Bosnian Serb Army since 1992.

Muhić, Fuad. Bosnian patriot, a supporter of the 1974 Bosnian Constitution, who best predicted what would happen to Bosnia if Izetbegović prevailed. Fuad Muhić was one of the few intellectuals brave enough to stand up against Serbs regarding the important political issues *https://hr.wikipedia.org/wiki/Fuad Muhić.* Dr. Muhić died under mysterious circumstances at the beginning of the war in Bosnia.

Orić, Naser. Leader of the Srebrenica defenders from the beginning of the war. Before the fall of Srebrenica, Naser Orić was removed from Srebrenica, on Izetbegović's command, to "attend military school in Tuzla." That Izetbegović's move left Srebrenica without its leaders, in disarray. That was the tragic "mistake" that cost eight thousand lives in Srebrenica.

Owen, David. EC mediator who removed (?!) Dr. Duraković and Dr. Filipović from the Bosnian negotiating team in Geneva in the fall of 1993, Bosniaks who did not accept the partition of the country and had the trust of the Bosnian Assembly and the Bosnian people.

Paraga, Dobroslav. Founder of the Croatian Party of Right. The main characteristic of that party is the doctrine that Croats should fight together with Bosniaks against the common enemy, the Serbs. That is why they were against Tuđman's conspiracy with Serbs to divide Bosnia. *https://ba.boell.org/de/2019/03/25/karadordevo-und-die-territorial-ethnische-teilung-bosnien-und-herzegowinas*.

Plavšić, Biljana. "Vice president" during Karadžić's presidency of the Republika Srpska, when all the crimes were committed. She was a hard-liner in the Karadžić government. After Karadžić was indicted as a war criminal, she became the president of the Republika Srpska.

Pohara, Armin. Bosniak-Croat, who worked for Izetbegović, Tuđman, and Abdić as a special agent advocating among Bosniaks the division of Bosnia-Herzegovina along ethnic lines.

Pozderac, Hamdija. Bosnian leader before the Agrokomerc Affair. He categorically refused any possibility of changing the Bosnian Constitution. That is why the Serbian lobby set up the Agrokomerc Affair and removed Pozderac's government.

Račan, Ivica. Croatian Communist leader. He led Croatian Communists when they walked out from the last SKJ Congress after the Slovenians.

Ražnjatović, Zeljko (Arkan). Commander of JNA special units from Nis, accused of war crimes in Croatia and Bosnia. Biljana Plavšić publicly kissed him after he committed the first crimes against humanity in Bijeljina in April 1992.

Rugova, Ibrahim. Leader of the Kosovo ethnic Albanians since 1989. He succeeded to keep Kosovo in peace until the Serbs finished the war in Bosnia. The Albanians had a better chance to fight for their freedom when the Serbs were in the wars in Croatia and Bosnia than in 1998, when the whole Serbian Army from Slovenia, Croatia, and Bosnia had moved in Kosovo. He played a similar role among Albanians in Kosovo as Izetbegović did among Bosniaks in Bosnia.

Šaćirbey, Muhamed. Bosnian foreign minister. His father, Nedžib Šaćirbegović, was Izetbegović's best friend since the student days. They changed the family name to the Turkish version *Šaćirbey*, which indicates that they felt as Turks rather than Bosnians. Recall the Turks occupied Bosnia for 4.5 centuries, and many ethnic Bosnians were assimilated with the Turks. Muhamed Šaćirbegović will be remembered among Bosnians as the man who on Izetbegović's request recognized Republika Srpska in Geneva on September 26, 1995 without the legitimate approval of the Bosnian Presidency. His anti-constitutional Geneva signature that recognized that 49 percent of Bosnia belongs exclusively to Serbs handed the necessary paperwork to Americans to legitimately stop the Bosnian Army at the moment when Serbs were in total disarray, losing one city a day.

Sapunxhiju, Rizza. Kosovo's representative in the Yugoslav presidency; he was illegally fired by the Serbs in 1991.

Selimović, Mehmed (Mesha). A writer of Bosniaks background who considered himself a Serbian author.

Šešelj, Vojislav. Serbian radical who became known for fighting against the Bosnian government and for Izetbegović's freedom in the 1980s. In the war, his units committed many crimes.

Silajdžić, Haris. One of Izetbegović's closest friends and allies. He was an unknown person to the Bosnians before the war, when he was brought in by Izetbegović into his inner circle to assist him with leading the party. Silajdžić was educated in Muslim religious schools and fluent in Arabic and English. These were his credentials, which were supposed to make Bosnian Muslims trust him. But we have to remember that despite his education, Silajdžić's previous career was in the Yugoslavian diplomatic corps, intelligence in Arabic countries. His many later actions to subvert and sabotage Bosnian interests show that he continued to be devoted to Yugoslav unity (i.e., greater Serbia).

Stonltenberg, Thorvald. UN envoy to the International Conference (1993–1995), replacing Cyrus Vance.

Tito, Josip Broz. The Leader of Yugoslavia from 1941 to 1980.

Tuđman, Franjo. Founding leader of the Croatian Democratic Union (HDZ) and the first president of the independent Croatia. He was general of the Yugoslav People's Army. In the seventies, he was prosecuted by Tito's government for his opposition to the 1972 change of the Yugoslav Constitution, which gave more autonomy to the Yugoslav Republics.

Ustaše. Croatian nationalists who considered the Serbs as enemies and the Muslims as allies against the Serbs. They committed genocide against the Serbs in the WW II, and after the WW II, "Ustasha" became a pejorative name used by Serbs to refer to all Croats.

Zulfikarpašić, Adil. Bosnian immigrant and businessman in Switzerland who signed the Belgrade Initiative (a.k.a. the Historical Agreement between Muslims and Serbs) with Milošević in 1991, on behalf of the president Izetbegović.

Preface

TWO PARTS BOUNDED AS ONE BOOK

Part I
This is a translation of the material that was published in the book in the Bosnian language "Rat u BiH 1992-1995" (The War in Bosnia and Herzegovina 1992–1995) in November, 1995. Note, it was published before the Dayton agreement was officially signed in Paris France, on December 14, 1995. In the present book we added references (links) to events that were well known then, but need to be documented for new generations.

Part II
Appendix consisting of some important, relatively unknown documents from the period after the war that reveal real-life effects of the Dayton agreement on Bosnia and Herzegovina.

First Military Commander
of the Bosnian Army

This is a testimonial about Bosnian President Alija Izetbegović, and his determination to destroy God's gift to the Bosnian people, the internationally recognized sovereign nation, The Republic of Bosnia and Herzegovina, and to create The Republic of the Serbs.

Dr. Borogovac, a mathematician by training, but also a patriot and witness, uses facts, logic and very direct writing cuts into the heart of the deceit upon which Izetbegović built his campaign against the Republic of B&H.

This work represents a definitive rejection of Izetbegović's big lies, including that "the world" conspired to divide Bosnia, that the Republic of Bosnia and Herzegovina would be defeated on the battlefield, and even that he, Izetbegović himself, was only well intentioned, but naive and helpless Muslim old man who could not withstand this conspiracy.

I recommend this book to all those who even after the Dayton treason still believe in those lies.

General Sefer Halilović
Chief of General Staff of the Bosnian Army

Introduction to the English Edition

The first edition of this book was published during the Bosnian War, in Bosnian language. It was titled *The War in Bosnia and Herzegovina 1992–1995* (*Rat u Bosni i Hercegovini 1992–1995*), and I wrote it in a hurry, to deliver a timely warning to the Bosnian people that President Izetbegović was collaborating with the aggressor and committing high treason that would have tragic and lasting consequences for the country. Along with a few other Bosnian patriots, I realized that President Izetbegović intended to divide the country's territory by signing over occupied and ethnically cleansed territories, thus making the occupation permanent. This was contrary to his oath as president, and to his explicit and public promises and assurances to the people of Bosnia that he would never agree to that. At the time, our accusation against President Izetbegović was considered as an extreme position, and we were called traitors by other Bosnians. This was expected, but it was important to deliver a timely warning, regardless. Later events confirmed that we were right, which exonerated us among Bosnians.

In 2000, I was approached by Zadarska Tiskara, a publisher in Croatia, to print an updated issue of the book, to be titled: *The War in Bosnia and Herzegovina: Political Aspects* (*Rat u Bosni i Hercegovini: Politicki aspekti*). Unfortunately, by that time the warning had come to pass, embodied in the 1995 Dayton Agreement, which created a Serbian puppet state called "the Republic of the Serbs" on territory that was ethnically cleansed by means of genocide during the war. It was an extraordinary outcome—that an aggressor should commit genocide, lose on the battlefield, yet somehow still achieve the criminal objectives of holding on to ethnically cleansed territories and get the blessing of democratic foreign governments. Our ability to foresee that outcome long before it happened, merely by observing the actions of one man, President Izetbegović, was strong evidence that our reasoning was correct; and it made sense to restate the case to the people. The second book also put in newer documents that further confirmed both prior warnings: a) that Bosnia will be divided, and b) that the divided Bosnia will be dysfunctional. The second book was also published only in Bosnian, because it too meant to educate and enable Bosnians to recognize and counter the continuing treachery of their leader and his cronies.

This third book is in English, because the lessons that Bosnians have been learning *are* applicable to other conflicts that are occurring in the world. First, it dispels the dominant narrative that has taken hold in the West regarding how the war in Bosnia ended. By that narrative, we refer to both the process and the outcome. You have heard the prevailing story: Bosnia was a success of hard US and EU diplomacy and negotiations that won the peace, as all sides compromised. Bad guys were arrested and punished. Bosnians of all kinds can now reconcile, forgive each other, and work together democratically on the path toward European integration. This story is parroted by certain current US and EU politicians who were on the scene in the 1990s, and are even using their connection to Bosnia's war as proof of their foreign policy and leadership credentials.

It is a false narrative. Instead, the extraordinary outcome we mentioned above, including Dayton's establishment of the Republic of the Serbs was a complete success for perpetrators of genocide and aggression. It embodied their stated goal for going to war in Croatia, Bosnia, and Kosovo—the creation of ethnically clean territories referred to as Greater Serbia. Incredibly, the US and European nations are guarantors of the Dayton agreement. It is akin to the Allies agreeing to be guarantors of Nazi German territories in Poland even after Hitler was defeated and his generals were on trial for genocide. We are astonished at how frequently we hear arguments for partitioning other countries without any legal basis or justification as a means for resolving any conflict that may have an ethnic, racial, or religious component. It comes up repeatedly in discussions of Iraq, Syria, Palestine, Ukraine, and Georgia; and inevitably, we hear advice from so-called experts and politicians to partition those lands in order to separate the groups that do not get along. And the false and naive narrative about Bosnia is used as the example of where that approach "worked."

Bosnia is a precedent, and even a recipe—but not for democracies interested in peacemaking but, rather, for dictators interested in carrying out genocide and conquest in the modern world, where they have to worry about creating an exit state that preserves the result of aggression, with some veneer of legality and acceptance by the international community. In fact, Russia's strategy in Ukraine and Georgia seems to closely mirror Serbia's strategy in Bosnia, with conquest under the guise of domestic ethnic rebellion. Ukraine, in particular, is progressing in a very similar way to Bosnia ever since Petro Poroshenko rose to power. I do not know as much about Poroshenko or Ukraine as I do about Bosnia; but his rhetoric and decisions, to, me are reminiscent of Izetbegović.

The dictators out there know the strategy, but it is my hope that now in these conflicts, the victims and defenders will be able to recognize it as well, with the help of Bosnia's experience.

Introduction to the First Issue

Boston, November 5, 1995

The war in Bosnia-Herzegovina is an unheard-of tragedy. Before the eyes of the entire world, a state is being destroyed, and the people were the victims of genocide and ethnic cleansing. All of the principles of humanity, morals, and international rules have been trampled. The question most often asked is, how could that happen today, when the genocide committed during WWII(the Holocaust) is so well known, and when the international community had the will and the means to protect the Republic of Bosnia-Herzegovina? The international community has shown that it is not the enemy of the Republic of Bosnia-Herzegovina and that it accepts this state into its membership when it recognized R B&H on April 7, 1992. With that act, the International community studs up against Serbian nationalism, which only started to bloody its hands in Bosnia-Herzegovina. So how come that in the fall of 1995, after the innumerable atrocities committed by the Serbs revolted the world, the international community crossed over to the side of the war criminals, giving them 49 percent of Bosnia-Herzegovina with its Dayton peace proposals? Who was the mastermind who succeeded to change the world's opinion, and what methods did he use? This book answers some of those questions.

This book has to be approached with having faith in no one but a common sense. Besides that, from the reader who comprehends what is truly happening in Bosnia, it is expected that he/she spread the truth. The ultimate goal is to help in the fight against the forces of betrayal and the division of Bosnia-Herzegovina.

Wishing to arm the Bosnian patriots as soon as possible with the knowledge of what is really happening, this book is being written in a hurry. I still hope that this book will reach Bosnians and friends of the Republic Bosnia-Herzegovina all over the world before it is too late, while it is still possible to say *no* to the division of a member of the United Nations.

Muhamed Borogovac

Part I

1

ETHNIC STRUCTURE OF
BOSNIA-HERZEGOVINA

1.1. The Serbs

The genocide in Bosnia did not happen suddenly, as an act of madness. It is not a product of a political situation. The Serbian antagonism against their neighbors is very deep. It is in the core of Serbian identity.

The cold war in the former Yugoslavia between Yugoslav republics intensified back in 1987 with the arrival of Slobodan Milošević to power in Serbia. Milošević was brought into the highest ranks of Serbian leadership by the liberal Serbian communist Ivan Stambolić, who considered Milošević to be a good banker. Stambolić dreamed that after the expected fall of communism in Yugoslavia, the Serbs would turn toward the improvement of their economy. He was wrong. He paid for his mistakes at the historical eighth conference of the Serbian Central Communist Committee (CK SKS) by being removed from all the positions he held by Milošević. He didn't know his people well enough.

Where did Stambolic go wrong? What makes the Serbs different from the other people?

The most important characteristic of the Serbs is their exaggerated collective conscience. The strong Serbian nationalism evolved from the Serbian Orthodox Church, which has always not only protected the souls of its disciples, but was also always active in politics. The reason for that is that it is a church of one people, the Serbs. There are many interesting consequences. One logical consequence is that there was never real separation between religion, ethnicity, and nationality in Serbian society. The other logical consequence of the Serbian religious postulates is the belief that Jesus Christ is a Serb. In the last years of Yugoslavia, it was a very

3

popular proposition among Serbian intellectuals. The outcome of that is that the Serbs talked more about the "Serbian bravery" and the "Serbian heroism" in their church than about religious issues. That trend intensified before this current war. Let's remember, for example, the ferrying of the remains of Tsar Lazar throughout the greater Serbian lands west of the Drina river. (Tsar Lazar was the last Serbian medieval ruler. After the defeat of his army on the Kosovo Field in 1389, Serbia became a part of the Ottoman Empire until 1812.) That "pilgrimage" with the remains of Tsar Lazar became the ritual marking of the Greater Serbia and the awakening of hate toward neighbors prior to starting the war.

Unfortunately, that hatred uncontrollably grew, and caused many casualties among the neighboring peoples, especially in Bosnia, where Serbs even committed genocide. Because of such strong showing of love toward Serbian ethnicity, the Serbs are known in the world as either great patriots or great nationalists.

How did such strong Serbian nationalism affect the *brotherhood and unity*? (Brotherhood and unity was a way of living, promoted by Yoguslav leader Joseph Broz Tito, based on tolerance among various ethnic groups in the diverse Yugoslav society.) I'll use the example of Bosnian universities. Working at different universities in Bosnia and Herzegovina, I noticed that most of the employees were Serbs, although the Serbs were a minority among the students. How did that come about? When a Serbian student appeared (although he might have been average), Serbian professors and instructors did everything possible to place him as a faculty member. To a Serbian professor, it was quite normal to sacrifice some of his own teaching hours just so that *their* faculty member would be hired by the university. The important thing was to employ as many Serbs as possible, in order to control the university. (All schools in Bosnia belonged to the working force of the school.) On the other hand, the Bosniaks and the Croatian professors were looking to maintain as many teaching hours in order to increase their own income. That's how it happened that the faculty was composed of average graduates while many excellent Bosniaks and Croats were forced to toil in some provincial industries.

The Serbian nationalism ensured that the favorite subject among Serbs was history, but mainly history that glorified the Serbian nation. There is a saying: "The Serbs live in the past."

The Serbian traditional epic literature that glorifies the "Serbian manliness and bravery" was always one of the most important topics of the curriculum in Yugoslav elementary and high schools. There was constant longing for a Greater Serbia, for a strong Serbian army, a strong police, and a strong Serbian football team, and everything else that could boost Serbian national pride. This meant that individuality among the Serbs was discouraged. In cases where the individual characteristics—such as morals, honesty, compassion, and conscience—clash with the Serbian nationalism, in the great majority of cases, the national interests will overrule individual sentiments.

That caused many tragedies within the Serbian neighbors. For centuries, Serbia was a diverse society, as long as it was ruled by the Ottoman Empire. The Ottomans built all the Serbian cities, in which they were also the majority. Under the term *city*, I consider the business and commerce centers, not some medieval castle, of which there were several even before the Ottoman Empire concurred Serbia. In those cities, there lived quite a few Greeks, Jews, Gypsies, Armenians, and many other peoples that comprised the Ottoman Empire. For example, in his work *Urban Development in the Western Balkans,* Francis Carter quotes the well-known Turkish historian Evlija Celebija, who wrote in 1660, "Belgrade is a port on the Danube, with 38 Muslim neighborhoods, three Serbian, three Gypsy and one each of Jewish and Armenian." But as soon as the Serbs took power in 1812, they eliminated all the non-Serbs and created an ethnically pure Serbia. The surviving Bosniaks from Serbia mainly escaped into Bosnia. However, no revenge against the Serbs living in Bosnia took place.

A very similar circumstance is taking place today. The massacred people of Bijeljina, Zvornik, Janja, Srebrenica are not avenged in places where the Serbs live under Bosnian Army control, such as Tuzla, Sarajevo, and Zenica. The Bosniaks explain that by their *Merhamet* ("honor, compassion and individualization of guilt").

As opposed to the Bosniaks, the Serbs in similar situations always act as a collective, as one entity, one people. If the Serbian soldiers are killed in fighting on the battlefield, the Serbs take their revenge on the Bosniaks in a city under Serbian occupation. Well known is the case of when Serbs buried alive tens inhabitants of Prijedor in 1994 after several Serbian policemen were killed in a battle near Bihać. Also, when the Serbs lost a battle in Croatia, the Serbs took it out on the Croats left in Banja Luka. There are many such examples. A better-known example was the Serbian revenge on the Croats in occupied Banja Luka because of the loss of Western Slavonia in May 1995. The world took more notice of that mistreatment of Croats living under Serbian control in Bosnia because the Bishop of Banja Luka, Mr. Franjo Komarica, protested by going on a hunger strike for the mistreatment. We will stop here listing such examples, because this book is not about the genocide but, rather, about political issues. I refer readers to the books *The Bosnian People Charge Genocide* by Francis A. Boyle and *Witness of Genocide* by Roy Gutman, who won the Pulitzer Prize for that book.

Let's go back to other events that took place in Serbian history. After the Second Serbian Uprising and liberation from the Ottoman Empire at the beginning of the nineteenth century, as Serbia was expanding, so were the Serbs ethnically cleansing the new Serbian territories of all non-Serbs, not only of the Bosniaks. That is readily apparent in Vojvodina (northern Serbia now). For many centuries, that region was an integrated, mixed society with a small Serbian minority, while it was ruled by Austria-Hungary. But since Vojvodina became a part of Serbia in 1918, almost all of Vojvodina's non-Serbs have disappeared. Completely gone are the Germans, most of the Croats, Hungarians, Slovaks, and others.

In the traditions of other people, a knight calls out an opposing knight to a duel. In the Serbian epic literature, it is considered heroism when a group of them kill a single opponent in an ambush, even in his sleep. This "heroism" is depicted in the historical poem "Death of Smail Aga Čengić." Two centuries have passed since that cowardly act took place, yet it is still celebrated as an act of heroism in Serbian schools.

Because the Serbs have so concentrated themselves on their nationalism, their culture is also exclusively nationalistic. Actually, the most important aspect of the Serbian artistic and cultural heritage consists of a few cycles of traditional epic poems, in which the Serbian "heroes" are honored for killing "Turks." In some of the poems, it is considered "heroism" when Serbian outlaws attack a Turkish wedding through an ambush and slaughter of its participants. The word Turkish is in quotes because in the Serbian mythology, the word *Turk* is the designation for all hated Muslims, no matter what ethnic group or nationality they are.

The best description of Serbian nationalism and culture is the madrigal "Gorski Vijenac" by Petar Petrović Njegos, in which he describes and glorifies medieval genocide committed against the Muslims during the reign of Vladika Danilo in Montenegro. The Serbs took"Gorski Vijenac" as the inspiration for all the later genocides they committed against the Muslims. The Serbs have constituted their nationality based on the genocidal ideas described in the "Gorski Vijenac." All children in regions of Yugoslavia inhabited by Serbs had to know "Gorski Vijenac" in details if they wanted to graduate. "Gorski Vijenac" has actuality been accepted as the Constitution of Serbs in the ethnic sense. Because of such reverence by the Serbs for the "Gorski Vijenac," Njegos is considered by Serbs as the Founding Father of the Serbian nation, even though he is from Montenegro.

It is interesting to note how the Serbs succeeded in developing such a strong nationalist view in their young. There are four pillars of the Serbian nationalism. I mentioned the first one: hate of the "Turks," a so-called Kosovo myth.

The Serbian hatred of the "Turks"— including Bosniaks, Albanians, and ethnic Turks—is the oldest and the most important pillar of Serbian ethnic culture. The second and third pillars of Serbian ethnicity are directed toward the Croats and the Germans. Lately, there has been the formation of the *Jasenovac myth* and of the *Kragujevac myth* in the Serbian culture, which are used to intensify the flames of hate toward the Croats and the Germans. All the government holidays in ex-Yugoslavia were occasions for reading from anti-"Turks," anti-Croats, and anti-German books, such as "historic" novels about the "Turks" from Ivo Andrić;

or the poem "Jama" by Ivan Goran-Kovačić, which depicts the Ustaše terror over the Serbs; or *Krvava Bajka* (The Bloody Fable) by Desanka Maksimović, which tells of the German mass execution committed in the Serbian town of Kragujevac during WWII. The fourth pillar of the "Serbian pride" is the love for fellow Eastern Orthodox Russians. Over the last few decades, as the result of the Russian confrontations with the West, there has been a development of hate toward the "decaying West." The west will never understand why Serbs killed so many French soldiers (more than thirty-five) by snipers in Bosnia, even though the French politics helped them so much. Killing by a sniper is not an accident. A murderer sees a victim clearly. The Bosnians will never understand why the French were so devoted to Serbs in this war.

Something like the meeting of 1 million Serbs on the Kosovo Field on June 28, 1989, could only happen to people who value collective feelings more than individual feelings. They gathered at the place of the greatest Serbian loss on the battlefield, so they could get incited toward one more "revenge" against the "Turks," their mythical enemies who defeated them in the Kosovo battle six centuries ago, 1389. After two days of travel and after half an hour of rallying around with their leader Slobo (Slobodan Milošević), they returned to their homes psychologically ready to launch a new reign of terror—killing their unarmed neighbors, robbing them, and raping their women, and even killing their children. To Milošević's followers, it wasn't difficult to make the two-day trip from Knin in Croatia to the Kosovo Field in Serbia, just so they could reconfirm their hatred of others. The "Serbian pride" that was reawakened on the Kosovo Field is responsible for some of the most gruesome sights ever seen in Europe. The Serbian soldiers loved to kill—whether using a knife, the garrote, the sledgehammer or the butt of the gun, or the string for cutting throats. In many episodes, they surpassed the cruelty committed by the Nazis. That is why the Serbs, who allowed to the worst scum to lead them for centuries in committing genocides against their neighbors, will have to carry their shame forever.

1.2. The Croats

Croatia wasn't occupied by the Ottoman Empire for as long as the Serbs were. In Croatian history, a much bigger role was played by Austrians, Hungarians, Venetians, and eventually the Serbs. There has never been as much hate toward the Turks and Bosniaks in Croatia, mainly because the period of occupation by the Ottoman Empire was relatively brief, and only a smaller part of Croatia was ever occupied (Slavonia and Lika). Somewhat more negative emotions toward the Austrians, Hungarians, and Italians have also pretty much evaporated, leaving the Serbs as the principal Croatian enemies.

Starting in 1914, many Croats have developed a sense of closeness and unity of purpose with the Bosniaks during their fight with their common enemy—Serbian expansionism. But there have also always been those Croatians who felt that an accord regarding Bosnia-Herzegovina should be reached with the Serbs, at the expense of the Bosniaks. However, toward the end of the 1980s and the beginning of the 1990s, there were many more of those willing to cooperate with the Bosniaks and work together against the common enemy—Serbian expansionism. The Bosniaks' bad luck was because of the fact that Croatia's current president, Dr. Franjo Tuđman, is a fan of the division of Bosnia, along the lines of Cvetković/Maček. (Cvetković/Maček was the deal between Serbs and Croats about the division of Bosnia-Herzegovina reached before the WWII in 1939. Bosnia-Herzegovina was reestablished by Bosnian anti-fascists of all ethnic groups on November 25, 1943.) Tuđman belongs to the small minority of those Croats who are convinced that an agreement can be reached with the Serbs, and thus they would get a large chunk of Bosnia-Herzegovina. Judging by the recent policy of the Croatian government, dividing Bosnia was more important than liberating all of Croatia. Because he couldn't find enough support in Croatia proper for the policy of aggression toward Bosnia while a third of Croatia has been occupied, Mr. Tuđman relied on the Herzegovina lobby, which he created himself in order to hand over many of the functions of the Croatian government and of his political party, the HDZ.

Why were the Herzegovinian Croats Tuđman's main supporters of the division of Bosnia? One of the reasons is that the Herzegovinian Croats were under the Ottoman rule before 1878 so that they have (just as the Serbs have) accumulated a lack of tolerance toward the "Muslims." The word *Muslims* is in quotation marks because in this case, it is the designation of the ethnic group rather than the religious group. Namely, in former Yugoslavia, the official name of Bosniaks was *Bosnian Muslims*. Working at the Džemal Bijedić University in Mostar, I learned that the Herzegovinian Croats had much more ill will toward the Muslims than toward the Serbs. Afterward, during the war, they properly conducted Tuđman's policy toward the Bosniaks. The second reason that the Herzegovinians were the headquarters for the division of Bosnia-Herzegovina is because in a few counties of western Herzegovina, Croats were in the majority, so it seemed natural that those regions become incorporated with Croatia proper, in case there was a division of Bosnia.

As opposed to the Herzegovinian Croats, the Croats of Bosnia were supporters of a unified Bosnia-Herzegovina. That occurred mainly because Croats in Bosnia are a minority, hence, they realized that if Bosnia-Herzegovina was divided into ethnically pure states, they would lose their homes and property. That is why they were in support of a unified civic state in which the rights of all would be protected equally. Another important fact was that there were many more Croats in Bosnia than in Herzegovina (because in Bosnia lives a ten times larger population than in Herzegovina). Additionally, many Croats from Bosnia-Herzegovina were real Bosnian patriots, especially among the intellectuals. The examples are Branko Mikulić, Hrvoje Ištuk, Stjepan Kljuić, Dr. Ivo Komšić, Dr. Miljenko Brkić, Dr. Ivan Lovrenović, Miljenko Jergović, and so on. That is why Tuđman has a lot of a hard time installing "his" people, the "Herzegovinians" in power among Bosnian Croats. The word *"Herzegovinians"* is in quotation marks because it here designates the political currents of dividers of Bosnia-Herzegovina among the Croats, rather than just the regional identity. We must remember that Davorin Perinović, Stjepan Kljuić, and Dr. Miljenko Brkić were one by one replaced by Tuđman until Tuđman's men, Herzegovinian, Mate Boban didn't finally take control of the Croatian affairs in Bosnia, i.e., until Mate Boban didn't become the leader of the Croatian Democratic Party for Bosnia-Herzegovina (HDZ BH).

1.3. The Bosniaks

In their insatiable hunger for a big and powerful Serbia, throughout all the wars, the Serbs have expanded their territories by eliminating their neighbors, while during the periods of peace, they tried to assimilate them. In that regard, the Serbs came out with a theory in which they claimed that all the Bosniaks were really just Serbs who converted to Islam. The strategy of that claim was to convince the Bosniaks that they are descendants of the Serbs who became separated from Serbs because of the betrayal by their ancestors. Generations of Bosniaks were forced to learn how, during the Ottoman Empire, their Serb ancestors were converting to Islam—some because of the incentives offered, some out of fear. According to that theory, only the staunchest and the most honorable Serbs stayed faithful to their religion. There are many clichés in the Serbian language that constantly keep insulting those who converted to Islam. Young Bosnians had been exposed to such humiliation and abuse since 1918.

During the Serbian language and history classes (the teachers were, in many cases, from Serbia, usually spouses to the Serbian and Montenegro officers stationed in Bosnia), the teachers were "explaining" to the little Bosniaks that they are descendants of the worst turncoats. Such education had as its goal to embarrass the little Bosniaks into abandoning any ethnic and national pride they might have been developing. To ease the loss of ethnic and national identity, during the period of communist Yugoslavia, a new ethnic identity was invented: Yugoslav.

To all the ethnically aware Bosniaks, it was clear that the name *Yugoslav* was invented just so that the assimilation of the non-Serbian people would proceed as painlessly as possible, hence, as successfully as possible. That kind of assimilation, which was taught in Bosnian schools throughout the Kingdom of Yugoslavia (1918–1941) and during the communist era (1945–1992), brought on the loss of any national identity for many Bosniaks. It is well known that the writer Mehmed Meša Selimović declared himself as being an ethnic Serb of Muslim descent. There were many Muslims who politically acted as ethnic Serbs but just didn't declare that publicly. It is also interesting to note that many Bosnian Muslim politicians and almost all the top leaders of the Bosnian Islamic community considered themselves as being ethnic Serbs. Why is it that only such Muslims were able to attain such high positions? That is explained by the fact that the Serbs perceived them as such and, under that condition allowed them to advance in their fields, where they were in a position to represent all Bosniaks (at that time called "Bosnian Muslims.") Many such "Muslims" were described by Alija Nametak in his book *The Sarajevo Necrology* (published in 1994 by Globus and the Bosniak Institute in Zurich). The best-known recent example of a Bosniak who converted to being a Serb is the movie director Emir Kusturica. Hiding behind his Yugoslav ethnic designation, he aligned himself to the Serbs, thus best proving that the new ethnic designation Yugoslav was only a synonym for Serb.

It is interesting to note that Alija Izetbegović also kept declaring himself to be a Serb until the 1970s. Before the 1990 elections (the first free elections after the fall of the communism) several documents from the 1960s were published in which Alija Izetbegović stated in his own handwriting that he was a Serb. It is also known that Izetbegović proclaimed himself to be a Serb during the population census in 1961. That discovery, made by Croats, could harm Izetbegović's nomination for the presidency of the Republic of Bosnia-Herzegovina in 1990. As on the eve of the 1990 elections, the Serbs were in charge of the national TV and radio. Izetbegović was given a half-hour program to explain to Bosnian voters his pro-Serbian statements from his past. He, unchallenged, defended his actions, claiming that the Bosniak ethnic identity wasn't recognized before 1970 as such, so he had to declare himself as a Serb. However, that is not true. He could have joined the majority of Bosnians who rather than calling themselves Serbs wrote: "Non-committed to any ethnic designation" on their census papers. Some Bosniaks had done it as a sign of protest, some as a joke; but many have written the following in the place where their ethnic designation is asked: Eskimo, Martian, Chinese, Japanese, and so on. Finally, the religious designation *Muslim* was allowed. He could simply declare himself as being a religious Muslim and leave blank his ethnic designation. Hence, Izetbegović declared himself as an ethnic Serb rather than a religious Muslim.

I've always declared myself as a Muslim, yet I too lived in the same state as Alija Izetbegović. All the Muslim descents that I know have declared themselves as being Serbs did so because of their affinity toward the Serbs. Realizing that

Alija Izetbegović was politically very knowledgeable, he was very conscientiously declaring himself to being a Serb.

Later, Tuđman's party, HDZ, withdrew those proofs that Izetbegović declared himself to be a Serb. That is, Croatian president Franjo Tuđman realized that, for his goal—division of the Republic of Bosnia-Herzegovina—it was better to have the Serb Izetbegović as Bosnian president than a real Bosnian patriot.

While I am still on the subject of the Bosniaks' identity, I would like to add a few more details. As opposed to the rest of the Southern Slavs who came to the Balkans toward the end of the seventh century and converted to the Eastern Orthodox Church, and who later in the nineteenth century identified themselves as Serbs, there were also those who accepted the Catholic faith and, later in the nineteenth century, identified themselves as Croats.

In addition to those two denominations, a third, albeit "heretic," church, spread its roots in Bosnia. It was the so-called Bosnian, or also called "the Christian" church. Their teachings sprouted from the contradiction of unity of God with the teachings of the Holy Trinity. They were strong believers in the afterlife. They believed there is only one God, and that God is good, that He is not the source of unhappiness on earth but, rather, that unhappiness is the result of the material world, the world of evil, which is the work of the devil. They believed that the death of a person frees that person from the material world, the world of evil, and into the eternal world of truth, which is the creation of God.

The Bosnian church and the Muslims alike do not accept the preaching of the Holy Trinity, which, according to them, destroys the image of the uniqueness of God. It was probably because of the dogma similar to that of the Muslims, that the members of the Bosnian church voluntarily accepted Islam later in the fifteenth century, when the Ottomans conquered Bosnia, some converting (to Islam) before Bosnia was even occupied by the Ottomans. Before converting to Islam, the members of the Bosnian church (sometimes also called Bogumils) were exposed to the Crusades against them directed by the Hungarians, and also by the Serbs, in order to force them to renounce their faith. As a result of those wars, the Bosnian kings formally accepted the Catholic faith in order to protect the population and the state, even though the majority of their subjects remained faithful to the Bosnian Church. The Bosnian academic Nedim Filipović proved in his research that the majority of the Bosnian Muslims originate from the Bosnians, who were converted to Catholicism only one generation before converting to Islam.

During the Ottoman Empire, they used to call themselves "Muslims" while they were in Bosnia, in order to differ from local Christians. Out of Bosnia, they used to call themselves "Bosniaks" in order to differ from Turks. As the result of such history in Bosnia-Herzegovina, we have Catholics, Eastern Orthodox, who, only much later in the nineteenth century, began to develop their Croatian and Serbian ethnic identity, respectively, and Muslims who rebuild old Bosniak nation. Hence, the truth is opposite from the teachings we have received in the Yugoslav schools: the ancestors of today's Serbs and Croats have, under pressure from "outsiders" and the Crusaders, abandoned their Bosnian church. However, those questions are of secondary importance. There shouldn't be any conclusions drawn from the ethnic backgrounds and history of different groups in Bosnia that would in any way impact any of their rights in Bosnia. All those who honor and respect the Bosnian Constitution and its borders have equal rights to live there.

It is completely unreasonable to claim that the Bosnian Muslims are descendants of converted (to Islam) Serbs or Croats. Until the later part of nineteenth century, there was only the religious identity in Bosnia and not any ethnic affiliation. Up to that point, the people of Bosnia considered themselves as being Eastern Orthodox, Catholics, or Muslims—not Serbs, Croats, or Bosniaks. In addition to their religious affiliation, the Bosnians also had a very strong sense of belonging to Bosnia-Herzegovina. During the period of the Austro-Hungarian rule, only after 1878 did the Bosnian Eastern Orthodox acquire their Serbian national identity, the Catholics their Croatian identity, and the Muslims rebuild their national identity and the name of *Bosniaks*, which was suppressed during the five centuries of Ottoman rule. However, this rule has many exceptions. There are well-known examples of Catholics and Eastern Orthodox people who identified themselves as Bosniaks. But there are many more examples of Muslims that acquired a Serbian or Croatian identity.

In 1918, the Bosniaks again lost their ethnic identity and traditional name *Bosniak* in Yugoslavia. Their ethnic identity and name *Bosniak* was forbidden. Officially, they were considered as Serbs or Croats of the Muslim faith. For the Serbian rulers of Yugoslavia, problems occurred during ethnic censuses. The great majority of unrecognized Bosniaks did not declare any ethnic designation. Those like Alija Izetbegović, Meša Selimović, Emir Kusturica, and some others who declared themselves as Serbs or Croats or Yugoslavs (in the ethnic sense) were only a few. For the formal recognition of their ethnic distinctiveness under the new name *Bosnian Muslims*, they had to wait until 1970. That recognition came about, thanks to the Bosnian patriots, formally members of the Communist party of Bosnia-Herzegovina, such as Džemal Bijedić, Hamdija Pozderac, Dr. Fuad Muhić, Munir Mesihović, and Avdo Čampara. That was a very delicate political fight in which no mistakes would be tolerated. A role of significant importance was played by the theoreticians Dr. Atif Purivatra, Dr. Muhamed Hadžijahic, Dr. Muhsin Rizvić, Dr. Kasim Suljević, and Dr. Fuad Muhić. The Bosniaks returned to their name of *Bosniaks* only during the current war, in October 1993.

Before the war, the Bosniaks were the most vital of all the ethnic groups in Bosnia-Herzegovina—but after the Albanians even in all of Yugoslavia. That is the direct result of being completely disenfranchised within the communist system. During the communist rule, all the doors were wide open to the Serbs in all the large, government-owned companies. The Serb who got tired of the hard life on the farm came down into the city. There he always found a fellow Serb who would always find some kind of employment for him. That is how it happened that all the factories were full of illiterate guards and unskilled security workers—Serbs who abandoned their farms in the mountains and came down to the easier life and state apartments in the city. (Having a state apartment was the greatest benefit. Rents were 5 percent to 10 percent of average wages, and nobody could evict a resident from a state apartment.) Getting acquainted with the city, they usually had only one or two children. Many of them, separated from their historical ambience—the farm—became alcoholics. The Serbian villages in the mountain became deserted. On the other hand, the Bosniaks didn't have those advantages and the possibilities of employment. That is how it happened that Bosniaks stayed on the farms. Living the traditional country life, they usually had quite a few children, like peasants usually do. As opposed to the Serbian villages, in the Muslim villages, life was on an upward path. The net result of that was the greater birth rate among the Bosniaks—fourteen per thousand, while Bosnian Croats had eight and the Bosnian Serbs seven. Only the Albanians had a greater birth rate in ex-Yugoslavia. The Bosniaks were by far the youngest of all the people of Bosnia-Herzegovina. During the prewar years, the number of Bosniak babies was two-thirds of the total number of babies born in Bosnia, although the Bosniaks composed only 44.3 percent of the population. That meant that eventually, Bosnia would develop into a predominantly Bosniak (i.e., Muslim) population. That is one of the reasons for the Serbian genocide and the insistence on the division of Bosnia into ethnic territories.

The Bosniaks in the city also didn't have many opportunities for employment. That is why they turned to creating small, private companies, as opposed to the Serbs who tied their future to the large, government-owned companies.

The Croats, along with the Bosniaks, turned toward the small, privately owned companies. The source of the starting capital was usually the savings or the money earned working abroad, usually in Germany. During the last twenty years before the war, the small, private sector enjoyed prosperity, but also the socialist downfall. That is how it happened that the economy of the Croats and the Bosniaks became more dynamic than that of the Serbs. That was the second main reason for the genocide committed by the Serbs. The Serbs couldn't stand that the "Turks" and the "Ustaše" again would become economically superior. The Serbs knew that power belongs to those who control the money. It was not by a coincidence that the greatest targets of the Serbian genocide were exactly those Bosniaks who succeeded in the business world. It was the strategic interest of the Serbs to separate themselves from the more vital and capable Bosniaks. That is why anyone who accepts the division of Bosnia is doing that for the benefit of the Serbian national interest.

On the other hand, because the Bosniaks lived so (almost) evenly spread throughout Bosnia, the division of Bosnia would certainly signify the disappearance of Bosniaks in the foreseeable future. That is why the mortal enemy of Bosnia is anyone who promotes its division. For the Bosniaks, there shouldn't be a higher and more significant goal of a unified Bosnia, because the alternative is the question of life and death of Bosniaks. That is why the unity of Bosnia cannot be bartered away for the promise of some economic aid, as is happening according to the Dayton peace process. Seeking economic aid in order to sign the peace agreement, in whichever form it takes, is the death blow to Bosnia, which can never be forgiven to those who committed it. The bases for the existence of a people—such as its sovereignty, territories, and the national dignity—are priceless. There is no compromise there. The country's leaders should not even bring into question such issues. That is why in all the countries of the world, during the inauguration, when the leader takes his oath, he swears that he will defend with his life the sovereignty, territorial integrity, and the constitution of his country. Bosnia is disappearing only because its president has abandoned those foundations, acquired through thousands of years of experience about the state.

2

BOSNIA AND HERZEGOVINA
WITHIN YUGOSLAVIA

2.1. Bosnia-Herzegovina before the Agrokomerc Affair

The 1974 Amendments to the Yugoslav Constitution are of such importance that they are usually referred to as the 1974 Constitution. Just as they have done for other republics, these Amendments have confirmed the statehood of Bosnia-Herzegovina. However, in order to keep those Amendments from becoming just some dead letters on paper, the Bosnian patriots who were a part of the then leadership were forced to fight a long political battle with the Serbian lobby in Bosnia-Herzegovina. Using the terminology of that day, the Serbian lobby was referred to as the *unitarists* (unionists), which means that they preferred the idea of a strong central government in Belgrade rather than the strong governments in republics, while the other side, which was fighting for a stronger statehood for Bosnia was referred to as the *separatists*. Working under the conditions of the communist rules (rubber stamping), that struggle was conducted using an intricate code language so that the majority of the Bosnians weren't sure who was who. The words *unitarists* and the *separatists* were used often, but only in a general context, without pointing to a particular person.

Among those struggling for the independence of Bosnia, the main protagonists were Mr. Džemal Bijedić, Hamdija Pozderac, Dr. Fuad Muhić, Dr. Ibrahim Festić. Among the Croats of Bosnia, the main activists were Mr. Branko Mikulić and Hrvoje Ištuk. There weren't any particularly noticeable opposition (Serbian) members. There was no need for them. The members of the Serbian community, on all levels, were working diligently toward the "strengthening of Yugoslavia." In reality, that meant employing as many Serbs as possible in the government, army, police, universities, schools, better and more prestigious companies, and so on. The Serbs kept control over the Yugoslav People's Army (JNA) and over the counterintelligence organization (KOS).

Prior to the 1974 Constitutional Amendments, the Serbs completely controlled all important Yugoslav institutions. Early in 1977, Mr. Džemal Bijedić, a distinguished Bosnian patriot, was killed while functioning as the president of the Federal Executive Council (the governing body of Yugoslavia). The so-called accident in which he died (near Sarajevo) has never been completely explained. The Bosniaks have never fully understood how much they have lost by the death of Mr. Džemal Bijedić. At a ceremony marking the fourth anniversary of his death, two documentaries about his life and works were shown to the faculty of the Mostar University, which was named after him. One of those documentaries was about Bijedić's diplomatic travels; the other was about his work in the Federal Executive Council.

During the second film, there were several of his arguments with Serbs that were presented without any editing and without any glossing over of the issues. Such open discussions have never been shown to the general public in Bosnia-Herzegovina. This documentary shows the courage and enthusiasm with which he opposed the Serbian lobby.

It became clear to me that particular film would never be shown on TV. The Serbs who ruled the Bosnian state TV network would never allow something like that in favor of Bosnian statehood to be seen by Bosnians. It turned out I was right. The powerful Serbian lobby in Bosnia-Herzegovina was able to keep under the informative blockade even the dead president of the federal government, Mr. Džemal Bijedić.

Soon after the death of Džemal Bijedić, the powerful Serbian lobby in Bosnia-Herzegovina tried to discredit and remove the next Bosnian leader, Mr. Hamdija Pozderac, who was also devoted to the Republic of Bosnia-Herzegovina. Today's Chetniks' supreme leader (Vojvoda) and the then professor at the College of Political Science in Sarajevo, Dr. Vojislav Šešelj, has learned that one of the students of Mr. Pozderac, copied (plagiarized) parts of his dissertation, but was not punished for it by Mr. Pozderac. Because the student, Brano Miljus, has risen to a very high position within the central committee of the communist party, a big controversy was born, whose goal was the removal from power of Mr. Hamdija Pozderac. However, at that time (1979), Mr. Pozderac succeeded in defending himself, and it was Šešelj who had to leave Sarajevo. What surfaced during that episode was the revelation as to what really irritated Šešelj: the national affirmation of the Bosniaks, whose ethnic self-determination was recognized in 1970, under the name Bosnian Muslims, and the ever-growing autonomy of Bosnia-Herzegovina. Šešelj pointed his finger at "Muslim nationalists within the Central Committee of the Bosnian Communist Party." I will mention a few of them: Mr. Hamdija Pozderac, Hasan Grabčanović, Dr. Atif Purivatra, and Dr. Fuad Muhić, among others. They enabled authors like Dr. Muhamed Hadžijahic, Muhsin Rizvić, Mehmedelija Mak Dizdar, Dr. Kasim Suljević, and Dr. Hamdija Cemerlić to publish their papers and books in which it has been proven that the Bosnian Muslims exist as a separate ethnic group—i.e., that they are neither Serbs nor Croats of the Muslim faith. It was the first crucial step toward Bosnian independence, because it stopped the ethnic assimilation of Bosniaks (a.k.a. Bosnian Muslims) into the Serbs and Croats.

During the spring of 1983, a group of so-called Muslim Fundamentalists was arrested in Sarajevo. They were accused of the conspiracy against the Bosnian Constitution. The trial lasted the entire summer, and the sentences were draconian. Among the accused were Mr. Alija Izetbegović, Omer Behmen, Hasan Čengić, Edhem Bičakčić, and Džemaludin Latić, today's Bosnian leadership. At that time, I was surprised by the fact that during the trial of those Muslims, the most active cooperation with the prosecutors came from Hamdija Pozderac and Dr. Fuad Muhić, men who were accused by Šešelj as being "the flowers of Muslim nationalism" and who were proven Bosnian patriots. (Namely, the so-called political trials were initiated by the government during the Communist rule if the accusation was "conspiracy against the Bosnian Constitution.") Many Bosniaks were convinced that they were witnessing "Bosnian Muslim" communists trying Muslim believers, and that they were playing into the hands of the powerful Serbian lobby in Bosnia-Herzegovina. (The term "Bosnian Muslim Communist" is not contradictory because "Bosnian Muslims" was the official ethnic, not religious, designation, hence, it was possible to have communists among the ethnic group of Bosnian Muslims.) That widely spread opinion about the trial separated Pozderac from many Bosniaks and also made him very vulnerable. That vulnerability would resurface when the Serbian clique tried again to remove Bosnian patriots from power, Pozderc's friends and followers, during the Agrokomerc Affair, which will be described later in this chapter.

The Serbian propaganda insisted that Bosnia was a "dark nation," where all those who opposed the Bosnian government would be persecuted and prosecuted, referring to Izetbegović's trial, where "Bosnian Muslim Communists were prosecuting Muslim believers." That kind of Serbian propaganda attracted many Bosnian Muslims to become sided with Izetbegović as a victim of communist rule, against Pozderac's government. Those who knew that Pozderac was a true Bosnian patriot were interpreting Izetbegović's trial as Pozderac's way of removing the political amateurs who could end up disrupting the process of Bosnian independence. At that time, no one could imagine that there could be Muslims willing to partition Bosnia, and that that was the reason why those Muslims were being prosecuted by Pozderac's government. It was well known that partition of Bosnia-Herzegovina has always been the Serbian goal, but it was inconceivable that there could be Muslims in Bosnia who had similar ideas. No one even noticed that Izetbegović's book *Islamic Declaration* was published by the Belgrade publishing house Srpska rec (Serbian Word), an unabashed Chetniks (Serbian extremist) business, and also that it was Šešelj, the Serbian leader, who circulated petitions to have the "Muslim intellectuals" released from prisons. At Šešelj's initiative, even a leftist-leaning group of European philosopher from the so-called Korčula School took a stand and protected the "Islamic intellectuals." No one among the Bosniaks (a.k.a. Bosnian Muslims) paid attention to the fact that Izetbegović kept repeating during the trial that in *Islamic Declaration*, he wasn't thinking about Bosnia-Hercegovina but about some other Islamic state in which the Muslims would be 80 percent of the population.

Much later in 1993, when he returned from Geneva, where he had just signed the Tuđman/Milošević plan of "union of three Bosnias" did Alija Izetbegović declare that the Muslims would get a state within former Bosnia-Herzegovina in which they would be approximately 80 percent of the population. It was only then that it became clear which state he had in mind when talking about a state with 80 percent Muslims in *Islamic Declaration*. It became clear and obvious that Alija Izetbegović had a deal with the Serbs and had been working for the division of Bosnia-Herzegovina since before the trial. It became clear why Bosnian patriot Pozderac prosecuted and Serbian nationalists as Šešelj supported Izetbegović. The partitioning of Bosnia in order to create a smaller Islamic state was in the best Serbian interest. In all of this, Pozderac committed a grave error. Thinking that he removed Izetbegović from political life by putting him in prison for fourteen years, he didn't explain to the Bosnian people who is Alija Izetbegović or that he was really helping the Serbs and that Izetbegović's goal was the same as the Serbian goal—the division of Bosnia-Herzegovina. Later, when during the Agrokomerc affair the Serbs removed Pozderac's followers, and when Izetbegović was released from prison ahead of time, Izetbegović emerged with the laurels of an anti-communist and as a "Muslim" victim of Communism. That enabled Izetbegović to emerge as the leader of the "Bosnian Muslims" during the crucial period in Bosnia's history, but more importantly, it enabled him to carry out the division of Bosnia. He made it possible for the Serbs to create a separate state of the Republika Srpska, which was recognized by Izetbegović and Muhamed Sacirbay (Bosnian Secretary of state at that time) on September 26, 1995, in Geneva. He pretends to the Muslim world that he is creating an Islamic state. In fact, he is creating a Serbian state Republika Srpska on 49 percent of the territory of Bosnia-Herzegovina. In order to get Croatian approval for it, he is giving a piece of Republic of Bosnia-Herzegovina (five counties) to Croats as well. The rest of Bosnia-Herzegovina, around 20 percent of the territory, will be futureless reservations in a few disconnected enclaves for the remaining Bosniaks.

Let's return to Izetbegović's trial of 1983. In the trial transcripts, there are unquestionable proofs that Izetbegović's accusers were those whose interest was the freedom of Bosnia-Herzegovina, and that Izetbegović was sided with Serbs fighting for the preservation of Yugoslavia. Here is a quote from the final speech by Mr. Izetbegović from August 16, 1983, during the trial, which was also called "the Sarajevo process."

"In conclusion, I would like to say that I didn't do any harm to the Yugoslav state. The harm was done by those who initiated this process. These narrow-minded and localized aspirations have already brought some heavy damage to this country (Yugoslavia, M.B.). That happened as a result of this case. This process was initiated only by those who could see no farther than the local (Bosnian, M.B.) interest.

While on the subject of Yugoslavia, I can only say that I loved it as much as one can love his homeland. I even loved the way it looks on the map."

Let us remember the Serbian terminology of those days, when "those who are narrow-minded localists can't see farther from their thresholds," and that they contribute to the disintegration of Yugoslavia.

Even Milošević would be proud of such (Izetbegović's) jargon.

Here, I have to digress a little. We can see that such code phrases were used long before Milošević assumed power. Dr. Nenad Kecmanović, one of the most devious politicians among the Serbs at that time, was the first to arm his fellow Serbs with such phrases and slogans. Actually, even before Tito's death 1980, Dr. Kecmanović started writing articles for the Serbian paper *NIN*, in which he started to dissect and discredit the last Yugoslav constitution from 1974. In this series of articles that were published for several years, he started to introduce the new, Serbian political terminology. He coined such phrases as "national oligarchy" (to describe states' governments), "autarkic economies" (to describe the different states' economies), "the narrow-minded localized views" (in describing local and state interests), "own domain" (for one's own republic/state), and so on. With those articles, Dr. Kecmanović became one of the key people in the Serbian nationalistic awakening, which, as always, ended in the genocide against their neighbors—the Albanians, Croats, and Bosniaks. It is not true that it was Milošević who has reawakened Serbian nationalism. Just the opposite is true—once their nationalist passions were awakened, it was the Serbs who chose a leader that fit their needs.

It would also be interesting to note that it was Dr. Kecmanović who hired Šešelj at the Political School of the Sarajevo University, and that he protected Šešelj during the later attacks on the Bosnian leadership. All that did not prevent Izetbegović from accepting Dr. Nenad Kecmanović to become a member of the Bosnian presidency in the war until Kecmanović escaped to Serbia!?

2.2. The Serbian Academy Fights for Izetbegović's Freedom

The Serbian Academy of Arts and Sciences (SANU) made, in 1986, a decisive motion to change the Yugoslav Constitution. That was the first step toward the war. Namely, in that document, they determined what the Serbian national interest is—i.e., they proclaimed that "all Serbs should live in one state." That meant a changing of borders of the neighboring states Croatia, Bosnia-Herzegovina, and Macedonia, where Serbian minorities lived; and that meant war.

The Serbian academics knew that according to the international laws, borders cannot be changed by force but by negotiations with the legal representatives of the neighboring states. That is why they needed somebody who was willing to negotiate the new borders. Having in mind that Dr. Franjo Tuđman in Croatia, Alija Izetbegović in Bosnia, and Dr. Ibrahim Rugova in Kosova are leaders who are willing to negotiate with Serbs about everything, including changing borders and constitutions, the question arose: was this just a coincidence, or did the Serbian secret police help those three men to become national leaders in the states that would be targeted for Serbian expansion? Thanks to those three men, the victims of the Serbian aggression were never unified; hence, the Serbs were able to massacre them one at a time. Is this also a coincidence?

I don't know the answer regarding Croatian leader Franjo Tuđman, the Kosova leader Ibrahim Rugova, but it is evident that Izetbegović had a secret agenda with the Serbs.

An illustration of how the Serbian academics were determined to let Izetbegović out of jail can be found in the book *Sarajevski Process* published by the Bosniaken Institute in Zurich in 1987. On pages 271 to 272, there is a letter that Serbian academics sent to the Presidency of Yugoslavia and that of Bosnia-Herzegovina requesting for Izetbegović's group to be released from the jail years ahead of time. Why were Serbian academics so worried about Izetbegović's freedom of speech when at that time there were hundreds of prisoners of all ethnic backgrounds, including Serbs, sentenced for "anti-constitutional propaganda and activities"? The leading Serbian academics were known as hard-liners. According to Serbian propaganda, Izetbegović was the example of Muslim fundamentalism rising in Bosnia. Their fight for a "Muslim fundamentalist Izetbegović" was surprising, indeed. Can somebody imagine members of Likud party helping the leader of Hamas to publish his book, and then fighting for his freedom? Here are the names of Serbian academics who were the members of the SANU's body, called Committee for Freedom of Speech, who wrote the letters lobbying for Izetbegović's freedom:

Matija Becković
Professor Dr. Dimitrije Bogdanović

Dr. Kosta Čavoški
Dobrica Ćosić
Professor Dr. Andrija Gams
Dr. Ivan Janković
Professor Dr. Neca Jovanov
Professor Dr. Mihajlo Marković
Dragoslav Mihajlović
Borislav Mihajlović - Mihiz
Professor Dr. Nikola Milošević
Tanasije Mladenović
Dr. Gojko Nikoliš
Professor Dr. Predrag Palavestra
Misa Popović
Professor Dr. Radovan Samardic
Mladen Srbinović
Professor Dr. Dragoslav Srejović
Professor Dr. Ljubomir Tadić
President of the Committee, Ljubomir Tadić

2.3. The Agrokomerc Affair

The Agrokomerc Affaire started in 1988, when it was published that large amounts of noncovered and worthless checks and promissory notes were issued by the Agrokomerc company from Velika Kladusa. In fact, those notes were covered by the company's property in domestic animals. The Agrokomerc setup started when the Belgrade "independent" daily *Borba* published that Agrokomerc promissory notes are not valid. Suddenly nobody wanted to sell food for the animals. That caused the deaths of millions of animals within a couple of weeks. Then the Agrokomerc promissory notes really become worthless. The fact that its CEO, Mr. Fikret Abdić, was placed in that position by Mr. Hakija Pozderac, a brother of the Bosnian leader, Hamdija Pozderac, was used by the Serbian lobby in Bosnia as a weapon to expel the followers of Mr. Pozderac from any leadership positions in Bosnia-Herzegovina. During the conflict with the Bosnian patriots, many members of the Bosnian bureaucracy were used, of whom most had Muslim names and supposedly represented the Bosniaks' (Bosnian Muslim) interests in Bosnia but in fact were pro-Serbian politicians, or simply corrupt by their own well-being. They completely forgot about the people they came from.

Their homeland was Yugoslavia (instead of Bosnia-Herzegovina). Those corrupt politicians took side after it became clear who would be the winners. Once they sided with the winners, they helped them to finish off the victim. Mr.

Hamdija Pozderac made a crucial mistake when he resigned his future position as the head of the Constitutional commission of Yugoslavia. He knew that his position and function bothered the Serbs, who wanted to change the Constitution of Yugoslavia and the return of a strong central government (unitarists). He thought that by removing himself from "the Yugoslav scene," he would be left alone in Bosnia. However, by resigning, he showed weakness, which meant the Serbian lobby, followed by all the scavengers with Muslim names but Yugoslavia at heart, turned against him and his followers. Usually, a man doesn't remember these insignificant corrupt people, so even I remember only three of them: Nijaz Dizdarević, Raif Dizdarević, and Seid Maglajlija.

On the other (Bosnian patriotic) side, there were, in addition to Mr. Hamdija Pozderac, Munir Mesihović, Ferhad Kotorić, Avdo Čampara, Hakija Pozderac, Sadi Čemalović, and Jole Musa, just to mention a few. These patriots are some of the people removed from high positions in the Bosnian government during the time of the Agrokomerc affair and the anti-bureaucratic revolution. There were several young and well-educated Bosnian politicians who surfaced on the political scene during that period: Dr. Fuad Muhić, Muhamed Abadžić, Nijaz Skenderagić, Fatima Zubović, and Edina Rešidović, the prosecutor from the Sarajevo process in 1983. It is interesting to note that except for Skenderagić and Rešidović, all others later offered their support to the SDA (Izetbegović) government. They didn't do that as a career move but because they saw what peril awaits Bosnians. If they were only interested in their careers, during the Agrokomerc affair, they would have sided with Milan Uzelac, Savo Čečur, Miroslav Jančić, Milanko Renovica, and other protagonists of the Serbian lobby and "antibureaucratic" revolution, as was done by Raif and Nijaz Dizdarević and Seid Maglajlija. As opposed to the SDS (Serbian political party) and the HDZ (Croatian political party), who gladly accepted all the ex-communists into their ranks, the SDA (mostly Bosnian Muslim political party) didn't accept all—only a few chosen ones, whose criterion was characterized by a statement from Mr. Izetbegović at the party's second Congress in 1994: "It is better to choose those who are honest than those who are capable." When you observe the behavior of his current collaborators, such as Dr. Kasim Trnka, Džemaludin Latić, Edhem Bičakčić, Kemo Muftić, and others, you will notice that the part of his "motto" that says "honest" actually means completely obedient.

After the "Agrokomerc affair, the things started changing fast. The Bosnian Constitution was changed in order to facilitate free elections in Bosnia. Alija Izetbegović and his followers were easily released from jail. Mr. Adil Zulfikarpašić, the leading Bosnian decedent to the communist role, talked about that to me during his visit to Boston in spring 1995: "Two days after Izetbegović's release from prison, he was in Zurich visiting me. I remember that during the 1983 trial, he lost all his civil and constitutional rights and that these rights cannot be restored without due process. When I asked Izetbegović how he got his passport so fast, he could not find better answer in the moment and said, "Oh, they just gave it to me." If one is familiar with the situation in Bosnia at that time, and when one knows who can issue a passport on such short notice, (namely, the police that was completely under Serbian control), the question arises: "Who is Alija Izetbegović?" Why would the Serbs facilitate the creation of a Muslim" political organization (SDA)? Our suspicions increase when we remember the support to Izetbegović made by Karadžić just before the elections: "If Duraković is elected, there is going to be war, if Izetbegović is elected, we'll negotiate." (Dr. Nijaz Duraković was a leader of the Social-Democratic Party of Bosnia-Herzegovina (former communists) in which equally participated Serbs, Croats, and Bosniaks. They were devoted to the civil society, as it was described in the Constitution of The Republic of Bosnia-Herzegovina, rather than ethnic partition.)

Today, after all the "peace" proposals that Izetbegović signed so far, it is clear that Karadžić needed Izetbegović, primarily so that he could conduct the war more successfully, specifically, so he could have someone in the opposing camp who would with his signatures legalize for Serbs the conquered territories of Bosnia. There was a clear attempt by the communist organizations in the predominantly Serbian parts of Bosnia, to neutralize Dr. Nijaz Duraković, before the elections. In other words, those patriotic Bosniaks who could gain in popularity had to be silenced in order to ensure Izetbegović's assuming the title as the head of all the Bosniaks.

2.4. Izetbegović's Party of Democratic Action—SDA

Izetbegović's political party, the SDA was established on March 27, 1990. That certainly was a surprise. Under the laws in force at that time, every participant of that organization could have received ten years in prison. According to Bosnia-Herzegovina laws, it was forbidden to organize political parties based on ethnic agenda. Besides, to the large majority of Bosnians, who were brought up in the spirit of brotherhood and unity, the subject of ethnicity was taboo in public relations. As opposed to the Serbs, the Bosniaks didn't have a strong sense of ethnic or national identity. Even the Serbs in Bosnia-Herzegovina contained their ethnic and nationalistic sentiments, at least in public. That is why it seemed unbelievable to see forty Bosniak men and women sitting in front of TV cameras as proof that it was the Muslims who were the first to initiate the division along ethnic lines in Bosnia. That was a strong point in favor of the Serbs. From that moment on, a whole series of unusual and strange events for the communist rule took place. Although the SDA was several months away from being registered as a political party, from that moment on, the meetings and conventions of the local branches of the SDA were not stopped anywhere in Bosnia, except in Travnik. In the most beautiful hall of the Holiday Inn in Sarajevo, the constitutional convention of SDA was held on June 9, 1990. Izetbegović's people freely carried green (Muslim) flags throughout eastern Herzegovina, Majevica, Grmec, and in many other predominantly Serbian regions of Bosnia where Bosniaks were attacked, or even killed, for transgressions much smaller than the green flag. It was clear that the creators of the "anti-bureaucratic" revolt allowed Izetbegović and his followers to create a lot of attention for themselves and emerge as the leaders of Bosniaks. I suppose that Izetbegović had that honor because in *Islamic Declaration*, he wrote that Pakistan was our "dress rehearsal." With that statement, he acknowledged that he agrees to huge shifts and transfers of population in order to divide the Republic of Bosnia-Herzegovina along the ethnic lines. Maybe that was the reason he had the attention of the British administration. Namely, it is known that representatives of Great Britain visited Izetbegović twice in the prison in Zenica. Those ideas of moving the population in order to create "ethnically clean territories" were promoted publicly just before the 1990 elections by protagonists of the Greater Serbia project.

My first encounter with Izetbegović took place several days prior to the referendum on Bosnia's independence, at the end of February of 1992. That happened at the meeting in the amphitheater of the Sarajevo city ward of Old Town. The meeting was called with only one item on the agenda—"preparations for the upcoming referendum." Every Bosnian municipality president and secretary of the SDA party was invited. I was the president of the public relations department of the Tuzla chapter (and not actually invited), but I was sent in place of the Tuzla president Dr. Salih Kulenović, who had another engagement that day. The elite of the SDA party was present at that meeting. The reason for the meeting—preparations for the referendum—was taken care of quickly. That part of the agenda was taken care of by good organizers Mr. Hasan Čengić and Ms. Amila Omersoftić. It wasn't planned for Izetbegović to appear at that meeting. We were all pleasantly surprised when we were informed that Izetbegović would like to address the meeting. Dr. Ejup Ganić, a member of the Bosnia-Herzegovina presidency, accompanied him.

Izetbegović addressed us with approximately these words: "Maybe we will be asked to negotiate the internal division of Bosnia-Herzegovina into ethnic cantons. Maybe it wouldn't be so bad to define those areas where the Muslims are in the majority. That doesn't mean that there would be a major shift in population—only those cantons with the predominantly Muslim population would be called Muslim cantons, those with predominantly Serbian population would be called Serb cantons, and, of course, those with a Croat majority would be called Croat cantons.

The delegates spoke one by one, and it became clear that the great majority of them wasn't interested in accepting any partition of Bosnia-Herzegovina.

The delegate from Gacko was the clearest on the subject—I think his name was Bajro Greljo—who said, "Let's not fool ourselves. If Gacko was proclaimed a Serbian canton, there wouldn't be a single Muslim left there." The only one out of two hundred who supported Izetbegović's suggestion was the delegate from Gračanica. It might have been because the Bosnian Muslims were over 80 percent of its population. I also got the floor. I told the delegates that under no circumstances should there be ethnic borders within Bosnia. If they were drawn, Bosnia would eventually be divided along those lines, just as Yugoslavia disintegrated. Hearing those words, Eljup Ganić turned and approvingly nodded his head. I concluded at that time that Ganić was a true Bosnian patriot, and I didn't suspect him of any wrongdoing for a long time.

At the end of the meeting, realizing that he couldn't get the division's approval of his idea, Izetbegović took advantage of the mentality of the "little" people who were always in the majority and didn't want to confront the leaders—he got permission to at least negotiate with the Serbs, but not to agree on anything. The idea of the negotiations was to buy time. Although I didn't agree with any negotiations about our Constitution, negotiations could be somewhat justified by the fact that we were unarmed compared to the Yugoslav People Army, so every day of negotiations could be used to better organize and arm ourselves. Besides, up to that point, the Serbs and the Croats hadn't committed any atrocities against the Bosniaks yet, so the negotiations didn't seem so far out of line, out of dignity.

2.5. The First Congress of the SDA

I received my invitation to the First Congress (Convention) of the SDA that started on November 29, 1991, from Ms. Amila Omersoftić, then member of the Central Committee of the SDA, and later the wartime director of the Bosnian Radio and Television. She had tried earlier to start an action of connecting the Bosniak intellectuals with the SDA party. The enrollment of new intellectual members was stopped by Izetbegović himself by handing over the membership affairs to a cleric, Hasan Čengić. Amila couldn't accept the rejection of intellectuals at such a crucial moment of the Bosnian history. That is why she sent the invitations to the First Congress (of SDA), hoping that some new intellectuals would influence and improve the SDA.

All those attending would remember that congress because of the fighting between Izetbegović and Fikret Abdić. (Abdić is a very ambitious man, with a big ego, who does not have any other political agenda, except to become a leader. Later in the war, he collaborated with Serbs in order to reach his selfish goals and become a leader in his region.) I realized back then that Abdić wasn't a very clever politician. Izetbegović played him like a little child. But Abdić didn't know when he had had enough, so he kept trying until he had completely lost any stature he held with the SDA.

I took part in the work of the Commission for economic questions. By that time, Croatia and Slovenia had already introduced their own currency, and they had huge amounts of unusable Yugoslav dinars. Besides that, Belgrade was also still printing huge amounts of dinars. These worthless dinars were being spent in Bosnia for the purchase of German marks and many of the goods manufactured in Bosnia. I decided to initiate that question at the SDA Congress. On a piece of paper I turned in to the commission, in addition to my name, I also explained what the question was going to be about. The president of the commission was the minister of industry for the state of Bosnia, Dr. Resad Bektic, and the vice president was Dr. Hasan Muratović, later, during the war known as the minister of the Bosnian government in charge of the UNPROFOR relations. Because I was sitting in the front row, I noticed that Dr. Muratović, upon seeing the subject that I wanted to address, placed my request on the top.

However, when the president of the commission, Bektic, read my note, and when he was supposed to call on me to present my concern, he quietly took my slip and placed it at the bottom. I became upset and strongly objected. Later, I did get the opportunity to speak. At that moment, continuing to use the Yugoslav dinar as the official currency was only beneficial to Serbia. Bektic's behavior could have only been indicative of a Serbian supporter. That day, I was watching on TV news that delegates to the other commissions were also demanding the introduction of a Bosnian currency. The proof that I was right and that that was a crucial question in Bosnia-Herzegovina was the fact that all those delegates requesting the introduction of Bosnian currency independently came up with the same conclusion. However, Izetbegović didn't pay attention to any of that. Bosnian currency was introduced much later, during the war. At the time, I thought that Izetbegović simply didn't realize the importance of the question of currency for a newly independent state. However, from some of Izetbegović's statement, it was clear that he was very intelligent and well informed, so I couldn't understand his reluctance to introduce Bosnia's own currency. That really did confuse me, but I do admit that at that time, I didn't yet realize that even Izetbegović was working against Bosnia-Herzegovina, and that that was the reason there was room at the SDA leadership level for people like Resad Bektic.

3

YUGOSLAVIA CEASED TO EXIST
BY LEGAL DISSOLUTION

3.1 The Yugoslav Fédération

Yugoslavia was a federation composed of six states (starting from the north-west to the south-east): Slovenia, Croatia, Bosnia-Herzegovina, Serbia, Montenegro, and Macedonia. The largest of the six states, Serbia, also contained two autonomous regions—Vojvodina on the north and Kosovo on the south. Those two regions were "awarded" to Serbia by France and England at the Versailles Peace conference at the end of WWI (1914–1918) as a reward for Serb cooperation. The reason those two regions were autonomous within Serbia was that the Serbian population in them historically was a minority, and Vojvodina was never even a part of Serbia before the WWI. The majority of the population in Vojvodina were Catholics: Hungarians, Croats, Germans, Czech, and Slovaks. The Serbs only started becoming the majority of the population during WWII, when they killed many of the Catholic people and colonized Vojvodina with hundreds of thousands of Serbs from economically undeveloped regions of ex-Yugoslavia. The Albanians still make up over 80 percent of Kosovo population. Every republic and both of the autonomous regions had their presidency, government, and parliament. In addition, each republic and autonomous region had an independent judiciary system, police, a school system, mail service, and railroads.

3.2 The Yugoslav People's Army and the Territorial Defense

After the 1974 change of the constitution, it is very close to the truth when stating that of all the "federal" institutions in Yugoslavia, only the army (JNA) was totally under a single control and not divided and influenced by the state lines. Besides the federal army in Yugoslavia, there was also the territorial defense, which somewhat resembled the American National Guard. Every republic (state) had control over its own territorial defense. Since the territorial defense in each republic had its own arsenal, it would be reasonable to say that such territorial defense units were, in fact, the republics' armies. The weapons for those territorial units were purchased by the local companies and the republic governments.

With the development and maintenance of such units, Tito's goal of a true people's army and the defense was realized. Although Tito justified the concept of the Territorial Defense by stating that such an all-inclusive force was needed to fend off an external attack, he had a different goal in mind. He was more concerned with the Serbian expansionism within Yugoslavia. By creating the Territorial Defense, Tito enabled every republic to protect itself from the Yugoslav People's Army, which was controlled by the Serbs. The concept of such territorial defense was totally successful in Slovenia and completely useless in Bosnia-Herzegovina. Unfortunately, Bosnian socialist government before Izetbegović did not offer any resistance to the Serbian disarming of the Bosnian Territorial Defense forces. They accepted the offer of the Serbian-dominated Yugoslav People's Army (JNA) to safeguard arms of the Bosnian Territorial Defense forces. Izetbegović's government continued the suicidal policy of trusting to JNA, even when the war broke out?! For example, many of us still remember when the JNA hauled away some fifty truckloads of the Territorial Defense weapons from the old center of Sarajevo at the beginning of the war.

Although the total command of the JNA was completely centralized on the federal level, the recruiting was done on the local, usually municipal, level. That meant that the lists of the potential recruiting candidates were in the hands of the local governments. That fact had a crucial effect on the future of Yugoslavia. For example, during the war in Croatia, Macedonia used its constitutional right and made a decision to remove (hide) from the JNA all the recruiting candidates' lists. That is how it happened that Kiro Gligorov (Macedonia's leader) succeeded in preventing the recruiting and sending of young Macedonians to the Croatian front.

But the government of Alija Izetbegović refused to do the same for the Republic of Bosnia-Herzegovina (R B&H). I remember when Tuzla's members of the Muslim Intellectuals Society Preporod (Rebirth) met in an effort to contact Izetbegović so they could ask him to do the same for his people that Gligorov had done for the Macedonians. I personally went to the SDA Izetbegović headquarters and, together with the party's secretary, contacted Osman Brka, who immediately forwarded Tuzla's request to Izetbegović. Izetbegović made an appearance on the TV news that evening. But instead of using his constitutional right in ordering the local governments to remove the list of recruits from JNA access, he only said, "Some (people) notified me that the JNA is mobilizing Muslims in order to send them to the Croatian war. My message to the Muslims is that I wouldn't send my son to serve in the Yugoslav army." That was one more sample of betrayal of the R B&H Constitution. The JNA used the fact that those lists weren't removed and, in a lightning action, came into possession of them, thus giving them the necessary information to enlist young Bosnians. Every young man from R B&H who was recruited from that point on is the responsibility and the fault of Alija Izetbegović.

There were a few places where by the simple reaction of the local people, those lists were hidden and kept away from the JNA. I remember the grand rally in Bratunac, where the JNA was prevented by the people of Bratunac from acquiring those lists from their municipality. The embarrassed JNA withdrew, but returned several months later, in April of 1992, and took revenge for the earlier embarrassment and slaughtered those present at the prewar rally. The stadium and the gymnasium in Bratunac became known for the Serbian massacre of the people of Bratunac.

Even in Tuzla, the mothers tried to prevent the JNA from taking recruiting lists from the municipality building. A strong resistance was also put up by the head of the recruitment center, Mehmed Žilić. Only when the soldiers of the JNA pointed their guns at him did he give them those lists of potential recruits from Tuzla. What followed was the wholesale recruiting of young Bosnians for the Serbian war in Croatia, especially the drivers, who were taken by force into the Croatian war, instead of being protected by their own Bosnian government, which had the constitutional right to remove those lists from the access to the JNA. Only after the JNA came into possession of the R B&H recruiting lists was there an announcement by the SDA (Alija Izetbegović) to the local governments to organize demonstrations against the JNA. It is obvious that these protest meetings didn't have any effect except to show that Izetbegović was "upset" about the JNA taking these lists and, with that, trouncing the constitution of the Republic of Bosnia and Herzegovina. To those of us who knew that Izetbegović refused to protect those lists, it became obvious that Izetbegović was just trying to fool the Bosnians in order to cover up one more of his "mistakes." But even then, I still didn't realize that all his actions were just a part of the elaborate plot of his betrayal of Bosnia and Herzegovina.

Maybe someone will wonder how come no one started to suspect any wrongdoing on the part of Izetbegović, even after that many mistakes. The answer is simple: a human being simply has to believe someone. One has trouble suspecting his own president of betrayal, and besides, a human being cannot imagine such level of dishonesty—the betrayal of the president.

3.3 The Assembly, Presidency, and the Government of Yugoslavia

The Socialist Federal Republic of Yugoslavia had its presidency, assembly, and government. The presidency was composed of eight members—one from each of the states, plus one from each of the autonomous regions (Vojvodina and Kosovo). There were also two houses of Parliament, the Federal House and the House of Republics and (autonomous) Regions. In the Federal House, the decisions were made by a simple majority vote of the representatives. In the House of the Republics and Regions, decisions regarding the equality of states and autonomous regions were reached by consensus. This last fact was of tremendous importance in the ending of Yugoslavia. We will be referring to it later.

There are many examples in the modern world that show that the disintegration of a modern state is almost impossible. Lebanon, Iraq, Afghanistan, Estonia, and Cambodia are all states that didn't disintegrate despite the fact that many of them have been occupied for a long time, or that there were conflicts and long wars between the different groups living there. What is it that doesn't allow for a disintegration of a country? It is the international law that prevents disintegration. By the principles of the international law, the borders of a country can't be changed by force—that is, the world cannot recognize borders changed by the use of force. That principle of the international law (UN charter) was introduced in order to discourage eventual aggressors. A country's borders can only be changed by the agreement of the concerned legal authorities. Lebanon wasn't divided into different religious states because none of the Lebanese presidents was willing to break their oath of the presidency and start negotiating the changing of their country's borders, or even the total division.

Now a question arises: How was it then possible for Yugoslavia to come apart? Yugoslavia fell apart because even without war, it could no longer function *legally*. In other words, within the legal framework of the Yugoslav Constitution, it became impossible for any decisions to be made at the federal level. When Slovenia and Croatia withdrew their delegations from the House of the Republics and the Regions, a permanent veto was instituted into that assembly body. The only constitutional solution to that crisis was a declaration of a state of war. However, the presidency has already lost four of its eight legally elected members: Janez Drnovšek (Slovenia), Stjepan Mesić (Croatia), Boško Krunić (Vojvodina), and Riza Sapunđiju (Kosovo). Boško Krunić (Vojvodina) was illegally replaced by Branko Kostic and Riza Sapunđiju (Kosovo) was illegally replaced by Sejdo Bajramović. The world did not recognize Kostić's and Bajramović's legality as members of the Yugoslav Presidency. That is why the Yugoslav Presidency couldn't make any legal decision at that time, and hence, couldn't declare the state of war. The point is that after the collapse of the House of the Republics and Regions, even the presidency couldn't save Yugoslavia. Milošević understood that due to the crumbling of the House of the Republics and Regions, Yugoslavia would soon be declared dead by the world's community. That is why he did all he could to ensure that the disintegration happened along the new borders favorable to the Serbs. In reality, that meant that in this new Serbian-dominated entity, there would also be Montenegro, the Republic of Bosnia and Herzegovina, Macedonia, and a large part of Croatia. In that regard, he encouraged the Slovenians to leave (Yugoslavia) as soon as possible, "the sooner the better."

The United Nations (UN) gave a mandate to the European Community (EC) in 1990 to resolve the Yugoslav constitutional crisis, according to the international laws. Due to the fact that the federal government of Yugoslavia didn't function but the states (republics) did, the Europeans demanded that the states come to some sort of agreement on a new constitution. That is why toward the end of 1990 and the beginning of 1991, meetings were called between the presidents of the republics and the regions. At these negotiations, the representatives of Croatia, Slovenia, and Macedonia insisted on a confederation of the Yugoslav states, while Serbia and Montenegro wanted a federation (a much stronger central government, more favorable to the Serbs). Actually, they too (Serbia and Montenegro) really wanted the collapse of Yugoslavia, since after the 1974 Constitution, Yugoslavia stopped being the Greater Serbia. The problem was that they wanted to change the borders of the republics in order to form Greater Serbia. The Serbs also wanted Serbia to be recognized as a legal continuation of ex-Yugoslavia. The president of the R B&H presidency was behaving very strangely during all these negotiations. It was known that two-thirds of Bosnians wanted separation and independence (from Yugoslavia), or a loose confederation. All the Bosniaks (Muslims) and Croats wanted independence. That was later proven during a referendum on independence held on March 1, 1992. However, Izetbegović was coming out with some very strange proposals. One of them was an "asymmetrical" federation. According to him, that meant that Serbia, Montenegro, Macedonia, and B&H would constitute the federation, which would then enter into a loose confederation with Croatia and Slovenia. That meant he placed B&H and Macedonia under the control of a Greater Serbia.

Fortunately, in the R B&H at that time existed unrestricted public opinion, which strongly criticized Izetbegović for that proposal during the negotiation of presidents of the Yugoslav republics. He was forced to spend many days defending himself from that proposal. He learned that any move to place B&H into the Serbian sphere of influence could cost him his popularity—maybe even his position. The best proof that he has learned his lesson was reported in the book by Milovan Djilas and Nada Gace: *Bosniak Adil Zulfikarpašić*. There, from Zulfikarpašić's conversation with Izetbegović regarding the so-called "historical accord between the Muslims and the Serbs," we see that it was Izetbegović who influenced Zulfikarpašić to reach the accord with Milošević. Hiding behind Adil

Zulfikarpašić and Muhamed Filipović, Izetbegović again tried to realize his project of connecting B&H with Serbia, without risking his own integrity and credibility but that of Zulfikarpašić's and Filipović's."

Let's return to Izetbegović's proposal of an "asymmetrical federation." When introduced to that proposal, Macedonian president Kiro Gligorov rejected it outright, even though Izetbegović introduced it as a joint Izetbegović/Gligorov proposal. After Gligorov's statement regarding that proposal, it was clear that Izetbegović made up the story that Gligorov supported the proposal. The question is asked: "If Izetbegović didn't get an agreement from Gligorov for such a motion, why did Izetbegović propose something like that for Macedonia? Why would a Bosnian try to push Macedonia into the Greater Serbia? There is only one answer possible: Izetbegović was concerned not with the well-being of the Republic of Bosna and Herzegovina but with that of the Greater Serbia.

The third prewar attempt by Izetbegović to deliver B&H to the Serbs was done with the help of the prewar member of the Yugoslav federation assembly— Irfan Ajanović. Ajanović was an important ally of Izetbegović from before the war. One relative of Irfan Ajanović, a Dr. Ekrem Ajanović, professor of the School of Medicine at the University of Tuzla and a representative at both the Republic of B&H Assembly and at the Yugoslav Assembly, told me that Irfan Ajanović was "sacrificed by Izetbegović" in order to give strange and unusual proposals for "tactical reasons." Irfan Ajanović had been a prisoner of Karadžić since the spring of 1993. Since then, there were many negotiations and meetings between Izetbegović and Karadžić on many different subjects, but never about Karadžić's prisoner, Irfan Ajanović. So many of Izetbegović's "diplomats" went undisturbed through the Serbian lines, but an ex–vice president of the Yugoslav Assembly is languishing in Serbian jails, even though in poor health. Looking from the morality point of view, Izetbegović's negotiations with Karadžić, while his key pre-war envoy is in Karadžić's prison, points to his total moral bankruptcy and lack of dignity.

Let's return to Izetbegović's prewar "tactical" proposal to the Federal Assembly. The proposal created by Izetbegović and then presented by Irfan Ajanović was that the Yugoslav Assembly should continue to work with only four federal units. It should adopt a bill that will define a new quorum, without Croatia and Slovenia, in the House of the Republics and Regions and that a simple majority would be enough to render any decisions. All those who followed the Yugoslav political scene knew that since the days of Ranković (a Serbian politician who tried to overthrow Tito in 1966 in order to form the Greater Serbia), such a constitution, where decisions would be made by simple majority, was always a dream of the unitarists (unionists)—that is, the Serbs. It was the possibility of a veto in the House of the Republics and Regions that kept the Serbs from total control of Yugoslavia.

That proposal that favored the Serbian control of Yugoslavia, which would include the R B&H, raised many suspicions about Izetbegović. Unfortunately, these suspicions were related to his ability as the president and not his loyalty to or the betrayal of the Republic of B&H. It is unfortunate that none of the Bosnian people raised an alarm after so many mistakes in favor of Greater Serbia. There were those who believed that it was all about some clever tactic that simple mortals couldn't understand. Some thought that Izetbegović was too naive for politics, but they hoped the others from the government would correct him in the future. No one saw a reason to worry because every time Izetbegović was corrected. It was done by the way of the public media and opinion. That fact also determined the tactic of the future war against the Republic of B&H. It became clear that without eliminating the free media, there would be no possibility of destroying the Republic of Bosnia and Herzegovina—that is, it would be impossible to get an agreement from the Republic of Bosnia and Herzegovina to change its borders and the Constitution. Just so he could eliminate freedom of the press and control the public opinion, and so that Izetbegović and a few of his followers are the only ones who have the authority to decide the future of B&H during the wartime, a total informative blockade was introduced, not only from Bosnian enemies from outside, but also from Izetbegović inside of B&H. The personnel of the B&H Army Second Corp knew that Izetbegović prevented them from installing the wireless telephone service from Tuzla. The equipment was donated by Germany soon after May 15, 1992, a day when Tuzla was liberated, and it could have connected Tuzla to the outside world, had it not been for an order from Izetbegović not to allow the equipment in from Slavonski Brod (Croatia). I can mention this particular case because I have an eyewitness to this event, Colonel Sefcet Bibuljica, of the B&H Army. There are others who wonder why Sarajevo did not have satellite TV during the siege, while every western media, e.g. CNN, had.

Let's return to the problem of the death of Yugoslavia. In addition to the already-mentioned Izetbegović's attempts to annex B&H to Serbia during the series of negotiations between the chiefs of the six Yugoslav states, nothing significant happened. When the negotiations became useless, the Europeans formed a commission of legal experts, the so-called Badinter Commission, whose goal was to resolve the Yugoslav crisis according to the principles of the international laws. The commission didn't have a very difficult task. All the Yugoslav republics kept all the state's institutions; and under those constitutions, the Yugoslav republics were defined as states—actually, countries. Considering that Slovenia and Croatia also held their referendums on their independence, and considering that Yugoslavia could no longer make any legal and legitimate decisions, those two states could have immediately been recognized as independent.

As far as The Republic of B&H is concerned, the opinion of the Badinter's commission was that it too could be recognized as an independent country if the majority of its inhabitants declare so in a referendum to be conducted according to the R B&H Constitution. Knowing that the R B&H civic constitution didn't differentiate between the different ethnic groups, in order for the referendum on the R B&H independence to succeed, it was necessary to only have 50 percent of Bosnian citizens plus one (person) vote for independence. The referendum was held on March 1 and 2, 1992. The voter participation was exceptionally high, over 64 percent voters chose independence. Regardless of the fact that Bosniaks are only 43 percent and Croatians 17 percent of the population, together they still number less than 64 percent. Besides, a few of the Bosniaks and Croats couldn't vote that day. That means that some Serbs and Yugoslavs also voted for Bosnia's independence. It took over a month before the EC agreed to extend the recognition to the R B&H. Despite the fact that the R B&H fulfilled all the legal requirements, it is still the right of any sovereign state whether or not to recognize any state it wants. That right was used by Greece not to recognize Macedonia—even worse, by using its EC veto, Greece succeeded in stalling the rest of Europe from recognizing Macedonia. Because the EC had the mandate from the UN to resolve the Yugoslav crisis, with the Greek veto, even the UN recognition of Macedonia was stopped. Then some might ask, how come so many friends and allies of Serbia recognized the independence of the R B&H? The answer will be given in chapter 5, "The New World Order."

4

THE WAR

4.1 The War in Slovenia

The clash between the JNA (Yugoslav Army) and the Slovenian Territorial Defense started on June 27, 1991, and ended with the ruin of the JNA in a war that lasted less than ten days. It was clearly demonstrated in Slovenia that the JNA didn't have much chance of success in a fight with well-motivated fighters of the Territorial Defense who are fighting for their freedom.

We should mention here that Alija Izetbegović didn't offer any resistance, political or military, when the JNA was hauling away the weapons of the R B&H Territorial Defense, as opposed to the Slovenians who refused to hand over their weapons to the JNA for "safekeeping." The weapons of the R B&H Territorial Defense have been hauled away in 1989 before the SDA assumed power. However, those weapons could have been prevented from leaving from the places where the Bosniaks were in the majority if they were only encouraged to do so by their government, as was the case in Tuzla. The fact that there was no organized attempt to save the TO (Territorial Defense) weapons from Sarajevo's Old Town, which was kept by only thirty JNA soldiers who were encircled by Bosnian soldiers who were willing to surrender, turned out to be a crucial mistake by Alija Izetbegović—a mistake that would cost the citizens of Sarajevo around ten thousand lives. During those times, Alija Izetbegović was meeting regularly with the JNA general Kukanjac, while the Serbs were using bulldozers to open a new road and circumvent the Bosnian Army blockade. Thanks to those Serbian tactics, they succeeded in hauling away over fifty truckloads of infantry weapons from TO Sarajevo—weapons that Izetbegović should have saved for the defenders of Sarajevo.

4.2 The War in Croatia

The war in Croatia started with the so-called log revolution in August of 1990. The Serbian population in certain Croatian regions rebelled by blocking the roads with cut trees, logs, and ambush. The cause for that was the new Croatian Constitution. In the old, communist Croatian Constitution, Croatia was a state of Croats and Serbs living in Croatia. Under the Tuđman's new Constitution, the Serbs became an ethnic minority. That was symbolized by the change of the banner. Instead of the communist flag of Croatia with the red star in the middle, the Croatian flag returned the historical Croatian coat of arms, or as the Serbs called it, the chessboard. Knowing that a state is characterized by its constitution, the Serbs knew well what those changes meant, so the Serbian rebellion was the expected outcome.

The war in Croatia would had started even without such constitutional changes; the Serbs intended to include large parts of Croatia, where Serbs were a majority, into the Greater Serbia. Those sudden changes of the Constitution were Tuđman's favor to Milošević, because the said changes made it easier for Milošević to mobilize the Serbs for war. The holding of free elections in the different Yugoslav states and the victories by the political parties whose goals were independence for their states signified the end of Yugoslavia as the country dominated by Serbs. The victory by Tuđman in the first free elections held in May of 1990 should have signaled to Tuđman that the Serbs were no longer in the full control in Yugoslavia. If they were, they certainly would not have allowed free elections in Croatia and the HDZ (the leading Croatian political party: Croatian Democratic Union) to be formed. However, Tuđman acted as if he didn't realize that Croatia was pretty much free from Serbian control. He should have stabilized the situation until he had consolidated the victory, and ensured Croatia stays within its AVNOJ borders (AVNOJ was the acronym the 1943 creation and mapping of the Socialistic Federate Republic Yugoslavia).

Instead, Tuđman was changing the constitution in the moment most favorable to the Serbs—when they needed an excuse to start the war. The almost fifty years of peace had an inertia of its own. To end this peace and to leave comfortable homes and apartments and go into the woods to fight needed something very provocative for Serbs in Croatia, something more substantive than Milošević's vague dream of a "Greater Serbia." Tuđman handed them that by changing the Constitution and waving the chessboard flag under their noses, which in Serbian mythology was synonymous with hell. The Serbs' problems of recruiting Serb rebels in Croatia ended when Tuđman tried to place the chessboard flag in Knin, the center of Serbian descent.

4.3 What Tuđman Considers "Logical" Borders

Tuđman is trying to place himself on the pedestal of the Founding Father of modern Croatia. However, it should be clear that the beginning of the independence came, thanks to the amendments from 1974 on the Yugoslav Constitution. The credit for the movement to amend the Constitution goes to the Mass Movement of 1971, the Croatian version of the 1971 spring (referring to the Czechoslovakian Spring of 1968 freedom movement). The credit for the start of those changes goes to the Croatians in power at that time: Dr. Savka Dabcević, Dr. Mika Tripalo, and Dr. Ivan Supek, as well as student leaders and other Croatian patriots such as Drazen Budisa, Ivan Čićak, Dobroslav Paraga, and some of whom are still politically active today. Although they had been removed from power by that time, Tito and Kardelj had fulfilled the requests of the Mass Movement and transferred many responsibilities from the federal government in Belgrade to the republics, giving each a central bank and a separate police, educational, and judicial systems. It gave the same to Serbia's two provinces Kosovo and Vojvodina. The two provinces were made a constituent member of the federation, giving them their own parliaments and governments, and giving their leaders seats on Yugoslav's rotating presidency, which assumed power when Tito died. In fact, the Constitution amendments give independence to Yugoslav republics and provinces from Serbia. The Serbs maintained control in the Communist Party of Yugoslavia, the Yugoslav Army, the secret police (KOS), and the police departments in all republics except Slovenia. Such strong Serbian grip on power on the local levels amortized the changes created by the constitutional changes in 1974; other ethnic groups still felt Yugoslavia as a version of the greater Serbia. So that those major changes in the Yugoslav Constitution wouldn't end up being just empty words on paper, we have to thank the effective battle by the Slovenian communists, led by Milan Kučan; Croatian Communists, led by Ivica Račan; Macedonian communists, led by Kiro Gligorov; Kosovo communists, led by Fadil Hoxha; and a part of the Bosnian communists, led by Dr. Nijaz Duraković. They succeeded in breaking up the "bonding cement" of Yugoslavia, the so-called "democratic centralism, in the communist league of Yugoslavia." That fight eventually led to the free elections in Yugoslav states (republics), which by definition meant freedom. Tuđman's policy toward the R B&H maintained his concept of a state—in Tuđman's doctoral dissertation, he stated that the Balkan countries' borders, which were derived from history, should be changed in order to get "logical" ethnic borders. (Dr. Ivo Banac, an American professor from Yale University, wrote about Tuđman's understanding of logical borders several times in the Croatian and Bosnian press during the war—e.g., the publication *Erasmus* in 1993.) That is why Tuđman was more interested in parts of the territory of the R B&H than in the AVNOJ (legal and, hence, internationally recognized) borders of

Croatia. Milošević and the Serbian Academy of Sciences and Arts (SANU) knew really well that the AVNOJ borders of the Yugoslav states and the autonomous regions and the international laws about the unchanging borders were the main obstruction in the creation of the Greater Serbia. That is why Tuđman's stand on logical (i.e., ethnic) borders was a welcome present to the Serbian expansion plans.

It shouldn't be any surprise, then, that Tuđman was prosecuted by Tito regime, right after the constitutional changes in 1974. We should also remember that Tuđman was undisturbed by the police (which was Serbian-controlled even in Croatia) prior to the free elections. The natural outcome of Tuđman's fondness for ethnic borders was his meeting with Milošević in Karađorđevo at the start of 1991, when the division of Bosnia was agreed upon *https://ba.boell.org/de/2019/03/25/karadordevo-und-die-territorial-ethnische-teilung-bosnien-und-herzegowinas*. That meeting eventually led to Tuđman's alliance with Milošević and Karadžić in their war against R B&H. By doing that, Tuđman spat in the face of thousand years of experience, which has led to today's principles of unchanging borders, and instead, he started by experimenting with Croatia and R B&H. The greatest victims of that experiment are the Croats of R B&H. They lost the best and most productive Bosnian lands in the Posavina region, so that the Serbs could create a territorial connection with the Serbian population in Western Bosnia and areas around Knin in Croatia. In return, the Serbs promised them some territories in the eastern Herzegovina, just so they could recreate the old Banovina Hrvatska—the pre-WWII deal between Cvetković (Serb) and Maček (Croat) of the division of Bosnia-Herzegovina.

The later association of Tuđman and Izetbegović is not contrary to his plan of partitioning R B&H. Actually, that alliance is also between two men wanting to divide R B&H, which will be described later.

5

The New World Order

Until the collapse of the Soviet Union, the world functioned in the order called cold war. That world was characterized by the "balance of the fear" because of the huge military of the Warsaw Pact, and the huge nuclear arsenal of the Soviet Union. Although the world was politically divided between two tremendously well-armed and mutually opposed political alliances during that period, Europe enjoyed the longest period of peace in its history. Why? Because Europe was of the greatest importance to both sides, and any military action there could have signified the devastation of interests of one of the two alliances, North Atlantic Treaty Organization (NATO) and Warsaw Pact. One of the characteristics of the cold war period was the lack of recognition of any international norms and standards when the interests of one of the blocks were in question. The best example of that was the constant misuse of veto power by the permanent members of the Security Council of the UN. There was no doubt that the Soviets would veto any resolution of the Security Council if it was directed against any Soviet ally in the world, regardless whether the chastised country was at fault or not.

On the other hand, the United States didn't hesitate to use its veto power if it became necessary to defend its allies, mostly Israel, whether or not Israel was at fault. That created the image of the unjust world where powerful countries do whatever they want, and international laws apply only to the third world countries. When the Warsaw Pact was dissolved, and soon afterward the Soviet Union itself, the question arose as to how would the world function when there was no longer a *parity* between the two blocks? Would the only remaining block, NATO, who economically defeated the other side, take the advantage of the situation? Would NATO dominate the world? Then the president of the United States, Mr. George H. Bush, launched a new theory called the New World Order (NWO). The formula was very simple: The new world order means governing according to the international norms and laws. That meant that all the members of the UN were expected to follow those rules and that breaking those rules meant certain punishment, usually in the form of UN economic sanctions—but if needed, in the form of military intervention as well. That meant that countries who were members of the UN were supposed to behave toward a member nation depending on how well it followed the international laws. Just as in the civil court where a judge was obliged to try the guilty and protect the victim regardless of the victim's color of the skin, nationality, and religion, the same should apply in international relations. It shouldn't matter whether a state was an ally or not, whether it was Muslim or Catholic, whether the population was black or white, or whether the political system was communist or capitalist. The only criteria should be whether or not a particular country was breaking any norms and rules of international behavior. That is how the United States of America behaved during the presidency of George H. W. Bush, who is, in my opinion, the greatest American president ever. Unfortunately, thanks to Clinton, it was a short-lived idea. Clinton diminished the rule of the law in international relations already in Bosnia by facilitating and recognizing Bosnian peace talks that included results of genocide as legitimate negotiating chips. That violated jus cogens norms of international law.

The New World Order doctrine played a significant role in the Gulf War. That war was led by the UN as punishment of Iraq for aggression against Kuwait and as protection of Kuwait's borders. For us, it is particularly interesting that the rule of international law played a significant role in the Yugoslav crisis. Thanks to the principals of the NWO, it so incurred that Russian, France, England, and many other Serbian allies and historical friends recognized the independence of the Republic B&H. It was thanks to the NWO that Russia didn't impose its veto on the economic sanctions that were imposed against Serbia, for its aggression on an internationally recognized country, the Republic of B&H. During the period of the cold war, it would have been unheard of for Russia to vote against one of its allies and historic friends. The Russian recognition of the Republic of B&H and its approval of the sanctions against Serbia and Montenegro are the best proof that the NOW—i.e., the universal acceptance of the international law—was taken seriously. It is precisely because of the NWO principles that the Republic of B&H could have, and should have gotten a much better outcome of the war. *How* and *why* did the R B&H miss that opportunity? That question will be answered in a later chapter of this book, "The Negotiations."

6

THE WAR IN THE TUZLA REGION

6.1 The Patriotic League in Tuzla

Tuzla is an industrial town of around 150,000 inhabitants in northeastern Bosnia. As was the case everywhere else in B&H, the Serbs also had complete control of the military and the police in Tuzla. That is why the Patriotic League (an organization of Bosnian patriots who formed military units in order to fight for freedom of the Republic of Bosnia-Herzegovina) functioned under illegal conditions. From the very inception of the Patriotic League (PL) in Tuzla, I was part of its leadership—a member of the presidency of the political wing. The start of the Serbian massacre of Bosniaks in the northeastern Bosnian border town Bijeljina on Eid, April 4, 1992, was also the start of our innumerable sleepless nights.

The headquarters of PL was in the SDA party housing. We had telephone communications with Bijeljina, and the orders were being issued by fax from Kemo and Halil from Sarajevo. I met Kemo only once, but I never learned his real name. Halil was Sefer Halilović, who eventually became Chief of Staff of the B&H Army. Our first commander in Tuzla was a very capable organizer by the name of Adnan, from Modriča. He was soon replaced by Vahid Karavelić-Vaha. Since we were, for a fact, working illegally, Vaha often hid at the house of our member, the surgeon Dr. Fazlić, in Solina. (Dr. Muhamed Fazlić was the man who later in the war organized field hospitals for the B&H Army in the area of the Bosnian northern stronghold Gradačac.) Because Solina was quite far from the center of Tuzla, and there was no fuel during those days, Vaha stayed at my house during the Bijeljina massacres. That was actually quite dangerous. The headquarters building of the Tuzla Corpus of the JNA was in a building next to mine, and the police headquarters were just as close, but on the opposite side of my house. Vaha was an interesting young man—quiet and very humble, and didn't fit the image of a commander. I remember one particular episode that perfectly characterizes Vaha.

During the massacres committed on April 1, '92 by Arkan chetniks (Serbian volunteers officially, who committed many horrible crimes; but in fact commando units from Nis, Serbia, directly under the command of Slobodan Milošević), a large group of young Bosniaks gathered in front of the SDA headquarters in Tuzla. We are not sure how, but two Serbs from the neighboring city of Lopare found themselves in the same location. Most likely, they came to the wrong place because the Serbian Orthodox Church and the SDS (Serbian Political Party) were located in the same park in Tuzla. One of these Chetniks was recognized by one of our men, who was beaten by the Serbs in the Ozren mountain, as one of the participants in the beating. The Chetniks had revolvers. After some confusion, we captured the two Serbs.

The capture of the Serbs occurred without anyone being in charge. Vaha observed all that as it wasn't any of his business. I asked him, "Why don't you take charge?"

He answered, "I handed over the command to Senad one hour ago."

Mehdin Hodžić, known as Senad, was an ex-policeman from Makarska, Croatia, who returned to R B&H in order to fight for its independence. Because Senad wasn't there at the time, in the general confusion, the two Serbs weren't even disarmed. If they were just a little more alert, they could have killed us all, because we did not have arms with us. When our men wanted to permanently remove the revolvers from the two Serbs, Vaha demanded that they be returned because (the Serbs) had all the necessary documentation to carry them. At that time, the Chetniks were slaughtering our people in Bijeljina, while we were releasing the same Serbs without even confiscating their weapons. I then told Vaha, "Let's make a deal that we will return the weapons to the Serbs if they ask for it when they will be released. If they don't ask, we will keep the weapons."

Of course, the Chetniks didn't even expect to be left alive, let alone to get their weapons back. Ecstatic, they jumped into their car full of meat and beer, and left. We should have at least kept them and exchanged them for some of the Bosniaks from Bijeljina. That way, we could have at least saved a few Bosnian lives.

Here, I would like to say a few words about Mehdin Hodžić, known as Senad, the policeman from Makarska, Croatia: He realized that the R B&H would be attacked, so he placed himself at the disposal of the Patriotic League. He had no family, so he devoted all his time to organizing our units. He lived without receiving any income, close to hunger. Although the SDA party had the legal right to employ in the regional police department, and although Mehdin was an experienced and qualified policeman, there was always someone "more important" for SDA leadership when hiring policemen. Finally, I tried to do

42

something about his employment. I went to see my then friend Mirsad Berberović, the son-in-law of the president, Alija Izetbegović. When I told him about Mehdin, he called someone by the name of Sabrihafizović. After he hung up, he told me that the matter would be taken care of. Unfortunately, Mehdin didn't see the resolution of his financial dilemma. The war broke out before he got the job. He died a hero at the very beginning of the war near Zvornik, while destroying two Serbian tanks.

From these examples can be seen how the B&H government formed—mainly through family connections to Izetbegović. As a matter of fact, Izetbegović was forming a private, not a Muslim, state. That is why members of the Bosnian bureaucracy are devoted to Izetbegović, not to Bosnia.

Let's go back to the PL (Patriotic League) of Tuzla. All the actions planned by Vaha (Vahid Karavelić) were unnecessarily complicated. He used his education acquired in the JNA, a well-trained and equipped army. These planned actions couldn't have been executed by civilians who had to buy their own weapons and had no military training. There was nothing we could do to help the Bosniaks of Bijeljina while the Chetniks buses were passing only a few hundred yards away from us on their way to Bijeljina town, where they were slaughtering Bosniaks at that time. We should have, and could have, placed a barricade on the road and stopped them. That probably wouldn't have saved the people of Bijeljina, but it would have done wonders for our national dignity. That was later communicated to us from the PL activists of the nearby town Živinice. These were truly dedicated fighters, who later formed a commando unit known as Živiničke Ose (Wasps of Živinice). They advised us that they were ready to erect barricades on all the major roads and also surround all the Serbian villages, as the Serbs did to Bosniak ones. However, nothing came of it. The Serbs (in fact well-organized JNA) continued to block our towns and villages while traveling unimpeded through them on to the battlefields like Kupres, Bosanski Brod, and others, where they were attacking other Bosniaks. Meanwhile, the only thing that we were accomplishing were useless and unenforceable grandiose plans of counteraction drawn on the military maps by our commander, Karavelić.

The "good guy" Vahid Karavelić (Vaha) was so incompetent at the start of the war that during some negotiations in his headquarters in Živinice, he was arrested by a Serbian officer and his two escorts. Later, the Serbs showed on Serbian TV Vaha's "confession." I saw that Vaha didn't give away some important details; he actually only told them what they already knew. The importance of that episode was in the fact that we had confirmation that Vaha wasn't "planted" by the Serbs. They would never treat one of their own in such a manner. During those days, everyone was a suspected traitor, especially the ex-officers of the JNA. Later, he was exchanged for a Serbian colonel. During 1994 and 1995, he was the commander of the B&H Army's First Corps. He had great successes in the Nišić and Treskavica battlefields, in the greater Sarajevo area. It looked as though the

B&H Army had reached the level of preparedness where it could execute the "textbook" action plans created by Vaha.

However, the PL also had some successes at that time. Some of our men were successful in taking weapons from Serbian guards and policemen. Besides that, some weapons were brought to Tuzla from Visoko. It was impossible to make the journey from Visoko to Tuzla without going through some villages in which Serbian rebel military units were already operational. I remember well that while the slaughter of Bosniaks in Bjeljina was going on, in April 1992, a professor from the School of Mining at the University of Tuzla. Dr. Sadudin Hodžić, transported a truckload of M48 rifles through Vozuča in the Serb-controlled territory. Professor Hodžić risked his life for the Republic of Bosnia-Herzegovina.

Later, during the "real" war, our PL-formed units became part of the Bosnian Army. They played a major role in liberating many towns and villages from around the Tuzla region.

Initial confusion, amateurism, and the lack of organization during the initial phases of Bosnia's independence characterized Bosnia-Herzegovina at that time.

6.2 The Attack on the SDA Headquarters in Tuzla

The attack on the SDA headquarters in Tuzla happened on April 5, 1992, the day after JNA slaughtered people in Bijeljina and surrounded the neighboring town Janja. But what led to that?

Because the SDA won the majority of votes in North-East Bosnia, by the agreement with SDS (Serbs) and the HDZ (Croats), it was entitled to install a certain number of personnel into the regional police departments. Despite the slaughter of Bosniaks in Bjeljina that started on April 4, 1992, some SDA affiliated policemen decided to take time off for the Eid holiday that started on April 6, 1992. When one of them, Alija Muminović, who was also the Representative in the Parliament of the Republic of Bosnia-Herzegovina, told us that he would not work during the Eid, I was shocked. He was employed in the local police department in order to help Bosniak during this critical period, yet he took time off during most critical times in the North-East Bosnia.

Because of the Eid holidays, there was no Bosniak authority on duty in the local police, except for county police chief Hazim Rančić and the commander of the Police station in Tuzla, Meša Bajrić. Meša Bajrić was the communist delegate in the local (municipality) Tuzla government, which was meeting that afternoon. I happen to be at the SDA Tuzla headquarters at that time. I remember that Mr. Salko Bukvarević was also there. He was the president of the young SDA members, called the "Muslim youth section" (Muslimanska omladinska sekcija - MOS). Our unit of PL was carrying weapons because of the situation in Janja.

In front of the building, there was an armed guard. Somewhere around 4:00 PM, the regional chief of police, Hazim Rančić, obviously very excited, came to tell us not to show our weapons in public because Serbs from Tuzla were calling the police station to protest the armed Green Barrettes, as the PL units were known. Because the municipal chief of police, Meša Bajrić, was absent from his positions in the police command, there was no Bosniak representation on the police force at that moment.

The Serb rebels on the police force used that error by the Bosniaks to issue an order to the police force to disarm the members of the PL. While we were talking to Rančić, a guard ran in and informed us that the police force was surrounding the SDA building. At that instant, I ran out from the SDA building and, using the confusion by the police, I escaped. Right away, I went to the Hall of the Workers University building where the Tuzla City Council was meeting, and I informed the president of the Tuzla chapter of SDA, Dr. Salih Kulenović, of the situation. The mayor of the Tuzla, Mr. Selim Bešlagić, immediately started a debate on the situation. The delegates decided to ask the JNA for help against the police, who were obviously under Serbian control. The continuing assertion by Izetbegović that JNA was not on the same side as the rebel Serbs played a decisive role. Alarmed and terrified people start to believe the words that give false hope. The same scenario, when Bosniaks under attack trusted JNA, happened several times before. For example, people from Brčko, surrendered their arms to the JNA and later became easy targets of the rebel Serbs and victims of genocide. Or, for example, the Bosniaks were going into the Bijeljina JNA barracks looking for safety and to hide from the "Arkanovci" (known as the most brutal of the Serbian extremists who called themselves the Arkan's Tigers), yet the Arkanovci were coming to the same JNA barracks to get additional ammunition. Actually, it was normal for the Arkanovci to get help from JNA since they were the special JNA units from Nis barracks in Southern Serbia, but just portraying themselves as being a paramilitary unit to hide Serbian involvement in the aggression.

But SDA headquarters in Tuzla were saved from the inside and by the people of Tuzla themselves. The men who stayed inside the building called the Bosniaks by phone from all of Tuzla's neighborhoods. From there, a huge outpouring of people dispersed the police surrounding the SDA building.

The whole episode was a decisive one for Tuzla. Up to then, Tuzla was divided into the left-leaning group (Reform Party and Socialist-Democratic Party) on one side and the SDA on the other. That night I realized that among both left parties of Tuzla, the reformers and the socialists (former communists), there is a majority of those supporting an independent and united Bosnia-Herzegovina. Mr. Selim Bešlagić, a "reformer" and also the president of the Tuzla City government (mayor) came to the SDA headquarters. He suggested that the question of the SDA paramilitary unit (PL) be resolved by joining them to regular reserve units of Bosnian police. He also offered a separate army post on a nearby hilltop. Realizing the importance of this decision, I worked very hard to influence the SDA leadership to accept that offer. There were some hotheads within the SDA, usually in the less educated who advocated war with the Commies, rather than with the rebel Serbs. Dr. Salih Kulenović, the president of SDA Tuzla, also took an interest in the Selim Bešlagić suggestion. When I later visited those new army barracks that Bešlagić secured for us, I realized that was the most strategic location in the entire area. It was overlooking all the major roadways connecting Tuzla with the rest of Bosnia. It also dominated the chemical plant, one of the largest on the Balkans and to the power plants. At that moment, I realized that Mayor Selim Bešlagić was a Bosnian patriot.

While these meetings were being held in the SDA building, there were people demonstrating in front. They chanted, "We want weapons!" Somehow they were convinced that our building was full of weapons. Things were getting so heated up that we were worried the people might try to storm the building. I went out to try to quell them. It was the first time for me that I was addressing a large group of people outdoors. I explained that the weapons of the TO (Territorial Defense) were theirs. I reminded them that it was bought with their money for just such an occasion—defending the people. The JNA cheated them and removed all the weapons from the TO and was storing it in the JNA barracks in Kozlovac, Tuzla. I told them that instead of demonstrating here, they should be demonstrating in front of the JNA Tuzla headquarters and demand the return of the TO weapons.

Because the market (a Balkan version of the Farmers' Market) was very close to the SDA offices, many of the merchants participated at that meeting. Many of these merchants and currency dealers had less-than-perfect reputations, some bordering on criminal, due to the former Yugoslav communist regulations restrictive to private businesses. However, that didn't prevent Selim Bešlagić from meeting with those merchants dealing in foreign currency. He suggested that they help him catch other black marketers that were coming from Serbia. The reason was simple: the Yugo money was printed in Belgrade, in Serbian hands, and under control. The purpose of the huge influx of these worthless Yugoslav dinars in Bosnia was their conversion into a stable Western currency, and also for the purchase of huge quantities of goods from R B&H.

I get upset when I remember that even then, Izetbegović refused to issue a Bosnian currency, even though the war against Bosnia had already started and Bosnia was recognized as a sovereign state.

During those days, Bosnian towns were falling into Serbian hands almost daily. These Bosnih towns weren't armed that poorly that they had to surrender so easily. The scenario was always the same: our people would take up defense positions, and the rebel Serbs with JNA muscles would ask to discuss the partition of the town. The SDA headquarters in Sarajevo would order locals to negotiate with

Serbs. The rebel Serbs would refuse to negotiate until the Bosniaks came down from the strategic positions in the town. Then the Bosniaks would come down, and at that moment, the rebel Serbs and JNA would attack and kill everybody. In fact, the same tactic was used by them during the disarmament talks in Srebrenica in 1993, which the Serbs then took in 1995. Someone might say, "What dumb people." However, people don't have a way of making any decisions, except through their politicians. In the case of R B&H, all the decisions were made by Alija Izetbegović. But when discussing Izetbegović, it is important to remember that it wasn't his stupidity but his intentional destruction of the Republic of B&H.

Using these same tactics, B&H was completely surrounded by the middle of April. The only road not controlled by the Serbs was the so-called road of Salvation. That was a net of dirt roads over the Vran Mountain. Using that road, on April 14, and 15, I took my family into Croatia and the relative safety there. I took a whole day, twenty-four hours, to travel the few hundred kilometers through central Bosnia. While traveling through B&H, I realized that the Croats were ready for the war.

On an untold number of checkpoints, we were controlled by the Bosnian Croats, dressing in camouflage uniforms. The Bosniaks had only a few checkpoints, and they still wore the uniforms of the police reserves. Those were also the moment of the terrific Croat/Bosniak friendship. Fear of the bloodthirsty Serb nationalists really brought the two victims together (the Croats and the Bosniaks). You can imagine how far the common misfortune had brought us together when a Croatian soldier (Catholic) on the Vran Mountain, looking at my ID card and seeing that my name is Muhamed but that I was born in Belgrade, told me, "Looking at your birthplace, I would normally execute you right away, but your name is *correct*. (That was a figure of speech, because nobody was executed because of his/her birthplace by soldiers on a checkpoint.) While driving the car, I didn't even hear when the nearby port of Ploce was being bombed by Serbian airplanes, so I drove with the lights on. While under the war conditions and while still under the fear of the spies, we were stopped by an annoyed Croatian patrol with their guns pointed at us. Again, the name *Muhamed* saved us.

I rested for only one day in Croatia, and right away, I returned to Tuzla. The parting with my family was sad and difficult, especially for them. We didn't know if we would ever see each other again. However, for me, there was no dilemma. My conscience wouldn't allow me to abandon my homeland under siege. At that time, that was still the case with the majority of Bosnians. It wasn't important that we didn't have enough weapons. We had a country that was recognized and independent, and that was worth dying for.

6.3. Tuzla before the Serbian Attack

When I returned to Tuzla, everything seemed different than before I left. During the few days of my absence, the people of Tuzla had aged. No one was laughing anymore. There was a tremendous sense of fear, but Bosniaks didn't retreat. I remember one particular detail that pictures the determination of the Bosniaks not to bow to the Serbs. It was an episode with a student of mine, Mirza Karamehmedović, who later died as commander of a military unit that was nicknamed Satans. At that time, he was a member of a unit called Posta (the Post Office). The unit was composed of different ethnic groups, and its orders were to guard the most important buildings in the city, such as the post office, power stations, government and media facilities, and so on. It was composed of 120 soldiers that were armed with the guns from TO, which Selim Bešlagić somehow "liberated" from the JNA by negotiations. Namely, back then the JNA still acted as if it was independent from the Serbian paramilitary rebel units. Using that tactic, JNA was able to occupy positions around Bosnian cities and those overlooking Bosnian roads. The cities of Brčko and Višegrad fell victims to those lies and later suffered some of the worst slaughter the Serbs have committed.

In order to be able to continue that game, JNA returned a small part of TO weapons to Tuzla and Jajce. In Tuzla, the conditions for the return of the TO weapons were that the unit carrying these weapons must be of mixed ethnic groups. That is how the unit Posta was created.

Now back to Mirza. In front of a small cafe, at the very end of October Revolution Street, four Serbs, in JNA uniforms, were sitting down. Mirza and one other soldier from his unit also happen to stop by to have a drink. They were sitting at the table next to the Serbs as if the Serbs were just tourists. The coffee house fell silent. I saw all that because I happened to be in the vicinity. At first, I thought that Mirza was a child unaware of the danger. I greeted him and joined him and his companion at their table. My intention was to warn him of the possible incident with the four Serb soldiers since they were well armed. After hearing my warning, Mirza told me, "I know, Professor. My finger is on the trigger. But this is our homeland. You wouldn't expect us to run, would you?"

God what a difference between the true, proud Bosniaks and their leader, Izetbegović—the man that kept destroying our dignity by dragging himself like slime behind Karadžić, traveling to all the capitals of the world negotiating the end of our homeland.

The Tuzla City Council was calling on the volunteers to defend Tuzla. I headed toward the regional office of the people's defense. I was pleasantly surprised. There was a huge line of those answering the call. Both young and old, fat and skinny, bearded and bold, peasants, workers, and intellectuals were quietly waiting in the hot sun, sweating, just so they could become soldiers in the defense of their homeland. I was so touched that for the first time during the war, I cried. I joined my people and stood in the line. I felt the overpowering strength of these miners, students . . . good Bosniaks. I felt as though we couldn't lose the war. No one can defeat people who are that motivated. Then I saw a neighbor. His name was Enes Bečić. Until then, I didn't know what his profession was. He asked me, "Where are you coming from, Professor?"

I replied, "In the army, I was the calculator in the artillery, and I know that there is a shortage of such soldiers in the artillery. That is why I came." It turned out that Enes was in charge of the recruiting station, so he took me directly inside. Because we still didn't have any artillery, there was no need for my services, but they told me they would call me when they needed me.

During the war, the men were not allowed to leave Tuzla without the permission of the military district. Being remembered as the man who stood in line to volunteer, I had no trouble getting the necessary passes. That is why during the first year of the war, four times I had the opportunity to visit my family that was living as refugees in Croatia. Unfortunately, last time I visited them (March 1993), the war between HVO and the B&H Army in Herzegovina erupted, and I couldn't return to Bosnia any longer, so I stayed in Croatia. Soon after the start of that conflict, HVO in Herzegovina massacred a convoy bringing some supplies (mostly food) for Tuzla. Dr. Šemso Tanković, the president of the SDA in Croatia, called on me to speak as someone from Tuzla at a news conference in Zagreb, Croatia. Among other things, I said that Boban (the leader of the wing of B&H Croats under the Tuđman control) was guilty for the war in Herzegovina between HVO and army of the Republic of Bosnia-Herzegovina because he had gotten greedy at the Vance-Owen plan, which awarded Croats ten B&H towns where the Bosniaks were in the majority. All of the Croatian newspapers carried my speech, and within few days, there weren't any Croatian newspapers where I wasn't attacked by the leaders of the HDZ (Croatian Political Party). Even Ivić Pašalić, a very highly ranked HDZ official, criticized my statement. I shouldn't even mention the anonymous letters and the anonymous calls to Dr. Tanković. Dr. Tanković answered some of this accusation in the press. For me, there was no more room in Croatia. I had to escape to America. That is how it happened that I am so far from B&H, while my thoughts are always there.

6.4. The Liberation of Tuzla

Again, we must return to the events taking place in Tuzla on Friday, May 15, 1992. I arrived at work at the Engineering School at the University of Tuzla, not suspecting that was an unusual day. As always, we all had morning coffee together: Serbs, Croats, and Bosniaks. At approximately 1:00 PM, all the Serbs left work. They had all asked the dean, Dr. Kapetanović Izudin, to let them start their weekends early. It was only later that we realized that the Serbs knew that Tuzla was going to be attacked later that day. Because there were some very close friendships between the Serbs and the Bosniaks, there was also a lot of disappointment. The Bosniaks were disappointed over how little they really knew the Serbs. The biggest disappointment came from a secretary from the student activities—Milenka Savić. She was very friendly with everyone, yet she didn't tell even one of her Bosniak friends to move their children to safety that day, while she left Tuzla before the attack, knowing what would happen. I am mentioning this because it was characteristic of things taking place in Tuzla in those days. Also, a defense education teacher at the Meša Selimović High School, was later caught as a sniper. Yet every firm in Tuzla had similar experiences that day, with some for their Serbian friends.

The clash between the JNA and Tuzla started at approximately 5:00 PM. That was the ending to a very tense several days prior to that. The people of Tuzla surrounded the Husinska Buna army barracks, one of the largest in Yugoslavia. The reason was that many units of the paramilitary Chetniks had moved in to the barracks over the last few weeks. The JNA generals were asking for Tuzla to be divided into the Serbian and the Muslim parts. They started the same thing that they did in Brčko, Zvornik, Bratunac, Vlasenica, and so on. What saved Tuzla was the fact that Izetbegović's political party, SDA, wasn't in charge in Tuzla, so Izetbegović's strategy of dividing Tuzla by the neighborhoods didn't work with the city mayor, Mr. Selim Bešlagić, Reform Party. SDA in Tuzla was advised from SDA leadership in Sarajevo to seek negotiations with Serbs, negotiating the division of Tuzla on "Muslim and Serbian towns." However, Bešlagić told the JNA officers to "f—— off." That telephone conversation was taped by the orders of SDA police leadership, who was spying on Bešlagić.

Mayor Bešlagić only talked about JNA leaving Tuzla. The corridor through which they were to leave was also decided on. The people of Tuzla, in only a few days, fabricated several armored transporters, which were used to secure the important junctions. Friday, May 15, the first part of the JNA column started evacuation from the encircled barracks in Solina toward a place called Sjenjak. The Serbs' signal for the all-out attack on Tuzla was the attack on the gas station in Slavinovići. A bomb was thrown at two of our policemen. At the same time, the second half of the JNA column left the corridor and headed toward the city bypass highway. That was a critical moment. If they were able to continue that way, they would easily occupy the city. A few weapons that the defenders had was able to secure the corridor, not the whole town. At that moment, our boys fired from the buildings in front of which the JNA column was moving. Our soldiers in the armored transporter also fired. The ammunition in JNA trucks started exploding. The battle was decided very quickly, JNA did not expect such good organization of the defense, and tried to take Tuzla, which they paid for by the terrible defeat.

The same night, all the TO weapons for eight northern Bosnian municipalities held at JNA barracks in Kozlovac, Tuzla, were liberated by the Tuzla's Bosniaks and distributed to their rightful owners. All of a sudden, it was many Serbian villages that were surrounded now. Almost every day, a Serbian village was disarmed. The Serbs had a very difficult time with the Bosniak fighters from Teočak and Sapna. The legendary Captain Hajro Mešić (pronounced *Me-shich*), just in one day, took more than ten Serbian villages in the Tuzla region. With that action, he connected Teočak, Zvornik, Kalesija, and Tuzla. Because sometime earlier, the Posavina Bosniaks and the Croats have liberated the Brod, Modriča and Derventa and Orašje, a big part of the North East Bosnia was not only liberated, it had a direct link with Croatia, and all the Serbian-occupied regions in Croatia and Western Bosnia were cut off. It became obvious that Serbia was quickly losing the war. (At that time that was stated also by Jonathan Ely, from the British Institute for Strategic Studies.) Although the Serbs had enough weapons, they offered no significant resistance. That was because the Republic of B&H was recognized within its borders, which couldn't be denied or changed by Serbian arms. They couldn't wait to go to Serbia, because a Serb couldn't survive where the Gusle (a Serbian traditional instrument for epic songs against the "Turks") will not be the main musical instrument and where there wouldn't be considered as heroism when Serbs slaughter an unarmed "Turkish" wedding.

6.5. First Negotiations about Territories

After the heavy Serbian defeats in the Posavina and Tuzla regions, the first person to return the fighting morale of the Serbs was the Croatian president, Franjo Tuđman. He started the secret negotiations with the Serbs about the division of B&H. One of the "middle men" was Boutros Boutros Ghali himself. He was asking Tuđman to let the strategic Posavina corridor in the northern Bosnia be given to the Serbs for "humanitarian" reasons. By negotiating Tuđman was badly hurting the Bosnians and Croats and greatly helping the Serbs. It was a big present for Serbs because they realized that by negotiations they will get something, that their dream of a greater Serbia is still not dead. That boosted their fighting morale. That created a vision to the Serbs of a successful conclusion to the war. However, Tuđman didn't just offer them that. He betrayed the Croats in Posavina region in return for a part of Herzegovina on the south of B&H. I met many HVO (Bosnian Croat) soldiers who testify that Croatian battalions were ordered to withdraw from Posavina without any apparent reason. The HDZ leaders in Zagreb were justifying the withdrawal of Croatian units from Posavina with the supposed fear of sanctions against Croatia because its troops crossed into another country. That was not true. Croatia couldn't be punished if the Bosnian Government consented to the intervention. The proof that was not true is the fact that Tuđman later allowed the Croatian Army to bombard B&H city of Mostar, and the Croatian troops were later helping B&H Croats to liberate Grahovo and Glamoč, without any fears of sanctions. Just as the Serbian troops were quick to retake the Posavina corridor (with almost no resistance), the Croatians hardly had any resistance while taking the left bank of the Neretva river in Herzegovina.

After the quick advances on the left bank of the Neretva river from where the Serbs withdrew too easily, the Croats stopped at the borders of Banovina Hrvatska, (refers to the 1939 division of Bosnia between the Croats and the Serbs). It is interesting to see how these agreements were enforced in the field. For example, Tuđman couldn't tell the Posavina Croats (on the Bosnian side) that he gave their homes and farms to the Serbs after they'd been defending them for so long. He simply stopped any logistics support, and he withdrew any HV (Croatian army) units from the region. The only ones left were the local inhabitants, who, vastly outnumbered and unarmed, succumbed to the Serbs. Examples of such behavior are villages of Kotorsko (Bosniak) and the Croatian village of Johovac, between Doboj and Modriče in Northern Bosnia. These two villages were abandoned and left to their own destiny. For many days, they resisted the Serbs from Western Bosnia, who had started to break through a corridor. Where the Croatian Army was supposed to offer resistance, there was no Croatian Army there. They had quietly withdrawn before the Serbian attack. Similarly, the Serbs withdrew without a fight from several Serbian villages on the left bank of the Neretva river in eastern Herzegovina. I know three soldiers in the HVO who swear that when their HVO unit got carried away and pushed the Serbs farther than the border agreed to between Tuđman and Milošević were, they were fired on by other Croatian units.

The fall of the Posavina region was the realization of Tuđman's politics relating to the ultimate goal of the division of B&H. At the same time, the close cooperation between the Bosniaks and the Croats was still encouraged wherever the Croats were afraid that Serbs might take more than was agreed upon. That is why they cooperated around Posavina corridor and at Bihać, the Achilles heel of Greater Serbia. On the other hand, those units of the Bosnian Army that were close to the territories controlled by the HVO were considered the enemies. That was the reasoning behind allowing weapons for Tuzla to pass through HVO-controlled territory, but not the weapons destined for Zenica. However, even the number of weapons for Tuzla was limited— enough to threaten the newly established Serbian corridor through Posavina, but not to cut it off. At that time, the commander of the Tuzla Corpus was Zeljko Knez, a Croat from Croatia and an obedient Tuđman soldier. The free territory of Eastern Bosnia, including Srebrenica, was only a few kilometers from the territory controlled by the Tuzla Corpus, yet not a single bullet was fired to connect Eastern Bosnia—including Srebrenica region—with the free Tuzla region. The people of Tuzla trusted Željko Knez and naively and greedily dreamed about Tuzla reopening its own South – North corridor to Croatia through Posavina, now closed by the Serbian East-West corridor through Posavina. That way, they would no longer have to depend on the HVO (B&H Croatians under Tuđman's control) gangsters in Herzegovina.

Unsuccessfully, I tried to warn them in the *Ratna Tribina* (the *War Tribune*) paper, then published in Tuzla, that those "gangsters" that were stealing the weapons destined for Bosnia were part of Tuđman's politics. That meant that even if Tuzla did create a northern corridor to Croatia, there would be other "gangsters" emerging on the north to steal the weapons destined for Bosnia. And that is beside the fact that it was unrealistic for the Tuzla Corpus to think they could cut the Serbian East-West corridor (and) hold it on their own. They didn't realize that the entire Yugoslav military would get involved in retaking that corridor. That is how it happened—that Bosnia's strongest Corpus ended up fighting in Posavina, keeping an eye on the Serbian corridor, while at the same time allowing the Serbs to "cleanse" Eastern Bosnia. Back in January 12, 1993, I wrote an article entitled "The Critical Battle for Bosnia" in the *Ratna Tribina*:

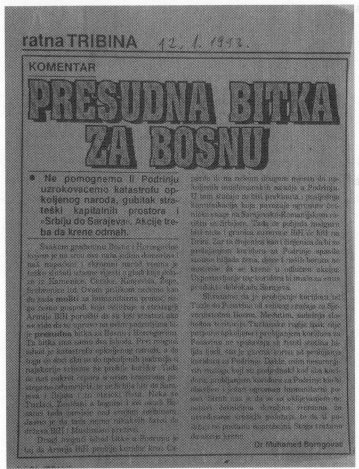

It is difficult for any citizen of BH who loves his homeland and its suffering people to hear the horrible news about the starvation in Kamenica, Cerska, Konjevića, Žepa, Srebrenica, and other Eastern Bosnian places. Yet this time I will not beg for humanitarian aid, but instead I would like to send a message to the people who are deciding the strategy of the B&H Army that they are poor strategists if they don't see that it is exactly in those places that the battle for B&H will be won or lost. There are only two possible outcomes to that Battle: the first possibility is the catastrophe of a surrounded people, and that will happen if a corridor isn't broken soon to connect them to the rest of Bosnia. Our resistance will crumble in those regions and Serbia will expand all the way to Sarajevo, and it will be 'ethnically cleansed.' When that happens, people of Tuzla, Zenica, and all other Bosnians better reflect on their prospects for any future. It is certain that if that happens, there is no way that B&H and the Bosniaks can survive. The other possible outcome to the battle around the Eastern Bosnia would be that the B&H army break a corridor through at Caparde or some other place that reached the surrounded Bosniak towns around Eastern Bosnia. That would also cut all the Serbian communications that connected the huge Serbian forces near Sarajevo with Serbia. The victory would then be ours, and the borders of the Bosnian state would stay on the Drina River. Isn't that fact and the fact that by creating a corridor to connect Eastern Bosnia with the rest of free Bosnia and the saving of hundreds of thousands of women, children, and our fighters, a good-enough motivation for such an action? A byproduct of creating such a corridor would be the liberation of Sarajevo.

We understand that the opening of a corridor from Tuzla, north to the Sava River would be of great significance for the North-Eastern Bosnia. However, the Tuzla region was not completely surrounded, and creating a corridor North would not save hundreds of thousands of lives, which would be the main reason for a corridor to Eastern Bosnia. The opening of the Eastern Bosnia corridor would be of a tremendous humanitarian use as well. I am afraid that any further postponing of such an action would allow the Serbs enough time to fortify their positions, and that the opening of the corridor becomes impossible. That is why I am asking for immediate action.

7

THE SDA CADRE POLITICS
DURING THE WAR

7.1. The Influx of New Members in SDA

I have already mentioned Professor Sadudin Hodžić, who risked his life to bring a shipment of weapons into Tuzla. Professor Hodžić was one of those Bosniaks who joined the SDA and the Patriotic League out of sheer patriotism. However, the majority of the later SDA leadership in Tuzla were those who joined after May 15, 1992, and who by joining saw their chances of promotion. It didn't matter to them that between 1990 and 1992 they were sworn enemies of "nationalist organizations", meaning the SDA. They were not ashamed that they publicly cursed God, in a typical communist manner, when former communist Dr. Fuad Muhić offered his services to the "Muslim party" SDA. Using the techniques learned from the communists, they quickly took the power from the true patriots, who were mostly in uniforms and were charging on the Serbian positions on Majevica mountains. As opposed to the actions of the original members, the new ones are charging the positions that were held by the Serbs in Tuzla, including abandoned, state-owned apartments in which Serbs lived before the attack on Tuzla.

Overnight, they changed their dresses from red (communist) to green (Muslim). The tragedy lay in the fact that they had brought their communist ways. We, the prewar members of the SDA, freely criticized Izetbegović whenever we saw him making a mistake. We were sending faxes to the headquarters in Sarajevo whenever we thought there was a need for it. Once the new members came, all the free discussions ended. They really weren't interested in politics, only in their self-promotion. That is why they never took a chance on anything. That created a climate of conformity and the "rubber-stamping" of everything coming out of

Sarajevo (from Izetbegović). Those people were opportunists who would follow whoever was in charge. They were ready to create a personality cult. I will not mention any of their names. I am only interested in them so I could answer the often-asked question: "If Alija Izetbegović is a traitor, why are Bosniaks, then, still following him?"

The answer was clear: Because of those opportunists in his government who created a personality cult from Izetbegović. They also created a Tito cult years ago, and later they spat on him. They would also turn against Izetbegović as they did during the "Sarajevo process," just so they could ingratiate themselves to whoever was in charge. I don't have a single person in mind but their whole way of thinking.

7.2. Izetbegović's Envoy Armin Pohara Arrives in Tuzla

A unique occurrence and very important for Tuzla, was the arrival of Izetbegović's special emissary, Armin Pohara. I will describe the first meeting between Pohara and the people of Tuzla—a meeting that I also attended. The meeting was held in the Islamic center of Tuzla, in January of 1993. Among those attending were imams Hasan and Adil; the president of the Muslim humanitarian organization Merhamet, Custović; the director of the weekly *Zmaj od Bosne* (the Dragon of Bosnia), Edib Kravić; Armin Pohara; and I. Later, we were joined by the secretary of the Tuzla City Council, Jasmin Imamović; the actor Emir Hadžihafizbegović; then an ex-soccer player and the organizer of humanitarian help from Turkey, Mersed Kovačević; and a few names I can't remember. One of the topics was the initiation of a Muslim TV station in Tuzla, for which large amounts of money were already secured by SDA. That is why actor Emir Hadžihafizbegović was also invited. The most important issue was who was going to be the leader of the newly created Northeastern County. That is why the City Council secretary, Jasmin Imamović, was invited to the meeting. Because Tuzla city was the largest free municipality in Northeastern Bosnia; it was natural for it to be the most influential in that region.

Actually, the true leader of the people was already Mr. Selim Bešlagić, the mayor of Tuzla. He objected to Izetbegović's negotiations with the Serbs in Geneva. Bešlagić and Ismet Hodžić (a candidate from the SDA for the Tuzla region's leadership) sent a letter to the Bosnian negotiators in Geneva, in which they opposed any negotiation about the future of Bosnia with the war criminals. That letter was published in the Tuzla paper *Front slobode* (the Freedom Front). Bešlagić, the man in charge of the largest free Bosnian city, wasn't fighting for a divided Bosnia but for a Bosnia free all the way to the Drina River.

On the other side, Izetbegović was manipulating the expanded B&H presidency into dividing the free Bosnian territories into "counties." Counties did not exist in the Constitution of the Republic of Bosnia and Herzegovina. It means Izetbegović illegally, contrary to the Constitution, reorganized the country and introduced counties. It does not matter how those counties would look like. Their sole introduction meant giving up the legitimate Bosnian Constitution and recognition of the occupation in the best Serbian interest. Izetbegović also ordered that all the municipalities in the regions would have an equal number of representatives in the county assemblies, regardless of their size. Although Tuzla was larger than any ten of the other municipalities in the Northeastern region, according to the new rules proposed by Izetbegović, it had the same number of representatives in the Assembly of the County. Because Izetbegović's SDA won in all the other much smaller municipalities, that meant that Bešlagić would lose his power. But because of the great popularity of Bešlagić, the people of the Northeastern region demanded that he stay in charge. Pohara came specifically in order to negotiate, cheat him, and to eliminate Bešlagić from the position of the regional leadership. At that meeting, through Pohara, Izetbegović was asking Bešlagić to join the SDA party. In other words, "you better give me your soul if you want power."

Bešlagić was not the kind of a man that would sell his soul for power, so he didn't make a deal with Izetbegović's emissary either, just as he didn't succumb to the Serbian (JNA), General Pracer. However, Izetbegović's main goal was achieved; he weakened Bosnian Constitution and legalized occupation by unconstitutional introductions of the counties (cantons) spreading only on the free territories. No wonder that after that, the international community started talking about the division of Bosnia by ethnic Cantons in the new Bosnian Constitution rather than defending the legitimate constitution of a UN member, the Republic of Bosnia and Herzegovina, from aggression. The Bosnian people were under the siege, informative blockade, and did not follow all of Izetbegović's tricks against the legitimate Constitution. People continued to fight for the Republic B&H.

Pohara tried one more action in Tuzla. He started with the following story: "Look, in Banja Luka, the Serbs are the majority, so Banja Luka is a Serbian city. In Mostar, the Croatians are the majority, so Mostar is Croatian city. In Tuzla, the Muslims are in the majority, yet Tuzla isn't Muslim but civic. In the B&H Army, Bosniaks are 90 percent of the manpower, yet the army isn't Muslim but is "Bosnian Army. Whose fault is that, and what can be done to change it?"

I immediately responded to him: "If we accept Tuzla as a Bosniak city just because the Bosniaks are in the majority, then we must also accept the "logic" that Banja Luka is Serbian because the Serbs are the majority, that Mostar is Croatian, and so on. That means that we would be accepting the Karadžić and Boban's logic of dividing B&H, which is in the best interest of our enemies." Because of my persistence on that point, Pohara's authority as the hero from Bosanski Brod and Izetbegović's special envoy was invalidated; and at least at that time, he didn't succeed in getting support for his views on the Muslim Tuzla.

Pohara, i.e. Izetbegović succeeded in eliminating Selim Bešlagić from the fight for the presidency of the newly created regional (county) government. However, Dr. Sadudin Hodžić became the president of the regional government, and Ismet Hodžić became the president of the regional assembly. Both of them were members of the SDA from before the war and just as Selim Bešlagić, they were fighting for a free and united R B&H, not their careers. That is why they were on the position of liberating all of Bosnia. A question asked here is, why did Izetbegović replace one true patriot (Bešlagić) so he could bring in another? Because, he could not always find the person that he would like. Therefore, by constantly replacing the leaders, he was diminishing their authority and creating a more controllable climate. Those were very smart moves by Izetbegović that helped him to achieve total control of the situation and, in the end, to divide Bosnia.

Later, Pohara was thrown out of Tuzla. Even the fact that he was a special emissary from Izetbegović didn't help. He (actually his sponsor, Izetbegović) created enough dissection and controversy in Tuzla. He started a battle for power that pushed the battle for the liberation of Bosnia on the second burner. In the battle for power created by Pohara, many of the ex-communists were given a chance, people who only know how to include themselves in the government, no matter what color it is.

8

THE NEGOTIATIONS

8.1. The Second Conversation with Izetbegović

Many Bosniaks had noticed the huge number of Izetbegović's "errors." People were rationalizing those in different ways. Some were convinced it was just his inexperience that led to so many mistakes. After all, he was just a lower-level lawyer in the judicial system until he was sentenced for "subverting the Bosnia-Herzegovina Constitution" in 1983. Some thought he was unqualified to rule Bosnia, and some thought he was too weak. There were others who were convinced that what appeared to be errors were just the *disguised* actions and intrigue of a superbly intelligent wisdom. However, none of it is true. Izetbegović knew diplomacy well, and he also knew enough about politics and the law to be a good president. I can personally testify to that. Being convinced at the time that he was just a misguided patriot and someone without enough political savvy, I spent almost one hour on the phone with him trying to explain to him the consequences of negotiating. Today it is clear that he already knew well what the consequences could be, but unfortunately, he abused that knowledge in order to partition the country of which he was the leader, not try to save it. He broke the sacred oath he took when assuming his office, an oath under which he swore to protect the Constitution and the borders of the Republic of Bosnia and Herzegovina, not to help our enemies to destroy it, as he had done.

The witness to my conversation with Izetbegović was a man with initials J.O., at that time the CEO of Tuzla's public housing company, which was one of the most important companies in the city. (In the previous communist system, public housing was much more important than one American could imagine, and that role did not change immediately in the democracy.)

I called Izetbegović immediately after his return from Geneva, after the first round of talks about the Vance-Owen Plan, in January of 1993. In order to explain some of his reasoning, I will cite some of that conversation:

I asked him, "Mr. President, will that be a unified B&H if Karadžić's Serbs are the police in Banja Luka, if we couldn't travel through Banja Luka or over the Romania Mountain, for example?"

His answer was, "Can you now travel through Banja Luka or over the Romanija Mountain?"

In other words, he accepted it as a done deal that everything the Serbs had conquered by force—i.e., by illegal means—should legally belong to the Serbs. Could Karadžić possibly have had a better negotiating partner than Izetbegović? Try to imagine Stalin regarding USSR cities of Kijev or Harkov as being Germans just because the Germans had occupied them. But that was the reasoning Izetbegović was using.

Among other things, I told Izetbegović that there could be no ethnic borders drawn anywhere in B&H. If they were not drawn, the war might last another ten years, but B&H would survive. If they were drawn, the war might again last another ten years, and when everyone was sick and tired of the war, the only thing remaining would be the new borders—i.e., several little states where B&H once stood, but there would no longer be a Bosnia-Herzegovina.

"But what will you do with the Croats? They too want us to divide up B&H," asked Izetbegović.

"Those Croatians who want to divide B&H are in the minority. Even in the HVO [the Croatian-run military forces in B&H], there are many Muslims. They [the Croats] are leaving the war zone in large numbers and would not cause a problem if they saw that we are determined not to divide B&H. The Vance-Owen Plan gives them almost one-third of B&H. That is influencing the Croats toward Bosnia's partition rather than a united country. The "peace" plan would eventually cause a war between the Croats and the Bosnian government.

That is why it would be much better if you didn't negotiate at all, but you should insist instead on preserving B&H in the shape and size that was recognized by the rest of the world. Croats wouldn't dare to attack us since that could mean sanctions against them as well. Besides, the Croats can't afford to let the Serbs overrun us, because without us Bosniaks, the Croats would be weaker than the Serbs. In other words, you must be tough with Boban [the then Croatian leader in Bosnia], because the Croats need us too," I told Izetbegović.

Here are a few more "pearls of wisdom" from our president, Izetbegović: "We must negotiate. If we don't, the world will consider us as the guilty ones."

To that, I answered, "That is not correct. A victim cannot become the guilty party in a conflict just because he refuses to negotiate with his perpetrator."

To that, he answered, "I know that our people would fight to save Bosnia, but I am also sure you are aware of the pressure that the world has put on us to negotiate. Vance and Owen are demanding it from us."

To which I answered, "We don't have to accept anything they ask. They are only the mediators. The mediators don't dictate or judge. Their task is to listen to both sides and find out on which points both sides can agree on. At that point, the mediator formulates a proposal that he thinks might be acceptable by both sides. Just as you can fire the agent who is trying to negotiate on your behalf a purchase of a house, you can do the same with Vance and Owen."

Vance retreated soon afterward. Izetbegović never fired Owen, who voluntarily acted as the one responsible for the division of R BH. Owen stoically carried the burden of the person responsible for the division of Bosnia, hiding from the Bosnians the fact that he could make proposals about Bosnia's division only because Izetbegović was willing to sign such proposals. Lord Owen had completely "forgotten" that he was only the mediator, yet he behaved as someone whose job was to decide and judge. That is how it happened that Lord Owen removed (?!) Dr. Duraković and Dr. Filipović from the Bosnian negotiating team in the fall in Geneva 1993—two Bosniaks who did not accept the partition of the country and had the trust of the Bosnian Assembly and the Bosnian people. Instead of immediately ceasing negotiations in such situations, Izetbegović continued as if nothing had happened. By allowing the mediator Owen to influence who would represent B&H, Izetbegović negated Bosnian sovereignty. That was one of Izetbegović's methods to help B&H enemies in breaking the Bosniaks' resistance to the division of R B&H.

The fact that we as a party to the negotiations had the right to let go of the mediator if we didn't like him was proven by Izetbegović himself when he fired Yasushi Akashi two and a half years later.

Let's get back to my conversation with Izetbegović. When he became restrained by the arguments about the role of the mediator (middleman) in the negotiations, he resorted to some dirty tactics. He said, "Can you gather a hundred intellectuals to back your stand?" He knew well that the correctness of a particular stand was not measured in numbers. The truth and lies were absolute categories, and they didn't depend on the number of votes. The role of a mediator is such, as I explained to him, that no matter how many supporters I had in Tuzla, he was still only the middleman.

Besides, Izetbegović tried to hide behind other "experts." He told me how many Islamic leaders urged him to negotiate. He mentioned only Jaser Arafat. Supposedly, Arafat told him to take whatever they were offering him because Arafat was sorry that he didn't agree to a Palestinian homeland that they offered him earlier. I don't know for sure if Arafat really told him that, but it is wrong anyway. The big difference is in the fact that Alija Izetbegović already was the leader of an internationally recognized country, meaning he already had that of which Arafat could only dream about. Whether Izetbegović only invented Arafat's advice or only used it as an argument, in either case, we can see Izetbegović even back then accepted the death of the Republic of B&H.

I concluded the conversation with Izetbegović by repeating, several times, "Stop the negotiations and any discussion on changes in B&H Constitution and borders.

His answer to that was, "Wouldn't it be better for us to accept the Vance-Owen Plan and that they [the Serbs] don't?" Soon afterward, the telephone connection with Izetbegović was lost. Obviously, Izetbegović's phone was tapped, and when he did not have any new arguments for division to offer, he was helped by the disconnection of the conversation.

During the first part of March of 1993, Izetbegović signed the Vance-Owen Plan in New York. Soon afterward, the war with the Croats started, because they eagerly accepted this Danaian gift by Owen. It was clear to me that Tuđman would eagerly accept the offer by Owen of ten major cities (in B&H) in which the Bosniaks were in the majority. That would help Tuđman to forget the fact that one-third of Croatia was still occupied by the Serbs. It was also very apparent that the Bosniaks in those cities would certainly not accept that deal, and war with the Croats was sure to follow. That is exactly what happened. The day after Izetbegović signed the Vance-Owen Plan, the HVO (Bosnian Croats) blocked any further deliveries of weapons to the Bosnian government. Less than a month after the signing, on April 10, a very bloody war started in Konjic, to the delight of the "peacemakers" Vance and Owen.

Alija Izetbegović is a very smart man, and I am sure he understood what I told him. I also know that the members of the B&H negotiating team in Geneva also told him, "If we sign the Vance-Owen plan, we will have a war with the Croats." Even General Stjepan Šiber, a Bosnian Croat and one of the three most important generals in the Bosnian Army, who was also a member of the BH negotiating team, told him that. Professor Muhamed Filipović, Harris Silajdžić, Kasim Trnka, and my brother Musadik Borogovac (from whom I learned about much of what went on) asked and implored Izetbegović not to sign the Vance-Owen Plan. Nothing helped. Within two months, Izetbegović distanced himself from the Bosnians' control and signed the Vance-Owen Plan in New York in March of 1993.

During a conversation with Ivica Mišić, at the end of 1993, a member of the BH Mission at the UN, I learned of one more facet of Izetbegović's methodology:

Izetbegović was to have arrived in New York, and I decided to write him a letter criticizing his role in the division of B&H. The letter was sent to the B&H Mission in New York by fax. I called Mišić and asked him to personally deliver the letter to Izetbegović. He told me he would do that because he liked the letter. "There is nothing in that letter that even I wouldn't sign." In addition, he said that even the members of the Bosnian Mission to the UN were urging Izetbegović to quit negotiating, to which he answered that he was being urged by the people of Bosnia to negotiate because "they can't take it anymore". According to Izetbegović, Bosnians were urging him to end the war under any circumstances.

In other words, when he was home in B&H, Izetbegović kept claiming that he was forced by the world to negotiate; and to his own diplomats, who knew that he was not forced by the world to negotiate, he was saying that it was the Bosnian people who were demanding the negotiations.

The reasons for my firm opposition to the negotiations will be explained in the sequel.

8.2 The International Law or the Negotiations

Every conflict between two parties can be resolved in two different ways. The first way is the established legal way. That basically means that according to the rules and the laws of the established authorities, by a due process, a determination will be made as to who is the guilty party and who is the victim. Afterward, the victim is exonerated and the guilty party is punished. In the case of the war in B&H, the overseeing institution was the Security Council of the UN, which determined that the aggressors (and the guilty party) were Serbia, Montenegro, and the JNA (Yugoslav Army), as stated by the UN resolutions 752 and 757, in 1992.

The other way of resolving differences between parties is by negotiating. If the opposing parties find a common interest and are willing to resolve their differences by negotiating, the eventual agreement is then signed by both parties. The signed agreement then becomes the legal basis for the solution of any future disagreement and conflict. The start of negotiations between the opposing parties also signals the suspension of legal proceedings against the guilty party. A major mistake was made on the part of the Bosnian government when Alija Izetbegović had agreed to negotiate with the aggressors at the very beginning of the war. That suspended the steps that the international community undertook to protect the Republic of Bosnia and Herzegovina from aggression and punish the aggressors.

Soon after B&H was recognized as an independent country on April 7, 1992, the Security Council had proclaimed Serbia and Montenegro as the aggressor on the Republic of Bosnia and Herzegovina. Then on April 15, 1992 President George Bush gave an ultimatum to the JNA, to withdraw from Bosnia by May 1, 1992. Even the sixth American fleet entered the Adriatic Sea preparing for intervention. But right after the ultimatum was issued, Alija Izetbegović went to Skopje, Macedonia, on April 24, 1992, where he started negotiations with JNA generals, including the Chief of Staff, General Blagoje Adžić, and Vice President of Serbia, Branko Kostić. During those meetings, he reached some sort of agreement with the generals, of which the only result was the tying of President Bush's hands. Namely, Serbs "complied" with Bush's ultimatum by renaming JNA into "Bosnian Serb Army" (BSA), and discharging all soldiers from Serbia (around 20%), without any Izetbegovic's objections regarding that deception. Alija Izetbegović even accepted that BSA (in fact JNA) could stay in Bosnia, if they withdrew to the "Serbian territories" in Bosnia and Herzegovina. As according to R B&H Constitution there were no exclusively ethnic territories, that meant that they were free to take whatever territory they could and call it a Serbian territory in Bosnia. How could Bush take any military actions against the Serbs if the Serbs and the Bosnians had reached an agreement?

President Bush immediately realized what kind of politician Izetbegović was, and he tried to distance himself from B&H and its problems. Bush understood that Izetbegović would take the path of compromise with the Serbs and that the legally simple situation in which there was a clearly defined victim and the aggressor would bog down in a tangled knot of agreements, which neither the lawyers nor the politicians would be able to untangle.

Because he distanced himself from the B&H quagmire, Bush was characterized as an enemy of Bosnia by many American friends of Bosnia who did not have our insider information about Izetbegović's moves. However, the truth is that he was neither an enemy nor a friend of B&H. He simply was a man who wanted to literally enforce the international law, which for R B&H

happened to be the only good path. Then-president Bush let the Europeans deal with the Yugoslav crisis by applying all the legal means available. However, because he verbally distanced the USA from the Yugoslav crisis, he also cleverly kept the Russians at bay, and thus made it possible for the New World Order principles to take hold and for B&H to be earlier recognized by UN, including Russia and China and many others of Serbia's friends and allies. Although Bush was proclaiming Yugoslavia a European matter, he nevertheless forced Tuđman (of Croatia) to recognize the sovereignty of B&H. As soon as Bush understood that Izetbegović was moving from the field of international law, which was clearly in B&H's corner, into the field of negotiations with the Serbs, he realized that B&H could easily become a quagmire for anyone attempting to help. Those are also the basis for the later greatly reduced USA involvement in regard to B&H.

Alija Izetbegović agreed to negotiate the Bosnian Constitution in the London conference in summer of 1992 and to talk directly with Karadžić about it as early as December of 1992, without any preconditions. For example, he could at least request the closing of concentration camps, stopping the genocide and ethnic cleansing, or a ceasefire. By that very gesture of accepting to negotiate, three major mistakes were committed: 1) agreeing to negotiate, 2) allowing for Karadžić to be the Serbian representative, and 3) opening the legitimate Bosnian constitution to changes by enemies of Bosnia.

8.3. The Decision to Negotiate

By the very decision to negotiate, any action directed at punishing the aggressor was suspended. It is not possible for the two sides to be negotiating at the same time that a legal process is initiated against one of the parties. Let's not forget that by the UN resolutions 752 and 757, Serbia and Montenegro were proclaimed as the aggressors and B&H as the victim. The punishing of Yugoslavia (Serbia and Montenegro) was initiated as a result of those resolutions. Economic sanctions were instituted against them by resolution 757, followed by a total blockade. The "new" rump Yugoslavia was not recognized as a country; it was expelled from the UN and all the European organizations. But by Izetbegović agreeing to negotiate with the Serbs, the punishment process was suspended. Later, during a lull in the talks, the no-fly zone was instituted, which was of great help to the B&H Army. All this proves that the "world" was not Bosnia's enemy but that it tried to protect it, starting with the recognition, on to the no-fly zone and the NATO's bombing of the Serbs in August of 1995. But any new action against the Serbs was always disrupted by Izetbegović's sabotaging move in the negotiations with the Serbs.

8.4. The Decision to Accept Karadžić to be a Partner in the Negotiations

With his negotiations, we went from a clear situation defined in the UN resolutions 752 and 757—by which the war in BH was a case of aggression by Yugoslavia with its army JNA on the independent country of Bosnia—to the Serbian claim that the Bosnian war was a civil war between the "Bosnian" Serbs, the "Bosnian" Croats, and the Bosniaks. With that, we made it impossible for our friends in the UN to fight for any military help to Bosnia, as the victim of aggression. The point is that the international law applies only to states and not different parties within those states. The UN has no right to get involved in the internal affair of a country, hence into a civil war. By qualifying the war in B&H as an internal, civil war instead of an aggression by the Serbs, any attempt of open military action under the UN umbrella on the side of R B&H was eliminated. There is nothing in the UN Charter that would justify military intervention by the UN against one side in a civil war. Just remember the bloody civil wars in Cambodia, Uganda, and Rwanda, in which the UN could not interfere.

At the very beginning, the war in B&H was looked at as the fight between the victim and the aggressor, which was in B&H's favor, since the whole world considered us to be the victims. But the strategic Serbian propaganda goal was to make the world forget that and look at that conflict as a war between the Muslims and the Christians. The Serbs had completely succeeded in that.

Let's take as an example of the success of the Serbian propaganda a battlefield map that appeared in a Detroit newspaper in the spring of 1995: all the Bosnian positions were marked with the Muslim symbol, the crescent moon, while all the Serbian positions were marked with the Christian crosses. It is natural that the mighty Christian West started aligning itself with the Christian Serbs. That Serbian propaganda victory was won the moment that Alija Izetbegović agreed to negotiate about the future of B&H with Karadžić and Boban (Serbian and Croatian rebel leaders in Bosnia, respectively). With that action, the president of B&H reduced himself to the level of the leader of the Bosnian Muslims (instead of the head of a state) and fulfilled the Serbian claim of the war in BH as a religious, civil war. In fact, when Izetbegović accepted to negotiate with the leaders of rebel Bosnian Serbs and Croats, he erased the UN resolutions that stated that Bosnia-Herzegovina was a victim of aggression of the foreign countries Serbia and Montenegro. It automatically cut off any possibility of a military intervention of the UN on the Bosnian side. Even worse, the identification of the Bosnian Army as group that is fighting for Islam made it more difficult for friends of B&H in the USA Congress to arm Bosnians. Those Bosnians living in the West realized how much have the Serbs had gained with that. In addition, Izetbegović's announcement of the six months postponement of the arming of the Bosnian

Army (see UN General Assembly on September 27, 1994, *https://undocs.org/ en/A/49/PV.7* , page 8), intended to prevent the last chance of protecting a unified R B&H by the UN.

Besides that, by agreeing to negotiate with Karadžić, Izetbegović helped to turn a war criminal into a diplomat who was now negotiating the new B&H Constitution with the legally elected president of Bosnia. We should remember that Lawrence Eagleburger declared in December 1992, in the name of the American administration, that Karadžić and Milošević were war criminals. Karadžić then left Geneva in fear of being arrested. That announcement of the American administration was a clear signal to Izetbegović not to agree to any further negotiations. However, in January 2, 1993, he resumed negotiations with the Serbs anyway. Because of that, everything that Karadžić and the Serbs had done to the Bosnian people received a sort of amnesty. The breakaway Serbs were recognized by Izetbegović as the legitimate Serbian authority in Bosnia, and those Serbs still loyal to the Bosnian government were left out. There is no precedent for such a speedy recognition of a rebel organization by the legitimate government.

Let's take as an example the Curds, Basques, North Irish, or the Corsicans. Many decades have passed, yet the legitimate authorities of Turkey, Iran, and Iraq do not recognize the rights of the rebel Kurd leaders to represent the Kurdish people. The Basques are only considered to be rebels by the Spanish and French authorities, with no legal standing. Izetbegović knew what he was doing. Even the simple, uneducated Bosnians realized the seriousness of his actions. The Bosnians were appalled by the realization that Karadžić could become a legal representative and leader in the future Bosnia, most likely as the president of that part of Bosnia that he had ethnically cleansed of the Bosniaks and Croats, and which he now called Republika Srpska.

I must also add that by recognizing Karadžić as the representative of the Serbs, Izetbegović gave stature to the man responsible for the deaths of around two hundred thousand Bosniaks (10 percent of the population), the rape of thousands of Bosnian women, and thus he also insulted the dignity of the Bosnian people. The dignity of a people is not just an academic question. You can enslave someone who lacks any national dignity, because without it, slavery doesn't hurt as much. To show that as a nation we have no dignity hurt us more than the occupation of over half of our country.

Our dignity was sold out in many ways. Here are just a few of them:

-   The signing of all the documents placed in front of Izetbegović.
-   Constantly agreeing to less and less.
-   One-sided acceptance of many documents and offers.
-   Honoring (implementing) of the agreements that the other side ignored.

8.5. Consenting to Negotiate the Constitution of the Republic Bosnian and Herzegovina

Opening the internationally recognized Constitution of the RB&H to negotiation with the rebel Serbs was the third, and the worst of Izetbegović's mistakes. It meant that despite the international recognition of the Republic of Bosnia and Herzegovina as an integral country, it is not a done deal. A state is characterized by its constitution and its borders. A constitution determines whether or not a state is democratic, communist or capitalist, efficient or not in business, and so on. After thousands of years of experience since the first states were formed, people came to recognize that the constitution of a state characterizes a state as a living entity. That is why in all the countries of the world, the president takes an oath to protect the constitution and the borders of his country. A country agreeing to negotiate its constitution is a lot like a man holding discussions that questions his very life. Imagine a man saying, "Take my life, but what will I get in return?"

Thanks to Alija Izetbegović, that is exactly what the negotiations on the B&H Constitution were leading to. B&H had agreed to renounce its own constitution by agreeing to all the offers of a partition based on the religious lines. Any new "Constitution" created by the negotiations was instantly accepted by Izetbegović, thus destroying a thousand-year-old entity called Bosnia. Whether it was the Cutillero Plan from early 1992, the Vance-Owen Plan from March of 1993, or the Owen-Stoltenberg Plan of three separate ethnic states from July of 1993, or the Tuđman-Milošević "Union" Plan from September of 1993, or the "contact" group plan from June of 1994, the part that changed the B&H Constitution was always signed by Izetbegović without any hesitation. The only "problem" Izetbegović had was with the maps of ethnic division. Karadžić always wanted part of Sarajevo, the wider corridor (at Brčko), and the enclaves Srebrenica and Žepa. Because of the fear for his position, Izetbegović couldn't announce to the residents of Bihać, Brčko, Goražde, Srebrenica, and Sarajevo that the parts of Bosnia they defended and died for would now be handed over to the Serbs. That is why the Serbs had always delayed the signing of any agreements, hoping that these strategic locations that they would like to see in Greater Serbia would be also militarily taken over by them, so that Izetbegović would have no trouble signing them over to the Serbs, just as he had done with Banja Luka, Prijedor, Kljuc, Drvar, Foča, Zvornik, and many other B&H cities. Before the betrayal of these Bosnian cities by Izetbegović, he usually held political rallies, where he stated that "what is ours is what the Bosnian Army controls," which he then used as an excuse to sign over to the Serbs the cities they occupied.

The negotiations on the future of the B&H Constitution had shown one more time that the very fact of negotiating about a nation's constitution with an enemy was deadly for that nation.

9

THE CONSEQUENCES OF NEGOTIATIONS ON THE BOSNIAN CONSTITUTION

9.1. Questioning the Recognition of Bosnia-Herzegovina

The question "What to do with Bosnia-Herzegovina?" has been opened again. That question has already been answered once with the international recognition of Bosnia-Herzegovina, but now it was opened once more. By agreeing to open the discussions on the Bosnia-Herzegovina Constitution, Alija Izetbegović practically annulled the recognition of B&H. Although it has not been stated and admitted publicly, all the international participants in the B&H affairs behaved as if B&H no longer existed as a sovereign state, and Izetbegović was looked upon as the leader of the B&H Muslims, instead of Bosnia's leader (which was the case in the first place).

Due to such conduct by the American State Department in a US Senate foreign affairs hearing on June 30, 1994, Senator Joseph Biden asked the Secretary of State Mr. Christopher, "How is it possible that you and President Clinton are engaged in the partition of a sovereign and internationally recognized state, member of the UN, Bosnia-Herzegovina?"

Mr. Christopher's answer was, "It is not true that the American administration is partitioning Bosnia-Herzegovina because neither the USA nor the international community has a right to do that. The representatives of the Bosnia-Herzegovina government had accepted its division during peace negotiations held a few months ago in Geneva." To that, Mr. Joseph Biden answered by stating that he was recently in Bosnia-Herzegovina and that he had reliable information that the Bosnians were ready to fight for the liberation of the remaining 70 percent of occupied territories. Senator Biden also stated that during that trip, he met with

Mr. Izetbegović and Mr. Ganić, and that both men told him that neither the Bosnian government nor the people had accepted Bosnia's division.

Mr. Christopher's answer to that was that Senator Biden must have been talking with different people, because he knew that Izetbegović's government had very close cooperation with the contact group on developing the maps of a divided Bosnia: "51 percent to the Bosniaks and the Croats and 49 percent to the Serbs." He also added, "The Bosnians are actually very cooperative in regards the division. It is the Serbs we are having trouble with."

After that response, Senator Biden did not speak anymore (as quoted on C-SPAN2). Senator Biden was naive enough to think that Izetbegović was like most of the leaders of state, and that he was trying hard to preserve his country instead of doing just the opposite. Senator Biden was unaware that Izetbegović had signed a document for Lord Owen in September of 1993 (in Geneva), where Izetbegović agreed to seek the end of the war in Bosnia by dividing it into three separate ethnic states. As a result of that signing, a new plan was developed by creating a "union" in B&H of the three states, which, fortunately, the B&H Parliament rejected. You might be asking yourself now, how it is possible that such an important signature and agreement by Izetbegović was unheard of by the American senators who otherwise played such an important role in the Bosnian war?

Who Izetbegović really is, and what does he really want is still a mystery to most people. That is one of the best-kept secrets in the Western diplomatic circles. Mr. Christopher revealed only a small portion of the truth, and even then, only when forced to do so. A similar thing also happened to Lord Owen, who when cornered by the difficult questions of reporters once admitted the same thing that Mr. Christopher did: "It is the Bosnians [read: Izetbegović] who are the ones who really want the partition of Bosnia." And that is the only part of that story that has leaked out so far. Bosnia's enemies knew that without Izetbegović's signatures, there could be no division of Bosnia and the creation of the Greater Serbia. That is why Izetbegović's true goals and aspirations are a closely guarded secret, especially by Bosnia's enemies and Serbia's sympathizers among diplomats involved in negotiations. By protecting Izetbegović, they are also protecting his stature in the Islamic world, from which Izetbegović was getting his financial support. Izetbegović was just one of "sold-out" souls to enemies. He was just one in the very long line of the Muslim leaders, presidents, kings, emirs, and sheiks who placed himself in the service against his own people.

9.2. Destroying the Motivation for the Struggle

The second very important consequence of negotiations to "reconstruct B&H," that is, the discussions about the B&H Constitution, was the drop-off in motivation to fight by the Bosnians and the proportionate increase by the Serbs. Before the negotiations and right after Bosnia's recognition, the situation was just the opposite. The Bosniaks received a goal that was worth fighting for, the independence of their country (which was even recognized as such by the rest of the world). That recognition was the guarantee of the Bosnia's victory in that war. The Bosnians knew that an international recognition could not just be reversed and its borders could not be changed by force; their territory could not be ceded to the aggressors.

On the other hand, those same reasons destroyed the Serbian fighting morale. That was best proven by a village recordkeeper from the Eastern Bosnian region of Zvornik, in Kamenica, a Bosniak (Muslim) village that had been fighting against the Serbs from the very beginning of the war. I met the record-keeper Bekir Omerović in Tuzla, in January 1993. He was a thirty-year-old man who was very interesting to the news reporters since he had kept a very meticulous and detailed log of the events that had taken place in his village, which was surrounded by the Serbs since the very start of the war. However, through a network of other villages and mountain roads, it was connected to other Bosnian-held villages and towns, such as Žepa and Srebrenica. The only thing separating the whole free region in Eastern Bosnia from the free Bosnian territory of Tuzla was the Serbian-controlled road from Zvornik to Sarajevo. That road was of great importance to the Serbs, since it was their only communication between the state of Serbia and the Serbian-held Romanija region of Bosnia—i.e., the Sarajevo battlefield. With the liberation of that road by the Bosnian Army, the whole Serbian-controlled portion of Sarajevo could have been cut off. So to keep the road from being cut off, and despite the shortage of men suffered by the Serbs, one section of the road was routed through a railroad tunnel through a mountain, five kilometers (three miles) long. By the Serbs "going underground," the Bosnians were using the mountain above the tunnel to supply their villages by transporting everything by caravans over the mountain. The existence of those paths across the mountain was such a well-kept secret that only a few people that actually used it knew about it. Their lives and the lives of their families depended on the secret paths. I was glad to know that the Serbian siege of those villages wasn't complete. It's by those mountain paths above the tunnel that the recordkeeper from Kamenica arrived in Tuzla.

At that time, I was a news reporter for the *War Tribune* (a paper directed at the fighters from the town of Zvornik), so my publisher, Hasan Hadžic, invited me to talk to the recordkeeper. My conversation with him explained why the Bosnians were winning the war, despite the poor weapons and hunger. It proved beyond any doubt that motivation was a far greater cause of victory than just the material advantages. Motivation is the deciding factor in a war. The fact is that a man values his life and will not endanger it if he really doesn't have to, and if he doesn't have a large-enough goal. The survival of their families was the motivating factor for Bosnians that created undefeatable fighting morale. According to the recordkeeper from Kamenica, that is how the numerically superior Serbs, who had unlimited supplies of ammunition, were running away from the defenders of Kamenica, who were given only five bullets each. The difference is that the people from Kamenica were defending their own families and property. By defending their property, they were also defending the source of their livelihood, since without their lands, they could not survive.

73

On the other side, the Serbs knew that their own families were safe and that they were dying for nothing since Bosnia-Herzegovina was already recognized as an independent sovereign state, while at the same time, the B&H Army was getting stronger by the day. However, when Izetbegović signed the Vance-Owen Plan in New York (March 1993) and when the Serbs realized that Izetbegović was recognizing as Serbian all the lands they took by force, their morale skyrocketed. But the same signature (of the Vance-Owen Plan) destroyed the B&H Army's morale. For example, I met some Bosnians from Banja Luka in the B&H Embassy in Zagreb who refused to fight in the B&H Army any longer, since as far as they were concerned, the war was over. Their city, Banja Luka, was given to the Serbs, and they no longer had the motivation or a reason to fight on. Also, the soldiers from Doboj that I met on the marketplace in Tuzla told me that they didn't want to fight and die in vain because Doboj belonged to Muslims according to the Vance-Owen Plan, and it would be given back by negotiations.

That reversal in the motivation of the two sides soon reflected itself on the battlefield. As early as April of 1993, a huge swath of B&H territory fell to the newly motivated Serbs.

According to the contact group plan, Srebrenica remained surrounded. The defenders of Srebrenica realized that there was no future in such a permanently surrounded place, so why fight and die for nothing? That is the same question that destroys the morale and the one that the Serbs were asking themselves after B&H was recognized; and it is the same moral killer that Izetbegović had sown among Bosnian defenders.

9.3. The Demilitarization of Sarajevo—Betrayal of Goražde

Just as he did it to President Bush, Izetbegović had succeeded in changing Clinton's B&H policy. Clinton had also enthusiastically started to help Bosnia-Herzegovina. We still remember the anger of Lord Owen, France, England, and the Russians because his administration had refused to pressure B&H to accept the "Union" plan, which Izetbegović accepted but the Bosnian assembly rejected. At the beginning of his time in office, Christopher had often repeated that pressure could be exerted against Serbia, the aggressor—but not against Bosnia, the victim.

We should also remember the frustration of the Serbian friends, the British, the French, and the Russians, who unsuccessfully tried to pressure Mr. Clinton into not dropping food from the air to the surrounded B&H enclaves. If those enclaves were supplied from the air, that meant that the Serbs could no longer threaten and blackmail them. Clinton decided anyway to supply them from the air. Later, Izetbegović agreed with the Serbs and the UN to supply those areas over land instead of by air drops, so the air drop operation ended. The Serbs could once again start blackmailing the people of the surrounded enclaves.

Clinton's support for B&H was felt all the way to the ultimatum issued after the February 1994 massacre at the marketplace in Sarajevo. The massacre of sixty-nine people in Sarajevo served as the opportunity for Clinton to give the Serbs an ultimatum. But instead of letting the Serbs be pressured by NATO and the USA, Izetbegović again jumped to the Serbs' rescue. His restart of negotiations with the Serbs at that time gave the Serbian supporters the argument that no foreign power should attack the Serbs militarily if the negotiation was going on, and the "peace process" was continuing. According to the so called Sarajevo Airport agreement, signed by Izetbegović, Bosnia-Herzegovina, which was not under any threats or ultimatums of the UN or NATO, also gave up their weapons in the Sarajevo region, just as the Serbs (who were under the NATO threat) did. By that agreement, which General Sefer Halilović refused to sign, lines of demarcation were defined between the "combatants," and the UN soldiers would take up positions in Sarajevo according to those lines. With that treasonous agreement signed by Izetbegović, it was, in fact, agreed that the UN would protect the areas conquered by the Serbs. That also gave the Serbs the opportunity to free up troops from the Sarajevo region they sorely needed on other fronts. For example, Goražde was endangered and attacked immediately by the same Serbian troops that Izetbegović helped to free up from the Sarajevo battlefield. The citizens of Sarajevo defined the agreement on "demilitarizing" Sarajevo as "changing the death sentence to a life in prison."

As a party to the agreement of dividing Sarajevo, the army of B&H could no longer undertake any actions to liberate their own territory around Sarajevo. As Goražde was encircled, the troops from Sarajevo couldn't help there. They could help only if they attacked Serbs on the Sarajevo battlefield, which was no longer possible because of the "Sarajevo Airport agreement." As a consequence of that Izetbegović's agreement Michael Rose, the UN commander in Bosnia in August of 1994, threatened the B&H Army with a bombing if it did not withdraw heavy weapons from within twenty kilometers of Sarajevo, and he also forced the B&H Army to withdraw from some of the most strategic points around the city. So instead of the Serbs being threatened by the NATO and the UN, they actually had gotten a better deal than the Bosnians.

After seeing what Izetbegović had done with the ultimatum he issued, Clinton finally realized that Izetbegović did not want a unified B&H. Similarly with Bush, Clinton changed his policy toward Bosnia after that failed ultimatum and gave up on any further efforts to keep B&H unified. Before the 1996 US Presidential Elections, Clinton had to resolve the B&H crisis because he promised to do so to the American people during the presidential campaign. If it wasn't for Izetbegović's betrayal and agreement that B&H should be divided; the only option would have been the protection of the unified state of B&H—the victim of the Serbian aggression. However, this way, Izetbegović gave Clinton the idea that the quickest and simplest way to remove pictures from Bosnian tragedy from American TV viewers and voters was the partitioning of Bosnia. That is why Clinton's administration finally started pushing in that direction. Clinton did not care that the partition would be the reward for aggressors rather than the punishment.

10

CONTROVERSIES OVER SOME OF IZETBEGOVIĆ'S STATEMENTS

I mentioned earlier how careful the Western diplomats were to hide who Izetbegović really was and what his true goals were. However, the best proof that Izetbegović wants to see Bosnia divided comes from him. With that in mind, here are some of Izetbegović's "thoughts" on Bosnia-Herzegovina's future:

In his book *The Islamic Declaration*, published in the 1970s by the Serbian publishers Serbian Word (Srpska Rec) in Belgrade, Izetbegović writes, "Pakistan is the general rehearsal for the introduction of Islamic regime under modern conditions and on today's caliber of development."

Izetbegović's thought unquestionably coincides with Karadžić's plan for Bosnia and Herzegovina. We must remember that from his very arrival on the political scene in Bosnia in 1989, Bosnian Serb leader Karadžić was unabashedly asking that the population be shifted in order to achieve ethnically "pure" regions of Serbs, Muslims, and Croats. Karadžić's main argument was the formation of India and Pakistan (after WWII) by the use of population exchanges. The above quote from *The Islamic Declaration* confirms that Izetbegović had the same thing on his mind, although he kept quiet about it since he knew that the Bosnians would have none of it. Knowing who and what Izetbegović really was, Karadžić and the Serbian political party, the SDS, supported Izetbegović in the November 1990 elections. Just before the elections, Karadžić threatened the Bosnians: "If Nijaz Duraković (another candidate for the B&H presidency) is elected, there will be war; but if Izetbegović is elected, there will be negotiations."

Ironically, Karadžić needed Izetbegović just so he (Karadžić) could conduct the war more successfully. He needed Izetbegović to agree to and endorse with his signature all the Serbian-planned conquests and ethnic cleansing. The really sad thing about the 1990 elections is that the Bosnians were actually electing their own executioners. In fact, Izetbegović's political party, the SDA, also endorsed the Serbian (SDS) candidates in the elections. That is how it came about that the Bosnians themselves made it easier for the Serbs to conduct the genocide they eventually committed because Izetbegović always agreed to and signed any Serbian expansion in Bosnia, and of course, Bosnia's ultimate demise.

Here is another quote from *The Islamic Declaration*:

> We would like to differentiate between the Jews and the Zionists, but only if the Jews themselves find the strength and make that distinction. We hope that the military victories, which they have achieved against embattled Arabic regimes (not against Arabs and not against the Muslims) will not cloud their judgment. I hope they will eliminate the confrontation which they themselves created so that a path could be opened to a joint life (with the Palestinians) in Palestine. If on the other hand, they continue with the path that their arrogance that is guiding them towards, which looks more likely today, for the Islamic movement and all of the Muslims of the world, there is only one solution: continue the struggle, expand it day by day, year by year, regardless of the victims and the sacrifices, regardless how long it will last, as long and until they (the Jews) are forced to return all of the lands they hold. Any negotiations and compromises, which could bring into question the basic rights of our Palestinian brothers signify betrayal, which could destroy the moral core of our world.

From this very quote from Izetbegović's writings, we can see that Izetbegović knew well how destructive the negotiations about vital questions could get, long before he himself started negotiating with Karadžić. There is no doubt that Izetbegović was not unintentionally making mistakes at the expense of Bosnia-Herzegovina but, rather, that he consciously acted to divide B&H.

In March of 1992, during the Serbian barricades in Sarajevo, Izetbegović said to the Bosnian people, "Sleep peacefully. There will be no war."

In April of 1992, when the Yugoslav Army took over the Bosnian communication rallies, when it burned Bosnian village Ravno, conducted war against Bosnians in Kupres and Brod, delivered ammunition to the Serbian extremists in Bijeljina, and was given an ultimatum by President Bush, Alija Izetbegović announced, "The Yugoslav Army is not the aggressor in B&H."

In September of 1992, Izetbegović accepted the London conference on Bosnia, in which the question "What will be with Bonsia?" was reopened after it had already been answered with the recognition of Bosnia, as the Bosnian people overwhelmingly wanted according to the referendum in 1992. His argument to Bosnians was, "Better a year of negotiations than a day of the war." We are all witnesses to the fact that the negotiations did not stop the fighting, but they had instead encouraged the Serbs, since it became clear to the Serbs that they could keep the territories they took by force. The fact that Izetbegović agreed even to talk about the partitioning of Bosnia-Herzegovina only gave encouragement to the Serbs to fight on.

In March of 1993, after his signing of the Vance-Owen Plan, Izetbegović declared at the B&H Assembly, "When confronted with having to make a choice between saving the country or saving the people, I chose to save the people."

Every schoolkid knows that the country is the basic entity for the protection of all its people. Without any state institutions, such as the army and police force, there is no protection for its people. Without the state, there is no mobilization of the army, no manufacturing, no health services—that is, there are no basic defenses of its people. Actually, the best way to destroy a people is to dismantle its country.

In September of 1993, after Izetbegović signed up for the Tuđman-Milošević plan of the "union of three states in Bosnia, he declared, "B&H will again become reunited one day, just as Germany became reunited." With that, Izetbegović compared B&H with Germany, which became reunited only because Germany had never agreed to its partition in the first place.

Also, after the signing of the "union" proposal in the summer of 1993, Izetbegović shamelessly announced, "It is important that we saved the state." A "union" of states is not a state by definition, but such statements were accepted by his followers. That was because by then, Izetbegović had succeeded in removing from government all the independently thinking patriots and intellectuals and brought in the moral scum, who asked nothing but who would pay them.

In his book *The Miracle of the Bosnian Resistance*, Alija Izetbegović describes how he sees a united B&H after his signing the "union" plan, by which B&H will be divided into three states. He writes,

> There are three possible paths to phases of the fight for a united BH. The first is the military one, which is now going on. A question is being asked, when will the war end? In my opinion, it could end when those regions where the Bosniaks were in the majority are liberated, either by military or political means. Before that, the war shouldn't end, and I think we should continue the fight until all the areas where the Bosniaks were in the majority were liberated. I think that the war should continue until that objective is reached. Regardless of the price we

might have to pay. The fascism cannot stay. We can't allow that Višegrad, Zvornik, Prijedor, Brčko, and other predominantly Bosniaks cities stay under the occupation of the Serbian forces or that the Serbs create some kind of a Republic in those regions. So accordingly, if they return our regions, only then there could be discussions on ending the war. Only then could the second phase begin, the phase of reintegrating and reuniting Bosnia. What does it consist of? On the 'liberated' territories, we should build a modern democratic society. And then when our army would enter, say, Drvar, those (Serbian) people cannot be educated by force. We would, God willing, if peace comes, try to create a modern Republic. Maybe we could do it in that way and that process could last 20 or 30 years, by which time Bosnia could be re-integrated.

So here we have another sample of Izetbegović's shameless lying. First, he openly admitted that he intended only to liberate those regions where the Bosniaks were in the majority, which by definition meant the division of BH. We must remember the open-air rally in Velika Kladusa, where he stated in front of hundreds of thousands of Bosnians that he would fight on for a united BH, and the Bosnians supported him in that. By lying that he was fighting for a unified BH, he also won the election as the president. His second deception was that in all the "peace proposals" Izetbegović signed (both before and after his book quoted above), he gave away many cities with predominantly Bosniaks population to the Serbs and to the Croats. Many times before and after he said the above words, he signed that Zvornik, Višegrad, Prijedor, Brčko, Rogatica, Foča, and many other cities with Bosniak majority belong to the "Serbian Republic." The third deception was that Izetbegović knew well that once B&H had been divided into ethnic territories, it could never be reunited and reintegrated. God, how could the Bosniaks follow such a man?

However, Izetbegović was not just a liar, he was a sickeningly manipulative man. He wanted the absolute and unchallenged power that would enable him to achieve an incredible goal—to divide a country that was never divided along any ethnic lines, because the population was mixed in every Bosnian municipality. We all remember American religious sects from the sixties and seventies, where such manipulative people were at the head. The ambitions of such leaders were to create their own sects where they would wield unlimited power over their followers. Some of these sect leaders even demanded suicide by their "disciples" just in order to quench their thirst for total control over others. Izetbegović used the same methods of manipulations with people. He succeeded in creating such a sect himself. Just look at some of his unquestioning followers, Mr. Džemaludin

Latić and the publishers of the Bosnian paper *Ljiljan* and media owned by the Islamic Community of Bosnia. Recall that Izetbegović illegally expanded his government's authority in order to place a cleric obedient to him, Mustafa Cerić, to become the Islamic leader of Bosnia. Recall how then, the illegally appointed Bosniak supreme religious leader Cerić preached in the Zagreb Mosque that Alija Izetbegović was the "lost" thirteenth friend of Mohammed a.s. Now, Cerić continued to use religion to promote Izetbegović's authority. That was probably the best explanation why Izetbegović did all those things against B&H and its people. His pro-Serbian agenda needed absolute obedience of his supporters in order to divide B&H.

In June of 1994, Izetbegović succeeded in convincing the B&H Assembly to accept the contact group's plan of dividing Bosnia: 51 percent to the federation of Bosniaks and Bosnian Croats and 49 percent to the Serbs as a "tactical" move. He told them, "We will accept the plan because the Serbs will reject it." When that plan, which was offered on a "take it or leave it" basis, was rejected by the Serbs, he came to the UN General Assembly on September 27, 1994 and asked that the weapons embargo against Bosnia *not* be lifted for another six months, but rather that the UN persuade the Serbs to accept the plan. (Detailed description of Izetbegović's behavior regarding the arms embargo is in paragraph 11.4, of this book.) That action on his part stopped the action of the US Congress, who already approved the lifting of the American arms embargo against B&H. Hence, the contact group plan (51 percent–49 percent) instead of being a *tactical* maneuver became the basis for the division of Bosnia.

After signing the contact group agreement, Izetbegović turned to his political party (SDA) with the following words:

> Karadžić's acceptance of the Plan will be the basis for further negotiations, the reason to extend the cease-fire, and one of the bases for reaching a permanent peace in Bosnia. Our goal is an undivided and democratic Bosnia. The federal arrangement is possible and welcome, but only as the federation of the cantons, and not national territories. This last would encourage further ethnic cleansing. Our goal is a democratic state, multinational and multiparty. This definition gives our political model a distinct advantage, over the retrogressive single nation, single religion, and single political party concept of Karadžić and his SDS political party, or Boban's HVO party. Our democratic concept is a condition of our political and also military victory in this war. Without that concept, there is no unified B&H.

Bosnian patriots are asking themselves, how can the abovementioned Izetbegović's requests be justified? Even the very creators of the "Contact group plan" are calling their plan for the division of B&H as the creation of two distinct ethnic entities in the 51 percent–49 percent ratio, nationally defined, whose shaky connections would only be defined in a distant future. Not too long ago, in the spring of 1995, one of the members of the contact group, Mr. Michael Steiner, declared, "By enforcing the 'plan' in B&H, two distinct entities will have been created: the Federation shared between Bosniaks and Croats, and the Bosnian Serbs entity, from which one day a union might be possible."

It is important to note here that Izetbegović was aware that the division of B&H into national territories "encourages ethnic cleansing." That has been proven by the Serbs, since after every Izetbegović signature on some peace agreement, the Serbs intensified the expulsion of Bosniaks and Croats from the territories awarded to the Serbs. So, Alija Izetbegović conscientiously and knowingly participated in the ethnic cleansing. In the creation of these ethnic territories, the Serbian-controlled territories have developed into distinctly Serbian lands, where the territories controlled by the Bosnian government have remained multiethnic. That too is one of the key indicators that Izetbegović is more interested in the creation of a Serbian state than into the creation of an Islamic nation, his act for Muslim financiers as a Muslim who wants to create a Muslim state is merely a smokescreen that covers his true goal, a creation of the Serbian state on the half of Bosnia. In the future, Izetbegović's statements will be reexamined. His words and statements will be the proof that he was a willing participant in the Serbian-led ethnic cleansing of Bosnia, not just a naive, ignorant, feeble-minded politician. (He was a brilliant lawyer who finished law school in two years.) Izetbegović's words above prove that he was aware that his signatures of the plans dividing B&H encouraged the genocide, or as he calls it, ethnic cleansing.

While on the subject of ethnic cleansing, let me explain how that ugly term was created: In the international law, there is a clearly defined term for genocide, as is the case of genocide that the Serbs committed in B&H. The Serbs have created the term "ethnic cleansing" so that they would be held responsible for something not yet clearly defined by the international law, or even illegal. For the genocide they could be punished, but not for the ethnic cleansing. Who, if not the president of the victimized people, should be careful to use the proper terminology that would accurately describe the crimes committed against his people and help in indicting the criminals? Izetbegović uses the Serbian term of "ethnic cleansing" rather than the punishable and more descriptive legally defined term of "genocide."

Izetbegović further stated,

> We can't accept treating our enemies (the Serbs) in the same manner as they are treating us, or as our people would like

us to. Why? The first reason and the difference between us is a matter of principles. We are democratic, they are Fascists. The second reason is that they want a divided Bosnia, but for themselves want a portion of such a divided Bosnia, while we want a unified Bosnia within its internationally recognized borders. Besides, we are a state, they are not. We have an Army, they have 'paramilitary units,' and let us not forget that those are our differences.

At the same time, while he was telling his party members that he was only interested in an integral B&H, his own emissary, Ejub Ganić, signed an agreement with the Bosnian Croatian leader Zubak in which they agreed that the federation between the Croats and the Bosnians within Bosnia had to be strengthened and that the government institutions of the Republic Bosnia-Herzegovina should be dissolved. So there, where it was important, such as in the international agreements, Izetbegović and his government were not treating the Karadžić's Serbs and HVO as quasi-state. Izetbegović was giving them what they wanted (signatures and agreements), while he was telling wild patriotic stories to his own Bosnian people.

The Bosnian Croats, who supported an integral B&H, were especially tragically manipulated by Izetbegović and Tuđman. By "small" changes in the Washington Bosnia-Croatia agreement, he accomplished just the opposite of what Ivo Komšić, the president of the Croatian Peasant Party of Bosnia, and a supporter of a unified Bosnia, wanted. So now the Washington agreement recognizes half of B&H to Serbs and opens the possibility that the other half will create the union within greater Croatia. That is also how Izetbegović saved Tuđman's power. It was Tuđman's policy of dividing B&H with the Serbs, which was detrimental for Croatia, that brought his own power in Croatia in jeopardy just before the Washington agreement. The public display of displeasure over Tuđman's B&H policy by the true Croatian patriots Manolić and Mesić had brought Tuđman's own power in Croatia into questioning just before the Washington agreement. By Washington agreement, Izetbegović gave the Croatians possibility of gaining half of Bosnia, which then made it possible for Tuđman to win over Manolić and Mesić. Just prior to that, Tuđman, who needlessly started the war with the Bosnians while one-third of Croatia was occupied by Serbs and was on the way to losing the war in Bosnia was all of a sudden given a good deal and saved. By getting half of Bosnia into the federation with Croatia not only saved Tuđman but made him look like a smart politician who knew what he was doing. That is how Izetbegović used the Washington agreement to help those forces in Croatia that worked for dividing Bosnia with the Serbs rather than to strengthen pro-Bosnian forces in the fight to liberate the whole Bosnia.

11

THE BOSNIAN CONGRESS

As the reaction to the open treason of the Bosnian state, a group of Bosnians in the United States formed an organization which was named "The Bosnian Congress." It all started when Dr. Vahid Sendijarević and Stjepan Balog, dedicated activists and humanitarians from the "Bosnian Relief Committee," men who sent many containers of humanitarian help to Bosnia and had published dozens of articles and appeals asking for protection for Bosnia, in one particular exchange of correspondence with President Izetbegović became convinced that Izetbegović is actually the one who initiated the partitioning of B&H. Especially successful activist was Stjepan Balog. Both before and since "The Bosnian Congress" was organized, Balog had published dozens of letters in the New York Times, Washington Post and other newspapers of similar stature and importance. A large number of his articles were published in "Zajdnicar," the largest Croatian paper outside of Croatia. From one of Balog's appeal, the following exchange with Izetbegović took part, which convinced Balog and Sendijarević that with Izetbegović at the "helm," Bosnia had no chance of survival.

11.1. Balog's and Sendijarević's Correspondence with Izetbegović

In the open letter to Izetbegović after his signing of the union plan, among other things, Mr. Stjepan Balog states,

> However, if your goal is the division of Bosnia, then I hope you
> have considered all the possible consequences of that action. Do
> you want to be remembered as Bosnia's first and last president,
> as its undertaker? After many centuries of the existence of

Bosnia and its people, after over 200,000 Bosnians killed in this war, after millions driven from their homes, raped, and tortured, now you will tell them: all that was for nothing. When you start signing the end of Bosnia, remember that in addition to the news reporters and the TV cameras, there will also be the hundreds of thousands of souls of the slaughtered Bosnians who even in their death will lose their homeland.

If the sufferings of the Bosnian people are such that they can't go on any longer, if the Bosnian army has exhausted and is defeated to the point where it can't fight any longer, it is no shame to be defeated by the enemy who many times larger and better equipped and who is also supported by the so-called "civilized" West.

But you have no right to give Bosnia away at the negotiating table. Your objective must be the preservation of Bosnia, not to bury it. If you have no more strength to watch the suffering of the Bosnian people, then step aside and let others fight to preserve Bosnia. As a Croat, I am not proud of the role that Croatia has played in the destruction of Bosnia. But if you sign the agreement to divide Bosnia, you will not be any better than those Croats who betrayed not only Bosnia but their own people. You will be no better than those Serbs who are doing all they can to see the end of you and the Bosnian people.

Dear Mr. Izetbegović, Bosnia doesn't belong only to the Muslims but to the Bosnians of all religions who are willing to fight and defend it from its enemies. Those who love Bosnia would not divide it but would die defending it.

Respectfully,
Signed by: Stjepan Balog, Warren, Michigan, USA

The following is Izetbegović's reply in its entirety.

Dear Mr. Balog

Thank you for your letter of November 11, 1993.

I did not accept the fate of Bosnia as being inevitable, but I am not sure if that is of any importance. Tolstoy wrote 1,000 pages of one of his great novels just so he could prove (or at least try to) that people do not control history. Very often, just the opposite of what people want or strive for happens. What is happening in Bosnia is just our fate and destiny.

Two premises decided the future of Bosnia: The first, there is no Bosnia without the Serbs and Croats, and the second: Serbs and Croats do not want a united Bosnia. You can draw your own conclusions.

I am sure you will agree with the first premise but not with the second, otherwise, why would you have written to me.

The Serbs didn't surprise me, the Croats did. I will never understand their politics and motives.

The entire time they (the Croats) worked towards their own ruin, and I could have never predicted such a thing. A murder can sometimes be prevented, a suicide usually cannot. The Croats have attempted the later and have succeeded.

What is left now is for you to explain to me in a future correspondence (if you wish) how Bosnia can stay undivided without the Serbs and the Croats. I don't have that ability.

I suppose you will answer with mentioning several exceptions, and I will answer that exception do not make states, but that people make them, no matter how respectable, actually they can be just plain people.

If I don't sign some sort of peace agreement, it very likely that Bosnia would be totally occupied. There are those who think that even occupation is better than signatures, and as an example they cite the Baltic states, which even after 50 years of occupation were resurrected as independent states (because there was no signing of a peace agreement, capitulation).

But comparing the Baltic countries to Bosnia is totally unreasonable. The Baltic countries were occupied for fifty years, but their people survived. My people wouldn't survive not 50 years, not even 50 days. We (the Bosnian people) would be completely eliminated, along with our Mosques and all other traces of our existence. That is why the Baltic example doesn't apply to Bosnia.

Unfortunately, those are the facts.

That doesn't mean that there is no hope for a unified Bosnia at this time. At the moment, that would be just a utopian dream, but sometimes even these utopian dreams come true.

Thank you for your love of Bosnia.

Respectfully,
Signed by: Alija Izetbegović, Sarajevo, December 6, 1993

The same day Stjepan Balog sent his reply to Alija Izetbegović. Here is a part of his letter:

One of the reasons I am writing to you asking to preserve Bosnia as a unified country is the fact that a unified Bosnia would be a guarantor of a unified Croatia and buffer between its worst enemy. In your letter you ask:

"How can Bosnia be preserved as unified without the Serbs and the Croats..."

My question is, what are the alternatives to a unified Bosnia and are there other alternatives but a fight for survival and freedom? Who can guarantee you that regardless what agreement is signed, it will be implemented or that the Bosnian people will be saved. In the case of Bosnia, for the international community, the changing of the borders is acceptable even if it was accomplished by force and involved the use of Genocide and ethnic cleansing. Do you expect the same international community to protect the borders of a little "Islamic" state in the middle of Europe? Just as the promises made by the international community were broken in Croatia, they would be broken in Bosnia. Remember the American Indians. After every battle that the Indians lost, a peace was signed which lasted only until the whites needed more land. Then another battle, another "peace" and loss of land, then another battle and peace and the loss of land, until the Indians have lost everything. For the love of Bosnia and for the future of Croatia, do not make the job of your enemies any easier. Your signature will only give legitimacy to the ethnic cleansing and genocide committed against the Bosniaks, but it will not stop it. Does anyone still remember the Bosniaks from Belgrade, Sabac and other Serbian cities in which the Bosniaks were a majority at one time?

You should know that there are many Croats who see the hope for Croatia in the saving and preservation of Bosnia. You are not alone in this war. Those of us who love Croatia are convinced that Croatia will not be liberated from the Serbs without a military fight with Bosnia as its ally.

Although the establishing of closer ties with Croatia looks impossible now, your persistence and the persistence of the Bosnian people in the struggle for a unified Bosnia will force the Croatian government that without a unified, sovereign Bosnia, within its internationally recognized borders, there will be no totally liberated Croatia within its internationally recognized borders.

I ask you not to go to the negotiating table ready to divide Bosnia. By even agreeing to negotiate on Bosnia's borders, you will eliminate all those Croats and Serbs who want to live in the unified Bosnia homeland.

When the Afghanistan chased the Russians, when a Somalian General, who controls only a part of a city succeeded in stopping the American forces, when the Palestinians, after 40 years, are succeeding in the creation of a homeland, why is it then that Bosnians couldn't win the fight against their aggressors.

Respectfully,
Signed By: Stjepan Balog

In a letter to Alija Izetbegović, Dr. Vahid Sendijarević (among other things) states,

> I will agree with you that majority of the Serbs and Croats were manipulated by their own leaders, but what Mr. Balog doesn't know is that you haven't done anything to convince the Bosnian Serbs and Croats to fight for the independent Bosnia. You are also doing everything you can to eliminate even those Muslims who are fighting for an independent, multi-religious sovereign state. Mr. Balog didn't follow your election campaign in which you call for the unification of all the Muslim people of Bosnia, not for the unification of all of the Bosnians. In your program there is no place even for the Muslims, Bosnian patriots, so is it any wonder that the Serbs and the Croats would not fight for "your" Bosnia.

From the above letters, we can clearly see that those two future members of the Bosnian Congress were still convinced at that time that Alija Izetbegović could still be influenced and that his mind could still be changed. However, they soon realized that Izetbegović already knew everything they were telling him—he just didn't care. He wanted Bosnia divided in the best Serbian interest.

That is *why* and *how* the Accusation by Bosnian Congress against Izetbegović for High Treason came to be. Its effect was phenomenal. Many Bosniaks were familiar with the signers of the accusation and knew that they were honorable men with no ulterior motives; nor were they traitors. The accusation had such an effect on Izetbegović that even the Serbian news agency SRNA came to his defense. In the accusation, Izetbegović was criticized for negotiating Bosnia's division with the Serbs. However, the Serbian propaganda machine reported exactly the opposite. The signers of the accusation (and the members of the Bosnian Congress) were praised by the Serbian media as Muslim intellectuals who were criticizing Izetbegović for *not* negotiating with the Serbs. According to the Serbian SRNA news agency, "The reasonable and smart Bosnian intellectuals are criticizing the extremist Izetbegović."

Knowing that Bosnians would oppose anyone who was praised by the Serbs and support anyone who was attacked by them, the Serbs continued to fabricate Izetbegović as a Muslim extremist. With its "support" of the Bosnian Congress, the Serbian SRNA news agency actually was supporting and helping Izetbegović. Such wholehearted Serbian support of Izetbegović is the best proof that he was helping them to accomplish the Serbian project of a divided Bosnia.

It is important to note that at that time, there were no e-mail and World Wide Web in Bosnia; and the mainstream media, controlled by Izetbegović's government, was in full control of Bosnian public opinion.

11.2. The Accusation by Bosnian Congress against Izetbegović for High Treason

Below is the accusation in its entirety:

The Accusation against Alija Izetbegović for High Treason of the Republic of Bosnia and Herzegovina

The Bosnian Congress the USA

May 4, 1994

TO ALL THE CITIZENS OF BOSNIA-HERZEGOVINA, IN THE HOMELAND AND ABROAD

The Bosnian Congress, an organization of Bosnians and friends of the Bosnian people who fight for integral Bosnia-Herzegovina as it was recognized by the UN, feels compelled and duty bound to initiate the following:

ACCUSATION AGAINST ALIJA IZETBEGOVIĆ FOR TREASON COMMITTED AGAINST THE PEOPLE OF BOSNIA-HERZEGOVINA.

1) The Bosnian people are forced to live in an information blockade since the war started, in an implementation of which are involved all of the Sarajevo's media, which in turn are controlled by Izetbegović. The Bosnian people are denied access to the information about the goals and the status of negotiations which are conducted between Izetbegović and the Serbian and the Croatian-controlled portions of B&H. Alija Izetbegović has very smartly gained the trust of the Bosnian people, which is completely cut off from the outside world and is fooling them into thinking that he is really not dividing Bosnia but only deceiving Bosnia's enemies. Actually, the only ones who are really fooled are the Bosnian people and the state of B&H. Also fooled are those Serbs and Croats who are still fighting on the side of the Bosnian government into thinking that they are sacrificing their lives for a unified, multiethnic country of B&H.

It is this unified, civic Republic of Bosnia and Herzegovina that the majority of the Bosnians have voted for during the referendum on Bosnia's independence. The goals of Alija Izetbegović completely coincide with the goals of those who want to divide Bosnia and create the "Greater Serbia" and the "Greater Croatia."

2) Isn't it ironic that it is the Serbian leader Karadžić who is the biggest supporter of creating a "Muslim" state within Bosnia and of the so-called Federation of Croats and Muslims and the CO-Federation of this new entity with the state of Croatia? With the creation of the Muslim - Croat Federation, Izetbegović has in fact guaranteed the creation and existence of the Serbian state within Bosnia. With the recognition of the Serbian and Croatian entities, Izetbegović has also brought into question the existence of the internationally recognized state of B&H and its constitution. By creating the Muslim - Croat federation, Alija Izetbegović has acknowledged the aspirations of Bosnia's enemies, which was to end the existence of B&H and in its place to create several new states. Isn't Alija Izetbegović the one who in his presidential oath took on the responsibility to defend the Constitution and the sovereignty of The Republic of Bosnia-Herzegovina. With the "goal" of creating the "Muslim" mini-state within the confederation with Croatia, Alija Izetbegović has brought into question the existence of Bosnia-Herzegovina and the existence of Bosnian people.

3) Step by step, Alija Izetbegović is realizing the division of B&H by converting the free areas of Bosnia into "protected" zones and thus denying the Bosnian Army and the Bosnian people to continue the struggle and the fight to liberate and connect with other Bosnian territories. On the majority of the battle lines, such agreements have been negotiated, the last one being in the Brčko region. Based on the Brčko agreement of May 3, 1994, the United Nations will now protect the Serbian corridor between Belgrade and the city of Banja Luka. In all of the areas where such agreements have been reached, the UN are serving as the buffer between the warring sides and in some cases, it was the Bosnian Army that was disarmed. During the war, the Bosnian Army was the only one that was forced by Izetbegović's signatures to permanently give up its weapons,

in places such as Žepa, Srebrenica and the newest example, Goražde.

4) Alija Izetbegović knows very well that the UN forces have been separating the Turkish and the Greek sides on Cyprus for over twenty years. Although the division of Cyprus has not been internationally recognized, no one is even questioning the Turkish control over a large part the Cyprus Republic. Izetbegović's goal is to freeze the existing borders until that time when the Bosnian people and the rest of the world will accept the division of Bosnia-Herzegovina as the final and only solution to the Bosnian conflict.

5) Alija Izetbegović knows well that according to the international laws it is not possible to partition a country by force, but only by negotiating. Because of that, his willingness to negotiate with the enemy has given courage to the enemies of Bosnia. Let us remember how large a portion of Bosnia controlled by the Bosnian Army was prior to the January 1993 and how much territory has fallen into the enemy hands since then. The start of negotiations in January of 1993 has returned the fighting morale of the Bosnia's enemies. It is with the start of these negotiations that they realized that Izetbegović will legalize them the occupied territories.

6) By accepting Karadžić and Boban as representatives of the Bosnian Serbs and Croats, he reinforced our enemies "truth" that what is going on in Bosnia is not a war of aggression against a sovereign state but a civil war. We must remember that the UN Resolution 752, in the summer of 1992, clearly stated that Serbia and Montenegro were the aggressors in the Bosnian war and that Bosnia-Herzegovina was the victim of that aggression. By agreeing to negotiate, that resolution practically dismissed by Izetbegović and the process of punishing the aggressor eventually stopped.

7) As the result of the division of Bosnia-Herzegovina, Alija Izetbegović has accomplished the following: there is no more talk of aggression on B&H and about the B&H Army but about the civil war, Muslim Government, Muslim Army, and so on.

8) Many other states were occupied in modern history, but none of them ceased to exist. Some of the examples were France during WWII and many states occupied by the Soviet Union. Why is it that only in Bosnia-Herzegovina the occupation is being accepted as a "done deal"? Because, any negotiations about borders and constitution of a country translate into a death blow for that nation. There must not be any discussions about such sensitive issues as the borders and the constitution of a country, and the protection of these sacred points is sworn in during the presidential inauguration. Alija Izetbegović was duty bound to protect those two sacred things, constitution and the borders of Bosnia.

9) It is not true that we must negotiate. No one can punish us for not wanting to talk to the occupiers of our homeland. It is the right of every victim to refuse to talk to its aggressors and executioners and to demand their punishment. The victim cannot be turned into the "bad guy" just for refusing to negotiate with its assassins. By often repeating the lie "If we don't negotiate, we will be accused of prolonging the war" Alija Izetbegović has tried (and succeeded) in DECEIVING his people, and with the help of negotiations he is beginning to realize his dream of a division of the country with a "Muslim" mini-state on a part of what was Republic of Bosnia and Herzegovina. The price of his betrayal is the loss of most of the Bosnia-Herzegovina and the creation of the Greater Serbia and the Greater Croatia.

10) The Army of Bosnia-Herzegovina is responsible for protecting the Bosnian constitution and the entire territory of Bosnia-Herzegovina, as recognized in its internationally recognized borders. Because of that, the BH army is not responsible for honor the negotiations made by politicians that lead to the destruction of Bosnia's constitution and into the partitioning of the state.

11) For the hundreds of thousands of Bosnians killed in defense of our homeland, for the dignity of Bosnia-Herzegovina and its future generations, Alija Izetbegović must be tried in front of all of the Bosnian people for the crime of treason.

Signed by The Presidency of the Bosnian Congress USA:

Dr. Vahid Sendijarević
Dr. Muhamed Borogovac
Mr. Sven Rustempašić
Mr. Stjepan Balog

The fifth signer of the accusation against Izetbegović could not stand the barrage organized by Izetbegović's people, apparently by Izetbegović's personal emissary in America, Nedžib Šaćirbey (the closest ally and personal friend of Izetbegović's, and also the father of Bosnia's UN representative, Muhamed Šaćirbey). He asked us to omit his name from the document in this book, not because he changed his mind, but because "Bosnia is already divided and any action reversing Izetbegović's betrayal is too late."

11.3. Who Are Indeed the "Young Muslims"— Izetbegović and Šaćirbey

The two very close families of Izetbegović and Šaćirbey are the protagonists of the Bosnian politics for which the Bosnian Congress is sure that they know what exactly is happening to Bosnia-Herzegovina and for whom they know that the goal of their political activities from the very start of the conflict was the division of Bosnia-Herzegovina. It wasn't that they were fulfilling the demands of the international community—it was that this community (more precisely: Owen, Stoltenberg, the Contact Group, etc.) was fulfilling their (Izetbegović's and Šaćirbey's) ambitions and goals. True, the international community was glad to do it. The vast majority of Bosnians dedicated to Izetbegović were manipulated by the very able manipulators Izetbegović and Šaćirbey. The Bosnians who worked for Izetbegović, such as Besim Velić, had placed themselves into the function persecuting the members of the Bosnian Congress. Besim Velić is a lower-level clerk from California, pro-Serbian oriented, who started a paper called *Bosniak*, which would supposedly write against Izetbegović. The plan was to put Velić at the head of Izetbegović's opposition in America. Izetbegović had been doing that often; he himself created opposition to his government so he could then control it. Izetbegović's man, Velić, had tried everything to discredit the Bosnian Congress—from lying about in Izetbegović's Bosnian press to making false accusations against members of Bosnian Congress. But the Bosnian Congress survived it all. We knew that little people blindly follow the authority and suck up to the authorities, so we weren't too surprised.

The question remains: how could Izetbegović and Šaćirbey so successfully manipulate the Bosnian people? One of the answers has already been given: people tend to follow the authority figures and suck up to them. However, there was something else that helped them to fool the intellectuals also. Alija Izetbegović and Nadžib Šaćirbey, were friends since childhood. As many other Muslim high school students, they were imprisoned during the communist crackdown on the organization called "Young Muslims" after WWII. That gave these two the laurels of the victims of the Communist persecution and insured for them the trust of the Bosnian people. However, that title doesn't really guarantee that they are dedicated Muslims and Bosnian patriots as they are being portrayed. Here is why: Post WWII Serbian Communists didn't treat Bosniaks much better than they are doing today. Just as the Serbs are killing all the male Bosniaks that they can get their hands on, so the Serbian-controlled UDBA (Yugoslav version of KGB) nonselectively captured all the young and educated Muslims from Bosniak noble families, regardless of whether they were dedicated to Islam. Then in the prison, the experienced UDBA agents could identify the true, dedicated Muslims or Bosniaks. Those Bosniaks were killed in jails, or they stayed for many years.

All the other "young Muslims" were being recruited into the UDBA service. Many of them did not accept the offer to work for UDBA, but some did. I am particularity familiar with this facet of Bosniak persecution, because my uncle, Ahmed Borogovac, from Zvornik was arrested as a "young Muslim." He was never involved in politics, which also proves that the Serbs, parading as communists, were arresting not only dedicated Muslims. The names of Avdo Sidran, Alija Karamehmedović, and Husref Bašagić were well known in Bosnian prewar emigrant circles. They are the men who agreed to work for UDBA (the Yugoslav secret police) just so they could get out of prison, but afterward, while risking their lives, they succeeded in escaping from Yugoslavia. They would rather abandon their homeland than dirty their hands working for the secret police. How many of the "young Muslims" didn't succeed in escaping from Yugoslavia? How many of them did start working for UDBA? Of course, we would not find them among the ones who were killed in prisons or the ones who served more than ten years, such as Alija Bečić, Hamzalija Hundur, or Teufik Velagić. How come that some of the Bosnian Muslims served as little as one or two years while others served ten years or longer? It is very intriguing that Alija Izetbegović had served his short sentence in prison at the same time when he would have to serve the obligatory three years service in the Yugoslav army!?

For Muslim "fundamentalist" to serve only a short sentence, and simultaneously with military service, is highly suspicious. Why would the Serb dominated communist regime do such a favor for a "Young Muslim"?! Interestingly, two young, dedicated and highly educated Muslims, Hasan Biber and Halid Kajtaz, were discovered as members of the organization by the Yugoslav secret police in 1949, only after Izetbgović contacted them when he returned to Sarajevo after serving simultaneously in the Yugoslav Army and his "sentence" for being a "Young Muslim". They were quickly convicted to death and executed. It would be important to remember that many years later, in nineteen eighties, Bosnian patriots led by Hamdija Pozderac have accused and convicted Izetbegović on a fourteen-year prison sentence for the conspiracy against the Constitution of the Republic Bosnia and Herzegovina.

It is very interesting to note that Izetbegović's minister (secretary) of the interior, Alija Delimustafić, who was described as a Yugoslav secret police spy by both General Sefer Halilović (the first commander of the Bosnian army) and by Dr. Nijaz Duraković, (a member of the Presidency of BH) was hiding from the public what happened with the archives on "young Muslims." Here is what Dr. Duraković had to say about that in the Bosnian newspaper *Ljiljan* on August 9, 1995. I quote, "Muhamed Abadžic was the manager of the newspaper *Oslobođenje*, and on one occasion, he told me that the biggest mystery are the "young Muslims." Who are they, what are their goals, and could I write a book about them? He also told me that we were all just naive children in this questionable game. He asked me if I would write the book for a lot of money. "Of course," I said, knowing that the archive about them and about all those unfortunate trials was being held by UDBA, whose chief at that time was a Dusko Zgonjanin—a chief of the Bosnian police who played the key role in the Agrokomerc setup when Bosnian patriots were removed from power. But since they gave Dervis Susic the job of writing that unfortunate book *Parergon* (a book about Muslim politicians in Bosnia-Herzegovina during WWII), which he did by using the "archives" held by UDBA, I told him to also let me have those "archives" so I could also write my part. We agreed, and I started to work on the project. However, suddenly and very mysteriously, the entire project collapsed, mostly because the UDBA had gotten involved; but most importantly, those archives disappeared, and the Secret Police closed the project. The biggest mystery was the disappearance of the "archives." Do they still exist anywhere? I don't know. That question should be asked of Alija Delimustafić, because I think that he "inherited" it. Was it destroyed during those critical moments? I think that the fingers of KOS (the Yugoslav military secret police, counterintelligence service) are in it, along with other secret services, whose goal was the destruction of our homeland, Bosnia-Herzegovina."

It is obvious that by hiding those "archives," the UDBA was protecting some of its important people. When one considers the fact that the only ones of the "young Muslims" who wielded a lot of power in Bosnia were Alija Izetbegović and Nadžib Šaćirbey, the obvious question that comes to mind is, is it possible that the UDBA was protecting these two?

Soon after "The Accusation of Bosnian Congress" was published, the Bosnian Congress started receiving words of encouragement from many Bosnian citizens. On the other hand, the attacks from Izetbegović's camp also started in the newspapers *Ljiljan* and *Bosniak*. Knowing that he couldn't win any arguments with the Bosnian Congress, because the truth was on our side, our answers to the attacks by Izetbegović's media were never published in those papers. We were publishing them on the Internet news groups.

11.4. Why the American Arms Embargo to Bosnia Was Never Lifted

On the web page of the American Congress *http://thomas.loc.gov*, it is easy to find all bills and votes regarding Bosnia and Herzegovina during the war in Bosnia 1992–1995, if you select 103th and 104th Congress, the corresponding "Legislation and Law Number", "Sponsor" etc. in the search form. Information for searches are listed in the sequel of this section.

The following are key actions in the House and the Senate regarding the lifting of the United States arms embargo on Bosnia:

> 54. S.AMDT.1695 to S.2042 To provide for the termination of the United States arms embargo of the Government of Bosnia and Herzegovina.
>
> Sponsor: Sen Dole, Robert J. [KS] (introduced 5/10/1994) Cosponsors: 33 Latest Major Action: 5/12/1994 Senate amendment agreed to. Status: Amendment SP 1695 agreed to in Senate by Yea-Nay Vote. 50-49. Record Vote No: 111. *https://www. senate.gov/legislative/LIS/roll_call_lists/roll_call_vote_cfm. cfm?congress=103&session=2&vote=00111*.

Quickly after that, in June, the Resolution passed vote in the House:

> 26. H.AMDT.611 to H.R.4301 Amendment requires the President to unilaterally lift the arms embargo on Bosnia and gives the President the discretion to provide up to $200 million in defense articles and services to the Bosnian government upon its request for such aid.
>
> Sponsor: Rep McCloskey, Frank [IN-8] (introduced 6/9/1994) Cosponsors: (none) Latest Major Action: 6/9/1994 House amendment agreed to. Status: On agreeing to the McCloskey

amendment (A025) Agreed to by recorded vote: 244 - 178 (Roll no. 222).

Procedure returned the Resolution in Senate on August 11, 1994. Senate votes, now with the significant majority of 56:44.

> 64. S.AMDT.2524 to H.R.4650 To express the sense of Congress concerning the international efforts to end the conflict in Bosnia and Hercegovina and to establish a process to end the arms embargo on the Government of Bosnia and Hercegovina.
>
> Sponsor: Sen Nunn, Sam [GA] (introduced 8/10/1994) Cosponsors: 4 Latest Major Action: 8/11/1994 Senate amendment agreed to. Status: Amendment SP 2524 agreed to in Senate by Yea-Nay Vote. 56-44. Record Vote No: 279.

At that moment, the USA was still in the position to help the citizens of the Republic of Bosnia and Herzegovina to preserve their unified country, and there was strong will on USA's side to do so, to be on the right side of history. Only one man could stop that—the Bosnian president, Izetbegović, if he declined the offer of help. And this is exactly what happened: Izetbegović came to the USA, to talk at UN General Assembly on September 27, 1994, and he asked for the postponement of the lifting of the arms embargo, see *https://undocs.org/en/A/49/PV.7*, page 8. To Bosnians, who were under the informative blockade and with media controlled by Serbs and Izetbegović, it was presented as a smart move that led to peace. Obviously, that was only another deception. Keep in mind, that genocide in Srebrenica will take place on July 11, 1995, a full year after Izetbegović's refusal to arm the Bosnian army. It never before happened that a country under attack refused arms from their friends.

Of course, many European and American media published the news about Izetbegović's "postponement" of arming the Bosnian army—unfortunately, without challenging Izetbegović's nonsense excuses for such an extremely unusual move. For example, Izetbegović claimed that arming Bosnians might make Serbs angry and that they could punish Bosnians with their powerful weaponry. Obviously, the Serbs never stopped using their weapons throughout. In fact, the situation on the battlefield was that Bosnians, even without the proper arms, were either holding their positions or advancing, because they did not have any other choice than to defend their families. For example, the Bosnians had around twice as many soldiers than the Serbs. And it was only the Serb advantage in weaponry that was maintained by the embargo that kept the Serb forces from getting swept away by the army of the Republic of Bosnian-Herzegovina.

As the war continued, American Congress returned to the issue of the arms embargo in January 1995, still six months before the genocide in Srebrenica. Here are the basic facts about the new resolution, which was vetoed by Clinton because "Bosnians preferred the peace process".

S.21Title: A bill to terminate the United States arms embargo applicable to the Government of Bosnia and Herzegovina.

Sponsor: Sen Dole, Robert J. [KS] (introduced 1/4/1995). Cosponsors: 18 Related Bills: H.RES.204, H.R.1172 Latest Major Action: 8/11/1995 Vetoed by President.

Text of this Resolution can be found on the web page of the US Congress. Here is a quote from the conclusion:

4. TERMINATION OF ARMS EMBARGO.

(a) TERMINATION - The President shall terminate the United States arms embargo of the Government of Bosnia and Herzegovina, as provided in subsection (b), following –

(1) receipt by the United States Government of a request from the Government of Bosnia and Herzegovina for termination of the United States arms embargo and submission by the Government of Bosnia and Herzegovina, in exercise of its sovereign rights as a nation, of a request to the United Nations Security Council for the departure of UNPROFOR from Bosnia and Herzegovina; or

(2) a decision by the United Nations Security Council, or decisions by countries contributing forces to UNPROFOR, to withdraw UNPROFOR from Bosnia and Herzegovina.

On July 26, 1995, right after the genocide in Srebrenica, both houses passed the bill S21 (Bosnian Herzegovina Self Defense Act) by two-thirds majority, 331 votes for the bill in the House of Representatives and 69 in the Senate.

http://www.senate.gov/legislative/LIS/roll_call_lists/roll_call_vote_cfm. cfm?congress=104&session=1&vote=00331.
See also the article in The Baltimore Sun

http://articles.baltimoresun.com/1995-07-27/news/1995208099_1_arms-embargo-bosnia-peacekeepers.

That meant that even a presidential veto could not stop arming Bosnians. However, the Bosnian president insisted on the "peace negotiations". That enabled Clinton's veto, which followed on August 11, 1995. According to the NY Times, published on August 12, 1995, Clinton explained that "he hoped that new allied diplomatic and military efforts in the Balkans would draw enough Congressional support to sustain the veto". Indeed, Bosnian government quickly made progress in August in the "peace process" by giving 49 percent of the country to Serbs, which was signed on September 8, 1995 in Geneva. The final blow to american attempts to arm Bosnians happened when Izetbegovic came to the UN, in the meeting of the General Assembly on October 24, 1995, and completely invalidated the large effort that Bosnian friends in the American Congress undertook in the long political battle to arm Bosnians.

In his speech, Izetbegović, while acting as a Bosnian patriot, refused to pose the necessary request to arm Bosnians. Instead, he did completely the opposite; he requested UNPROFOR to stay in Bosnia, in contrast to the American condition to arm Bosnians, see the above quoted Resolution S21. This time, he noted that Bosnians were winning the war anyways in order to conclude that arming them was not necessary. Note, that argument is in contradiction with his UN General Assembly talk on September 27, 1994 when he presented the Serbs as so powerful that he was afraid of their anger if Bosnians accepted American arms. This time, he said, "We approach this initiative, undertaken by the United States and its President, with the best of faith and with plenty of hope. Our people need and want peace. We have not started this war, and although we are winning, we have not dreamed of being victors in war. We have always worked towards peace and we would like to be victors in peace."

In addition, he now requests from Americans to disarm Serbs rather than to Arm Bosnians. He says:

> In order to achieve peace - and what is more - to maintain it, it is necessary to establish a balance in weaponry. This balance can be established on a higher or lower level. We give the preference to the latter, and we demand the reduction of Serbian heavy weaponry. (See "Statement by H.E. President Alija Izetbegović, the Republic of Bosnia and Herzegovina Special Commemorative Meeting of the General Assembly on the occasion of the Fiftieth Anniversary of the United Nations October 24, 1995", *https://undocs.org/en/A/50/PV.39*, page 14)

Everybody knows how complicated the procedure is to adopt a bill in the US Congress. Nevertheless, Alija Izetbegović threw away the long-awaited result borne from the persistent effort of our friends in the US Congress to arm Bosnians; and out of the blue, he requested that the United States should instead undertake the exponentially more difficult task of disarming the Serbs. Bob Dole, McCloskey, Lugar, Lieberman, Biden, and many others won a big political battle for Bosnia, only to be seen as naïve and to realize that Clinton and Christopher were right when they told them that Bosnian leaders participated with the Serbs in the division of the country.

After that debacle, our friends in the US Congress gave up their fight for a unified Republic of Bosnia and Herzegovina and let the administration search for peace in Izetbegović's terms, which was, in fact, exactly what the Serbs wanted.

As we explained, after the genocide in Srebrenica, the American Congress decided to push toward arming Bosnians. In the following link is a very interesting speech of Senator Olympia J. Snowe from Maine. She explained that, in fact, the UN arms embargo was never imposed on Bosnia, only on the former Yugoslavia as a political entity, not a geographic region. That is the reason that Slovenia and Croatia freely armed themselves, and that arming Bosnians would not be in violation of that arms embargo.

http://www.c-span.org/video/?66260-1/senate-session&start=12244

Unfortunately, Bosnian leadership did not want to behave like Slovenian and Croatian leadership and arm Bosnians. They rather chose to repeat to Bosnian people and to the world that Bosnia was under arms embargo. That was their excuse for not arming the Bosnian army, thus enabling the genocide to happen.

American intervention finally occurred in October 1995. Unfortunately, it was too late to save the Republic of Bosnia and Herzegovina, because Izetbegović's envoy, Muhamed Šaćirbegović already on September 26, 1995 in Geneva, recognized the Serbian Republic on the 49 percent of the Bosnian territory. The circumstances under which he quickly signed that document are described in section "12.5 "Serbs Are Defeated on the Battlefield." Therefore, Izetbegović did not object to American intervention at that time because that intervention secured the deal and as a result stopped the victorious Bosnian army in front of Banja Luka and Prijedor. After the Bosnian army liberated 51 percent of the territory, the Americans said, "Stop, you have to honor the deal that your government signed."

11.5. The Activities of the Bosnian Congress

All information and analyses that we wrote in the previous chapters, including our findings about Izetbegovic's suspicious behavior summarized in the Section 11.4 were made available to many decision makers in Bosnia, as well as to many others. Therefore, all the Bosnian politicians mentioned in this section are responsible for not standing up to President to prevent his treason of the Republic Bosnia & Herzegovina.

The Bosnian Congress was not fighting for a place in the Bosnian government for any of its members. It was not a classical political party. The members of the Bosnian Congress are patriots from all parties who are fighting for Bosnia-Herzegovina as it was defined in its last legal Constitution of 1993. For the Republic of Bosnia and Herzegovina, the Bosnian people voted on the Referendum for Independence, which took place on March 1, 1992, and the Republic of Bosnia-Herzegovina was recognized by the West on April 7, 1992 and became a member of the United Nations on May 22, 1992. That is why the Bosnian Congress can concentrate on spreading the truth about Bosnia without being accused of having ulterior motives. That can be confirmed by all those in the Bosnian government and in the opposition who had any contact with us, such as Alija Izetbegović, Dr. Haris Silajdžić, Stjepan Kljuić, Dr. Eljub Ganić, Dr. Nijaz Duraković, Milorad Dodik, Adil Zulfikarpašić, Dr. Rusmir Mahmutčehajić, Selim Bešlagić, Dr. Muhamed Filipović, Dr. Zlatko Lagumdžija, Krešimir Zubak, Sven Alkalaj, Nedžib Šaćirbey, Ivica Mišić, Dr. Ismet Grbo, Dr. Šemso Tanković, Hilmo Neimarlija, and so on. That means that the Bosnian Congress was fighting for Bosnia-Herzegovina by writing, which is distributed mainly through the Internet, but also by fax, mail, and independent magazines such as *Slobodna Bosna i Hercegovina* ("Free Bosnia-Herzegovina").

The Bosnian Congress had drawn up a mailing list of all the American Congressional Representatives and several hundred newspapers both American and Bosnian, and also other media. In that effort, a lot of help came from Prof. Francis A. Boyle, a professor of international law at the University of Illinois, the man who wrote many legal analysis about Bosnia, which we distributed in Bosnia, and Craig Hamilton from Boston, a friend of the Bosnian people. Craig volunteered primarily for proofreading of our English texts and "Americanize" them. We were closely working with Washington lobbyist Andrew Eiva, from the Washington Office for Bosnia; Frank Tigelar, a man who organized one of the most powerful websites in the 1990s about Bosnia and many others. The most important contacts were established through our online newsletters with both Bosnian politicians and with ordinary Bosnian citizens. That made us knowledgeable insiders of the Bosnian war and influential force on internet, while we were completely isolated by Bosnian regime-controlled media.

12

THE END OF THE WAR

12.1. The Betrayal of Bihać

The war in B&H didn't bring the military victory that the Serbs needed. Although they started the war against the unarmed Bosniaks, they didn't succeed in taking a wider corridor at Brčko, in taking the region of Goražde, the railroad center of Bihać or most of the city of Sarajevo, without which they couldn't create their dreamed-of empire called Greater Serbia. Without the control of the Bihać railroad junction, the Serbs couldn't have good communications with the Serb-occupied region of Croatia, the so-called Republika Srpska Krajina (RSK). Izetbegović couldn't sign Bihać away to the Serbs simply because the Bihać enclave successfully defended its region against the Serbian attacks, and signing it away to the Serbs at that point would be open treason.

But Izetbegović did find a way to help the Serbs anyway. During the heaviest Serbian attacks on Bihać in December of 1994, with mediation of the former USA president, Jimmy Carter, Izetbegović signed a cessation of hostilities with the Serbs throughout the rest of B&H, thus allowing the Serbs to concentrate their attacks on Bihać. The Serbs from the neighboring Croatia didn't sign that agreement, so they openly continued their attacks against the Bihać enclave. The cease-fire with the Serbs in the rest of B&H enabled the Bosnian Serbs from the rest of Bosnia to join in the attacks against the surrounded Bihać since, of course, no one could inspect the documentation of those attacking Bihać. On the other hand, Bosnians could not send enforcement to Bihać because Bihać was surrounded. They could help Bihać only if they tied up the Serbs by fighting them on the other fronts. The Izetbegović's betrayal of Bihać allowed the Serbs to concentrate tremendous powers on that surrounded and cut-off city. The Bosnian army in the rest of Bosnia respected Izetbegović's cease-fire while the Serbs from the different regions of Bosnia went to help the attacks on Bihać. During those days, Bihać was dying under the attacks of the Serbian shelling while the rest of B&H was dying from the shame of having betrayed that surrounded city. Alija Izetbegović hoped that with the fall of Bihać, one more Serbian strategic goal would be achieved, and thus one more obstacle removed for Karadžić to create the Greater Serbia. However, the defenders could not run away, and did not want to surrender.

Bihać became the Stalingrad of the Croatian Serbs from "Krajina." The international community decided to join in with its "protective" suggestions. They recommended that Bihać become a demilitarized zone like Srebrenica and Žepa. Of course, Izetbegović went along with this "peace saving" recommendation. However, General Atif Dudaković, the commander of the Fifth Corps of the Bosnian Army refused to sign that agreement and to disarm the Bihać enclave, stating that "the security zone is only that which the Army of the Republic B&H controls." Thanks to that decision, Bihać was saved, as opposed to Žepa and Srebrenica, which believed in Izetbegović's diplomacy, and thus fell to the Serbs after surrendering their arms to the UN.

12.2. The Fall of Srebrenica

We already saw how the negotiations with the Serbs during 1992 and 1993 had a negative effect on the fighting morale of the Bosnians defending the Drina region and how the same negotiations had lifted the fighting spirit of the Serbian soldiers. However, the collapse of the Bosnian defenders' fighting spirit wasn't by itself enough to bring them a total defeat. Three army corps from the Republic of Serbia, "Užice Corp", "Valjevo Corp", and units of "Niš Corp", were engaged in the Drina region in April of 1993. Several towns were taken by the Serbs, but not Srebrenica and Žepa. Large numbers of Bosnian soldiers had fled to those two towns, so the Serbs couldn't occupy them. If they had been able to, they would have taken those two towns. At that time, that still wasn't such a major "sin" in the eyes of the international community since those had not been declared safe havens yet. In addition, the Serbs knew that they couldn't keep three army corps in that region forever. They knew that the Bosnians would spread out again in that region as soon as the Serbs left (which is what happened to them later on in Bihać). The only way for the Serbs to hang on to Eastern Bosnia was to sign a peace treaty regarding Srebrenica and Žepa, which would then guarantee that the regions the Serbs have conquered will stay in Serbian hands even when most of the Serbian army left. Alija Izetbegović agreed to that. He even agreed to disarm the Bosnian army in Srebrenica and Žepa (all the heavy weapons were taken away by the UN). With that treasonous act by Alija Izetbegović taking place, the Serbs could then concentrate those same troops on attacking Goražde and Igman (Sarajevo). Our naive Bosnians thought that Izetbegović had cheated the Serbs, since most of the infantry weapons were not surrendered by the Bosnian army in those cities.

Actually, Izetbegović has betrayed his people since he forbade them to start liberating the areas occupied by the Serbs, while at the same time, the Serbs simply moved their forces and attacked other Bosnian towns. And that is how the Serbs, with Izetbegović's help, succeeded in politically, and not militarily, neutralizing the Bosnian army. If the Bosnians from Srebrenica and Žepa had General Dudaković instead of Naser Orić, Srebrenica, today would have been like another Bihać—free. As a matter of fact, in December of 1994, when a huge Serbian army came to within 700 meters of the Bihać hospital, General Dudaković refused safe haven, stating that the only "safe haven" could be the area controlled and in the hands of the Bosnian army. When the Serbs left the Bihać region to fight in other areas of Bosnia, the Bihać army liberated all its lost territories. I am not saying in any way to cast any blame on Naser Orić (the commander of Srebrenica) for any of the events taking place. He was young and inexperienced in politics. The one responsible for the losses is the person who was in charge of political activities. The people of Srebrenica will one day be witnesses to the trial of Alija Izetbegović for treason.

So just how did the fall of Srebrenica come about two years later, on July 11, 1995? The best units of the Bosnian army from Srebrenica, led by Naser Orić, were moved out of the region and into the Tuzla just before Srebrenica was attacked. At the same time, the neighboring Second Corp of the Bosnian army, from Tuzla, had an order not to attack the Serbs. In fact, all commanders of the Bosnian army outside Srebrenica were invited to Zenica for some celebration while the genocide in Srebrenica was happening!

A colonel of the Bosnian army, Sefcet Bibuljica, told me that the helicopters of the B&H army traveled back and forth to the surrounded Srebrenica region, and that Srebrenica could have easily been resupplied and rearmed. After the fall of Srebrenica, Kemo Muftić, an advisor to Izetbegović, admitted to my sister that Naser Orić was ordered out of Srebrenica before the Serbian attack. With that, Srebrenica was left without its leadership—i.e., in disarray. The logical question is, why weren't the Serbian weakness and men shortage used to resupply Srebrenica instead of being used to remove the most experienced soldiers and military leadership? Some Srebrenica fighters were even sent to help remove the blockade around Sarajevo, which was so pompously announced by Izetbegović. That raises another interesting question. Many military analysts have asked, why did Izetbegović make such an important action, the de-blockade of Sarajevo, so public? Even NATO forces would never undertake a military action without the element of surprise. That is why many people have asked, what was Izetbegović's "secret" plan?

Now his secret plan can be told. His plan was the fall to the Serbs of Srebrenica and Žepa. Izetbegović was hoping that with the fall of Srebrenica and Žepa, B&H would not survive. He hoped that the Bosnians would realize that Bosnia could no longer stretch to Drina, and that "small" Bosnia that he negotiated with Milošević and Tuđman in September of 1993 in Geneva would finally become a reality. However, this "small" (Muslim) Bosnia was only a bait that Milošević and Izetbegović are offering to uneducated religious Muslim people while they were destroying the internationally recognized state of the Republic of B&H. That small "Muslim" Bosnia, permanently surrounded by enemies, could not survive. That meant that Milošević and Izetbegović were offering them nothing.

12.3. The Betrayal of Žepa

At a news conference held on July 21, 1995, in Sarajevo, reporters asked the UN spokesperson, Alexander Ivanko, "Why is the UN talking only about helping Goražde, which isn't even attacked yet, while Žepa, which is under heavy attacks for several days is not even being mentioned?"

Mr. Ivanko answered, "The UN was officially informed by the Bosnian officials that Žepa has fallen. That means that we can do nothing for a city that has been officially declared as lost [by the Bosnian government]."

That day, Alija Izetbegović announced on TV B&H that Žepa did not fall yet. The question arises: "Why did Izetbegović officially inform the UN that Žepa had fallen and by that eliminated any possible help for the UN safe haven, Žepa, that might have been sent, when he knew that Žepa was still defending?"

Also, on July 21, 1995, during the worst of Žepa's fighting and during the massacres of Bosnians from already-fallen Srebrenica, Izetbegović arrived in Tuzla to greet the just-arrived women of Srebrenica. He stepped in front of the people raising his hands, expecting a huge ovation, as if he achieved some great victory. That reaction of his was picked up by all the international news and TV organizations. Actually, with the fall of Srebrenica and Žepa, Izetbegović did achieve one of his goals—he cleared the way for the territorial division of Bosnia-Herzegovina.

12.4. Political Consequences of the Fall of Srebrenica and Žepa

After the fall of Srebrenica and Žepa, the United States Congress started again the action to lift the arms embargo, to arm B&H. However, Izetbegović started taking new steps to ensure that the embargo is not removed.

Whenever the Serbs committed a new wave of atrocities in Bosnia, the American Congress would restart the action to lift the arms embargo. But the enemies of Bosnia would somehow always choose exactly that time to promote some new "peace agreement" or the creation of "protected zones," or even the bombing of the Serbs. Izetbegović would always jump at any such offer, making B&H friends think that it might be a better option from the lifting of the arms embargo. Izetbegović had stopped the lifting of the arms embargo against B&H many times in the past, as we explained in Section 11.4. For example, he would demand a military parity at a lower level, such as demanding that the weapons be removed from the Serbs, instead of the better option, and the Bosnian army being better equipped. Of course, not arming the Bosnians only helps those who want to see B&H permanently divided. The same thing happened after the fall of Srebrenica. While the American Congress demanded the removal of the weapons embargo, England, Russia and President Clinton were promising that there would be no more falling off the "protected areas" to the Serbs. Again, Izetbegović, with the help of his man, and the Bosnian secretary of State, Šaćirbey, accepted Clinton's offer. However, right after the genocide in Srebrenica, in July 1995, Bosnian Prime Minister and Izetbegović's key ally, Haris Silajdžić, apparently moved by the genocide in Srebrenica, sent a letter to the American Congress stating that B&H wanted a lifting of the American arms embargo.

After the genocide in Srebrenica, US Congress took a concrete action, and so on July, 26, 1995 two-thirds of the US Congress voted in favor of the lifting of the American arms embargo, which meant that even President Clinton couldn't veto it. Those were the unforgettable moments for the Bosnian patriots living in America. It became obvious that a majority of the American people were on the side of law and justice. However, just a few days after that historical vote in the US Congress, due to some shady maneuverings by Izetbegović, Haris Silajdžić was forced to turn in his resignation. Even President Clinton's veto on August 11, 1995, couldn't reverse the lifting of the arms embargo, but Izetbegović and Šaćirbey had succeeded in stopping it. With lightning speed, they made advances in the peace negotiations, first in August in the American embassy in Ankara, Turkey, and then in Geneva, on September 8 and 26, 1995, so that the lifting of the embargo became pointless. Therefore, the vote in the US Congress that would overturn Clinton's veto never took place. The deal was sealed by Izetbegović's speech in UN on October 24, 1995, as we explained in Section 11.4.

It is interesting to note that the president of Croatia, Franjo Tuđman, awarded a medal of Queen Jelena to Alija Izetbegović, see *https://www.youtube.com/watch?v=wy45UhKedZw&fbclid=IwAR2b5KRuQAcb GH2AHAbqqgW7lWSV07csQOp_o-6Z910C1bnh_JQpAohltjQ* and the "Medal of Zrinski" to Šaćirbey. If link does not work, you could copy it and paste in your browser. The acceptance of those medals by Izetbegović and Sacitbey was truly scandalous. First, it is very interesting that the president of the country that has a claim on the parts of Bosnian territory gives awards to the president of Bosnia. In addition, Queen Jelena was a Bosnian queen too. By claiming that Queen Jelena was only a "Croation Quin," Franjo Tuđman claims that Bosnia is just another province of Croatia, such as Dalmatia. That is a continuation of aggression of Croatia by other means and Izetbegović's acceptance of that medal is deprived of any dignity. In addition, it was interesting that Izetbegović accepted these medals on August 8, 1995, so soon after the genocide in Srebrenica, and while the massacres at Žepa were still going on. Such behavior by Izetbegović showed that he actually didn't consider the fall of those two cities as failures, but only the extension of his policies. After the massacre of over 8,000 Bosnians in Srebrenica, he had the nerve to accept medals. It isn't necessary to mention how much Tuđman contributed to the downfall of Bosnia. Bosnia's misfortunes had just reached a high point, and those most responsible for the downfall of Bosnia were accepting Tuđman's medals.

12.5. The Serbs Are Defeated on the Battlefield

The unsuccessful Serbian campaign on Bihać, called "Operation Shield 1994", (Operacija Štit 1994) exhausted Krajina Srbs in Croatia, and killed their motivation to fight. Bihać was their Stalingrad. In the beginning of August of 1995 a peace deal was offered to them. That was called Plan Z4. That plan gave a wide autonomy to Krajina Srbs, within Croatia. Croatian president Tuđman, accepted it and signed it, but Krajina Serbian leaders wanted full independence. That was used by Croatian generals to make an attack on Krajina (occupied territories of Croatia) from all directions. While fifty Serbian tanks were still on the Bihać front, and the UN again was ineffective in protecting the victims of the Serbian aggression, Croatia suddenly came into the fight. In a real record time, Croatia drafted thousands of soldiers and stormed all the Serbian strongholds in Croatia except in east Slavonia on the border with Serbia.

In the clash against armed men, the Serbian soldiers weren't as brave as against the unarmed civilians of Srebrenica and Žepa. Before the Croatian armed forces, they didn't even last three days. But even this fall of Knin wasn't the fastest that the "brave Serb heroes" lost a major stronghold. That record was set earlier in May of 1995 when they lost west Slavonia in only two days. The series of these lightning-fast Serb defeats continued in Bosnia-Herzegovina, when Bosnian ofansive against Serbs started on September 8, 1995, with Iranian arms suplied directly to Fifth Corp of Bosnian Army, on Izetbegoić's surprise. Toward the end of September and the beginning of October 1995, the Serbs lost enormous territories of Bosanska Krajina from Bihać and Bosanski Novi to Jajce and Donji Vakuf. On Ozren Mountain the

Vozuča stronghold in north Bosnia fell and the territories controlled by the Second (Tuzla) and the Third (Zenica) Corp of the Bosnian army became connected by roads. Before that, Tuzla and Zenica were connected only by narrow mountain military paths. The road to a strategic place Doboj (the main Bosnian crossroads) was open. The First Corps liberated vast lands near Sarajevo, on Treskavica Mountain and only needed to get ten more kilometers to reach Goražde. Republika Srpska was admitting defeat, and the president of the Bosnian Serbian Republic, Koljević, dramatically exclaimed, "If the offensive of the Bosnian Army is not stopped in thirty-six hours, you can except the Republic of Serbs in Bosnia to break.", see *https://www.facebook.com/ArmijaaRBiH/videos/609021342880681/?v= 609021342880681*

The Serbian forces were in disarray, and the Serbian refugees totally clogged up the corridor in Brčko (Posavina) as their tractors ran out of gas, so that the reinforcements from Serbia couldn't even reach the battlefields. Not that they could make a large enough force and send it fast enough into the distant Bosanska Krajina anyway. Besides, such a force coming from Serbia would be an easy target for the Bosnian and Croatian artillery on the thin Brčko corridor. Freedom was within reach.

But then Izetbegović urgently jumped to help the Serbs. In the negotiations in Geneva, on September 8, 1995, he recognized Republika Srpska on 49 percent of Bosnia. On September 26, 1995, he sent to Geneva his Foreign Secretary Šaćirbegović to sign that deal on behalf of Bosnian government, even though the deal was not approved by Bosnian Presidency. (Izetbegović became very sophisticated in hiding his treasons, after we from the Bosnian Congress started accusing him of high treason.) The cease-fire was signed on October 10. In two days, on October 12, Izetbegović succeeded in stopping the advancing Bosnian army, preserving around half of the territory of the Bosnia-Herzegovina under Serbs.

It is interesting to note that the Bosnian media blamed the Americans for stopping the Bosnian army. They knew only that the Americans stopped the advancing Bosnian army in front of the defenseless Banja Luka and Prijedor. The media did not know the important part—that Izetbegović's envoy, Muhamed Šaćirbegović, already on September 26, 1995 in Geneva, recognized the Serbian Republic on 49 percent of the Bosnian territory, and honoring that deal was the basis for the American request of the Bosnian Army to stop.

12.6. The Methodology of Deceit

All the given and supported reactions of Bosnian patriots didn't make Izetbegović change his policy on the division of Bosnia-Herzegovina. Neither did the fact that up to the day the truce was implemented, October 12, 1995, much more than 51 percent of Bosnia-Herzegovina was freed (the UN says 53 percent), and that the Serbs were in total ruin. Bosnian cities were freed daily, and General Dudaković was advancing even toward Banja Luka itself. Nevertheless, Izetbegović agreed to a truce with which he stopped our advances and saved the 49–51 percent formula.

Omar Šaćirbey, the younger son of Nedžib Šaćirbey, states for the *New York Times* from September 29, 1995, in the article by Chris Hedges that the Bosnian government was ready to give up territories that it conquered in the period of the past weeks if the Bosnian Serbs gave up Goražde and Sarajevo. The problem with this "logic" of Bosnian negotiators is that Bosnian Army already held, from the beginning of the war, both cities, Goražde and Sarajevo. Do not be surprised that experienced newsmen from the *New York Times* asked a young boy, Omar Šaćirbey, from Washington, who was only a son of Izetbegović's friend Nedžib Sacirbey, and not someone from the legal Presidency of Bosnia-Herzegovina. That is just because they were experienced, and so they realized who really had the power in Bosnia—the Izetbegovićs and their devoted friends.

Right after the large areas of Bosnia were liberated, the Croatian government intended to send Bosnian refugees from the liberated areas to their homes. Izetbegović protested and prevented it. Omar Sacirbey's statement for the *New York Times* revealed why the Bosnian government protested the Croatian efforts to return the Bosnian refugees to those newly liberated areas. If they returned to those areas, then it would be harder for them to turn those areas back over to the Serbs. Besides, at that time, both Sarajevo and Goražde were under Bosnian army control. Hence, according to Omar Šaćirbey's statement, our government would change areas that our army held for other territories that our army also already held Goražde and Sarajevo. So, it was enough that in some proposal which we didn't have to accept, it was proposed that Goražde was given to the Serbs, and then they used it as a fact that Goražde belonged to Serbs and trade other things for it. The Izetbegović-Šaćirbey clique was ready to give the territories that connected Bihać with the other Bosnian army–held parts of Bosnia-Herzegovina to keep Goražde, which we already held anyway.

Sometime ago, Izetbegović was convincing Bosnians that they should accept 51 percent of Bosnia-Herzegovina, because then 15 percent would be returned. Now, the non-obedient Bosniaks from Bosnian Krajina (western Bosnia), led by Dudaković, freed more than 53 percent of territories; he didn't have a better argument but to threaten with the Russian nuclear weapons. Namely, in many interviews and articles, one of those from the American Muslim magazine *The Minaret* (October issue, vol. 17, #7), he said that Republika Srpska could ask its ally Russia, who had nuclear weapons, for help if the war continued. That article was very important because in it, he completely revealed himself. He made all the possible arguments for the division of Bosnia, which I will not repeat because we already heard them from Karadžić many times. In that article, Izetbegović endeavors with an unseen determination to make a Serbian Republic on 49 percent of the territory of Bosnia-Herzegovina, which he finally succeeded in Dayton.

12.7. Army and Politics

Toward the end of April 1992, Tuzla was already filled with refugees, most of them from Zvornik. When Kula Grad (a stronghold of Zvornik municipality) fell, I met three soldiers who fought there. I welcomed them into my home and befriended them. I especially liked the eighteen-year-old Mevko Omerović. I gave him my "scorpion." I knew that they wouldn't stay with me for long because they yearned to return and fight for their hometown. That was then the only thing they lived for. Nobody should take away from anyone their right to fight for their homes and neighborhoods. In no way did they think that Zvornik was a Serb town just because the Serbs took it with guns. They knew that Zvornik was theirs, and that they could take it back only by force, as it was their right. They enlisted into the Bosnian army on May 16, 1992, one day after the liberation of Tuzla, when a big number of soldiers were armed with the weapons made available when they were taken from the JNA after the fight at Brčanska Malta. They immediately left for the battlefields into the Zvornik villages around Sapna (a free part of Zvornik municipality).

Later, I often saw them when they took leave in Tuzla. Izetbegović did to them a hundred times greater injustice when he signed that Zvornik belonged to the Serbs than the Serbs did when they took their homes with guns. Faced with betrayal, most people said, "The Army won't listen to him." However, slowly but surely, Izetbegović put the Bosnian army under his control. Every army is based on a strong hierarchy. An army is very easily controlled because it is enough to change a few high-ranking officers and gain a very strong influence on that army's actions and policies. That happened to the Bosnian Army. In July 1995, almost all the high-ranking officers who led the army and defended Bosnia-Herzegovina in 1992, were removed. I mostly regret that some of the greatest heroes were removed, including General Sefer Halilović (the first commander of the Patriotic League and the Bosnian Army), General Stjepan Šiber (who helped found the Bosnian army and successfully defended Sarajevo in the beginning of the war), Kerim Lučarević (who defended the Bosnian Presidency Building and freed Mojmilo Hill, thus ending the blockade of the Sarajevo suburb of Dobrinja), General Mustafa Hajrulahović-Talijan, (commander of the First Corps in time of its victories on Pofalići and Žuč), General Hazim Šadić (liberated Vijenac, a stronghold near Tuzla, and defended Olovo), General Arif Pašalić (broke the blockade of Mostar), General Ramiz Dreković (before Dudaković he successfully defended Bihać), etc.

Let's also add Naser Orić, who was taken out of his Srebrenica when it needed him the most. Those men were the ones who gave hope to Bosniaks by saying that the army wouldn't let Bosnia-Herzegovina be divided while Izetbegović journeyed around the world and signed such divisions. Before he removed Sefer Halilović, he criticized him by saying, "There are those extremists who say that the war will be over when the Bosnian flag flies in Banja Luka and Grude." So, for the president of Bosnia-Herzegovina, an extremist is someone who says that the army of Bosnia-Herzegovina has the right to liberate every square foot of its homeland. Their statements they paid for dearly. Izetbegović's secret police tried to kill Sefer Halilović with a bomb set in his apartment. He survived; but his wife, and brother-in-law didn't, see *https://www.youtube.com/watch?v=G4lq-zAsULw*.

The others lost their influence in the Bosnian army. In one interview in *Ljiljan* (1995), Sefer Halilović said, "From the beginning of the war, an invisible hand constantly makes the wrong moves."

He knew that many enemies of Bosnia-Herzegovina were operating as Izetbegović's special agents and advisors. In that interview, he mentioned Alija Delimustafić the prewar minister of internal affairs and the owner of CENEX; Armin Pohara; and Jasmin Jaganjac used against Bosnia-Herzegovina by the "invisible hand." Sefer Halilović was replaced by Rasim Delić, a man that just like Halilović "wants" an integral Bosnia-Herzegovina, but who finished all his speeches by saying: "The army is for an integral Bosnia-Herzegovina, but will implement whatever the politicians decide."

In that sentence is the fundamental difference between Halilović and Delić, and the explanation why Halilović was replaced by Delić. However, the Army is still a force composed of patriots and heroes. Commanders like General Atif Dudaković (Fifth Corps), General Mehmed Alagić (Seventh Corps) and all of those mentioned earlier are men devoted to Bosnia-Herzegovina. Their only weakness was that they never suspected that Izetbegović wanted the division of Bosnia-Herzegovina. Had they thought more about politics, maybe they could have prevented some negotiations and signatures that Izetbegović did, which brought great harm to Bosnia - Herzegovina. Remember the peace treaty from October 12, 1995, that Izetbegović made after the cry by Koljević that "if something isn't done fast, in 48 hours the Serb component in Bosnia will break."

That was after the total Serb collapse in September and October of 1995, when in a period of ten days or so, they lost Drvar, Sipovo, Jajce, Kulen Vakuf, Donji Vakuf, Bosanski Petrovac, Bosanska Krupa, Kljuc, Sanski Most, Mrkonjic Grad, the hydroelectric plant Bocac near Banja Luka, half of the mountains Ozren and Manjaca, and the great areas on the way from Sarajevo to Goražde. The total defeat of the Serbs was prevented by Izetbegović by recognizing Republika Srpska and signing the truce that stopped the Bosnian army from liberating a territory of the Republic. Why not defeat the aggressor and free the country? Why let the aggressors keep all that they conquered and let them escape their deserved punishment? To spare the Serbian Chetnik movement from breaking was to sign the death sentence for our homeland.

***

The End of the First Part.

Note: Writing of the First Part of the book was concluded on November 5, 1995. It was published in the book "Rat u Bosni i Hercegovini 1992-1995" at the end of November 1995, in Bosnian.

Part II

Part I of this book was written in Bosnia before November 5, 1995, before the Dayton peace agreement was reached on November 21, 1995, and officially signed in Paris, France on December 14, 1995. We wrote it only in Bosnian, because we were in hurry to do it before it was too late. We desperately wanted to explain to Bosnian people what Izetbegović was doing, hoping that the people would somehow prevent the division of Bosnia. Part I is a translation of the corresponding part in the book in Bosnian, published in November 1995, except that we now added references (links) to events that were well known to the war generation, but need to be documented for new generations. Part II pertains to the events that occurred after the Dayton peace agreement. This is the collection of documents that are not widely known.

As we saw, the Izetbegović-Šaćirbegović signatures converted the Serbian defeat on the battlefield into a victory on the negotiating table, and the Bosnian army victory was "rewarded with the division and disappearance of Bosnia-Herzegovina. That has been finalized and put into Constitution in Dayton (Annex 4 of the Dayton peace deal.). There wasn't anyone in the B&H delegation in Dayton who was defending integral Bosnia-Herzegovina—i.e., the internationally recognized Constitution of the Republic Bosnia-Herzegovina. People were hopeful of Silajdžić, but he caved in to Izetbegović; and so in Dayton, he didn't make any effort against the division of Bosnia. He was a bit uneasy when they gave up Srebrenica and Žepa. But Silajdžić did not care about Bosnia-Herzegovina; he was just another player of the same team. In Tuzla, he cried before the refugees from Srebrenica who had just fled their homes, but he didn't cry and he did not do anything for Srebrenica when Srebrenica was being given to Republika Srpska in Dayton. I am familiar with his position in Dayton because Dr. Vahid Sendijarević, Kasim Hadžović (a Bosnian businessman in the USA), and I spoke with him during the Dayton negotiations. Toward the end of our phone conversation, I appealed to him not to sign the breakup of Bosnia. He answered, "It is easy for you to be for an integral Bosnia from here, the USA. Why don't you return to Bosnia? Then you would talk differently."

I told him that my absence from Bosnia-Herzegovina was no excuse for one government leader to betray his homeland, Bosnia-Herzegovina, by signing its destruction. He hung up the phone. It seemed that the politicians in Bosnia, surrounded by yes-men, had lost the sense to listen to any criticism from the people whose fate they were deciding.

The following chapter is an analysis of A. Francis Boyle, professor of international law at University of Illinois. Professor Boyle sent this analysis to the Bosnian Parliament on time, to prevent ratification, but Izetbegović's people did not forward it to representatives.

13

THE DAYTON AGREEMENT

FROM: PROFESSOR FRANCIS A. BOYLE
SUBJECT: THE DAYTON AGREEMENT
DATE: NOVEMBER 30, 1995
TO: PARLIAMENT OF THE REPUBLIC OF BOSNIA-HERZEGOVINA

DEAR FRIENDS:

Introduction

1. I have now had the opportunity to study the Dayton documents. It is clear that Bosnia will lose 49% of its territory to the Serb aggressor forces. Even worse, however, the 30% of Bosnia now under the control of the Government and the Army will effectively cede its independence to NATO. NATO will become a belligerent occupation force that will be totally in control of the land where it is stationed. I can see why you might be prepared to give away 49% of Bosnia that you do not control. But I cannot understand why you would want to give away to NATO the 30% of Bosnia that you do control. In essence, the 30% of Bosnia that you do control will become the ward of NATO. You will have absolutely no independence at all. The NATO commander will have absolute dictatorial powers and the military force necessary to back up his decisions. The President, the Presidency and the Government will become nothing more than a puppet regime that will have to do whatever NATO tells them to do.

2. Thus, after all, these years, after all of your suffering, after all you have accomplished, you will be effectively surrendering 49% of your territory to the Serbs, 20% of your territory to Tuđman, and 30% of your territory to NATO. Of

117

course, this decision is for you to make, not me. But your Army was not defeated in battle. It controls 30% of the territory of Bosnia. It makes absolutely no sense for the Army to surrender to NATO under the terms of the Dayton Agreement. These conclusions become clear from an analysis of the following elements of the Dayton Agreement:

Proximity Peace Talks,
Wright-Patterson Air-force Base, Dayton, Ohio,
November 1-21, 1995

General Framework Agreement for Peace in Bosnia and Herzegovina

3. The General Framework Agreement refers to "the Federal Republic of Yugoslavia," not the Federal Republic of Yugoslavia (Serbia and Montenegro). This is yet another concession to the rump Yugoslavia that basically implies that the Federal Republic of Yugoslavia is the successor-in-law to the former Yugoslavia.

4. Article I already refers to "Bosnia and Herzegovina" instead of the Republic of Bosnia and Herzegovina. It appears from this phraseology that the Republic of Bosnia and Herzegovina will give way to something called "Bosnia and Herzegovina." In other words, the Serbs will have accomplished their objectives of dissolving the Republic of Bosnia and Herzegovina, while obtaining formal recognition of Republika Srpska.

5. Article III explicitly refers to Republika Srpska. This has been another Serb objective all along, to obtain formal recognition of Republika Srpska.

6. Article V. It is a bit strange and unprecedented for the Republic of Croatia and the Federal Republic of Yugoslavia to "fully respect and promote fulfillment of the commitments made" under the new Constitution of Bosnia and Herzegovina. In other words, Croatia and the rump Yugoslavia have basically been made guarantors for the Constitution of Bosnia and Herzegovina. This is similar to what happened in Cyprus, where Turkey, Britain and Greece were guarantors. Of course, the war ensued.

7. Article X says that the Federal Republic of Yugoslavia and the Republic of Bosnia and Herzegovina "recognize each other as sovereign independent states within their international borders." Yet, this language does not constitute formal diplomatic recognition. This can only be done by means of the two governments

exchanging ambassadors with each other. This is confirmed by the next language found in

Article X:
"Further aspects of their mutual recognition will be subject to subsequent discussions." Hence there is still not the establishment of formal diplomatic relations between the Republic of Bosnia and Herzegovina and the Federal Republic of Yugoslavia. I doubt very seriously that Milošević will ever exchange Ambassadors with, and thus formally recognize, the Republic of Bosnia and Herzegovina, which will be dissolved under the terms of the Dayton Agreement.

8. Article XI. The fact that this Agreement enters into force upon signature simply indicates that Holbrooke decided to ram it through immediately and then present it as a fait accompli to the Parliament of the Republic of Bosnia and Herzegovina.

Annexes:
Annex 1-A: Agreement on the Military Aspects of the Peace Settlement
Article I. General Obligations

9. Obviously, this Agreement attempts to treat NATO as if it were a "regional organization and arrangement" within the meaning of Chapter 8 of the United Nations Charter. But NATO is clearly not this. Rather, NATO is a collective self-defense arrangement organized under Article 51 of the Charter, which falls within Chapter 6. NATO has no authority under the terms of the United Nations Charter or the NATO Pact to engage in some type of international peace enforcement operation as described herein.

10. Arguably the United Nations Organization has authority to set up a peacekeeping operation such as UNPROFOR. But NATO does not.

11. 2(a). "Neither Entity shall threaten or use force against the other Entity and under no circumstances shall any armed forces of either Entity enter into or stay within the territory of the other Entity without the consent of the government of the latter and of the Presidency of Bosnia and Herzegovina." In other words, the Bosnian Army cannot attack the Srpska Army under any circumstances.

12. 3. "Both Entities shall be held equally responsible for compliance herewith..." In other words, the Federation of Bosnia and Herzegovina and Republika Srpska are being treated as if they were de facto independent states. The Republic of Bosnia and Herzegovina is nowhere to be found here.

Article II. Cessation of Hostilities

Article III. Withdrawal of Foreign Forces

13. This seems to require the withdrawal of military forces of the Republic of Croatia and the rump Yugoslavia within thirty days. And yet the Republic of Croatia and the rump Yugoslavia are not parties to this Annex. Rather, the only parties to this Annex are the Republic of Bosnia and Herzegovina, the Federation of Bosnia and Herzegovina, and the Republika Srpska. But there are side letters to that effect which will be discussed below.

14. There is established here a zone of separation between the forces that is four kilometers wide, that is two kilometers on either side of an agreed cease-fire line. Only IFOR is permitted in this agreed cease-fire zone of separation. In other words, this is a de facto carve-up of the Republic of Bosnia and Herzegovina along the cease-fire line that will be policed by IFOR.

III. Phase II, page 7

15. Here the document refers to "Inter-Entity Boundary Line." So it is clear that they are talking about a boundary line here. In other words, once again, both Entities are being treated as if they were de facto states requiring the demarcation of a boundary line.

16. 4. General, page 8. Notice here that IFOR will demarcate the boundary line between the two Entities. So, once again, you have NATO/IFOR formally demarcating a border, thus creating two de facto independent states.

V. Phase III, page 9

17. 6. "...the IFOR has the right and is authorized to compel the removal, withdrawal, or relocation of specific Forces and weapons from, and to order the cessation of any activities in, any location in Bosnia and Herzegovina..." In other words, IFOR is going to run the entire country of Bosnia and Herzegovina. The rest of paragraph 6 gives IFOR the right to use military force toward that end.

18. Basically, therefore, IFOR will be in charge of the entire country, with the right to use military force anywhere it wants. It is hard to see what will be left than of

the formal independence of the Federation of Bosnia and Herzegovina, let alone the Republic of Bosnia and Herzegovina.

Article VI. Deployment of the Implementation Force, page 11

The Security Council is supposed to establish IFOR acting under Chapter 7 of the United Nations Charter, which deals with enforcement action. Nevertheless, NATO still has no authority or competence to do this. Rather, it is simply a collective self-defense arrangement organized under Article 51, which is in Chapter 6.

3. IFOR can be called upon to assist the conduct of free and fair elections, to assist humanitarian organizations, to deal with refugees, etc. Page 12. In other words, it appears that IFOR will be drawn in to provide the military muscle necessary to do everything else in Bosnia and Herzegovina. This is directly contradictory to what Clinton is saying publicly about the limited role of NATO.

21. 5. Basically, the IFOR commander can do whatever he wants in Bosnia and Herzegovina. And paragraph 6 gives him the right to use military force. In other words, all of Bosnia and Herzegovina is going to be run by IFOR.

22. Page 13. Basically, IFOR will become the belligerent occupant of Bosnia and Herzegovina, with all the rights, privileges, and immunities thereof. And the IFOR commander has the right to use military force basically at his discretion.

23. Under these conditions, therefore, I do not understand how IFOR cannot get involved in so-called nation-building in Bosnia and Herzegovina.

24. Basically, under the terms of this Agreement, NATO will become the belligerent occupant of Bosnia and Herzegovina. It will, therefore, have the obligation under the Hague Regulations to maintain law and order. Consequently, the Bosnian government will be giving up whatever independence it currently exercises over the 30% of Bosnian territory that it now controls, as well as permanently surrendering away control over the 49% of Bosnian territory assigned to Republika Srpska. Under these circumstances, the President, the Presidency, and the Parliament will become nothing more than a puppet regime that will have to do whatever ordered by IFOR. Article VIII. Establishment of a Joint Military Commission

25. It seems to me that the Joint Military Commission will become the de facto government of Bosnia. Notice, however, that the Commission shall function as

nothing more than a consultative body for the IFOR commander. Therefore, the IFOR commander runs all of the Bosnia for all intents and purposes.

Article XII. Final Authority to Interpret

26. Basically, the IFOR commander has the legal authority to do whatever he wants to do. So, in essence, this Agreement is setting up a military dictatorship in Bosnia under the control of the IFOR commander.

Appendix B to Annex 1-A: Agreement between the Republic of Bosnia and Herzegovina and the North Atlantic Organization (NATO) concerning the Status of NATO and its Personnel

27. Basically, NATO personnel will be immune from the jurisdiction of the Republic of Bosnia and Herzegovina for whatever they might do. This NATO operation will be a law unto itself.

Agreement between the Republic of Croatia and the North Atlantic Treaty Organization (NATO) Concerning the Status of NATO and its Personnel I have not read this document

Agreement between the Federal Republic of Yugoslavia and the North Atlantic Treaty Organization (NATO) Concerning Transit Arrangements for Peace Plan Operations 29. I have not read this document.

Annex 1-B: Agreement on Regional Stabilization 30. This Agreement is between the Republic of Bosnia and Herzegovina, the Republic of Croatia, the Federal Republic of Yugoslavia, the Federation of Bosnia and Herzegovina and Republika Srpska.

Article II(i)

31. Notice that this only talks about a military liaison mission between the chiefs of the armed forces of the Federation of Bosnia and Herzegovina and the Republika Srpska. In other words, the Army of the Republic of Bosnia and Herzegovina disappears. And the Armies of the Federation and Srpska are treated as Armies of de facto independent states. There is no joint command, only coordination, which will never happen.

32. Article IV, page 4. These arms ratios are totally inequitable. Basically, the rump Yugoslavia will have 75% plus the 10% given to Republika Srpska for a grand total of 85% of the baseline. The Republic of Croatia will have 30% of the baseline whereas the Federation will have 20% of the baseline. I do not see how these ratios can create a stable peace in Bosnia or in the Balkans.

Annex 2. Agreement on Inter-Entity Boundary Line and Related Issues.

33. The establishment of an inter-entity boundary line between the Federation and Srpska will probably become permanent.

Article V. Arbitration for the Brčko Area

Basically, this puts the Brčko area on ice for the next year. Again, the whole purpose of this Dayton Agreement was for Clinton to get something in writing so that he could put the whole Bosnia issue on ice for the next year in order to move forward with his presidential election campaign without interference.

35. Also, right now I think it might be unlikely for the President of the International Court of Justice to appoint a third arbitrator when Bosnia has a case pending before the World Court against the rump Yugoslavia. Of course, if and when Bosnia is forced to withdraw this lawsuit, then perhaps the President of the Court might be willing to discharge this obligation. They should have provided for some other alternative here besides the ICJ President.

Annex 3. Agreement on Elections

36. Page 2. Quite frankly I do not see how there can be real elections within nine months after entry into force of this Agreement under the current conditions. This requirement is a joke. All the Pale Serbs have to do is stall. The elections will never go forward in Republika Srpska in accordance with these requirements and under these conditions.

Article III. The Provisional Election Commission

37. It is for the Commission to impose penalties "against any person or body that violates such provisions." But obviously, this means nothing without IFOR enforcement.

Article IV. Eligibility

"By Election Day, the return of refugees should already be underway, thus allowing many to participate in person in elections in Bosnia and Herzegovina." This is a ridiculous statement. How can anyone take this at face value.

39. There is absolutely no way anyone is going to be able to organize democratic elections in Bosnia within the next ten months.

Annex 4. Constitution of Bosnia and Herzegovina

40. Continuation. It does appear from the language used here that the continuity of the state as an international legal person will continue, including Bosnia's membership in the United Nations Organization. Of course, the Serbs will be able to claim that "the Republic of Bosnia and Herzegovina" no longer exists and that this Agreement explicitly recognizes Republika Srpska. But unlike previous versions, this language appears to protect the legal existence of the State and its UN membership. The first draft language is given by Holbrooke to President Izetbegović on 5 November 1995 would have dissolved the Republic of Bosnia and Herzegovina as a state under international law. So much for his good faith. It was just as bad as what Owen tried to do at the Owen-Stoltenberg negotiations.

Article III. Responsibilities of and Relations Between the Institutions of Bosnia and Herzegovina and the Entities.

41. Obviously, Defense is omitted from this list on purpose. Therefore, the central institutions will have no competence to deal with matters related to the defense of the State. Therefore, under paragraph 3, below, the two entities have responsibility for "defense". Hence, the two entities—the Federation and Srpska—will become de facto independent states.

42. Effectively, then, the institutions of the currently-existing Republic of Bosnia and Herzegovina will go out of existence, and a limited number of institutions with limited competence might take their place. All other institutions must be agreed upon by Republika Srpska, which will never happen.

43. Article IV. Parliamentary Assembly. The House of Peoples will never work here because the Serb Delegates from Republic Srpska will simply absent themselves as a block on instructions from Pale.

Since the Pale Serbs can veto the operations of the House of Peoples, then they can also veto the operations of the Parliamentary Assembly.

Since the Pale Serbs can order their delegates to the House of Peoples to absent themselves, there will never be a quorum in the House of Peoples. Since there will never be a quorum, the House of Peoples cannot act lawfully, and therefore the Parliamentary Assembly cannot act lawfully. Thus nothing will get done against the wishes of the Pale Serbs.

46. These other provisions do not change the situation. Since the Pales Serbs have the right to prevent a quorum, then no business can be transacted at all against their wishes.

47. Once again, by voting as a block, the delegates or members from Republika Srpska can effectively prevent any business from being transacted by the Parliamentary Assembly against their wishes.

48. Paragraph 4. Powers. Notice that the Parliamentary Assembly does not have the competence to actually levy, raise, or appropriate taxes or revenues. It can only do the "deciding upon the sources and amounts of revenues for the operations... ." In other words, it has no independent source of income. For this reason, it will be completely meaningless. It will be very similar to the first Articles of Confederation here in America that failed precisely for this reason. It was replaced by the Constitution of the United States of America that gave the Federal Congress the right to raise money by means of taxation, duties, imposts, etc. Without the power to tax, this Parliamentary Assembly will have no effective powers at all.

49. Article V. Presidency. Section 2(d) effectively gives the Pale Serbs a veto power over the operations of the Presidency. In other words, the Presidency will be able to do nothing against their wishes. It simply will not be able to operate.

50. Thus the Pale Serbs will even be able to prevent the Presidency from conducting the foreign policy of Bosnia and Herzegovina. Therefore, even that limited competence can be effectively forestalled by the Pale Serbs.

5. Standing Committee

51. Under this provision, the Bosniac member of the Presidency has control over the Bosnian Army. The Croat member of the Presidency has the control over the

HVO. And the Serb member of the Presidency has control over the Srpska Army. It does not appear that there will be any type of joint command or general staff for these three armies. Thus, the Srpska Army will remain intact as it currently is. If so, then that would undermine the paper guarantee of refugees and displaced persons to return to their homes. Why would a Bosniac or a Croat want to return to their homes under the occupation of the Srpska Army that is being commanded by the successors to Mladić and Karadžić? That refugee would have to be insane. The rest of the language in 5(a) guarantees the de facto partition of Bosnia and Herzegovina. The Standing Committee on Military Matters only has authority "to coordinate," not to command. Therefore, the three armies (Army, HVO, Srpska) will remain intact as is.

Article VI. Constitutional Court

54. This so-called protection in here giving the Constitutional Court the jurisdiction to decide on a "special parallel relationship" will not help. The Constitutional Court would certainly have to permit a "special parallel relationship" between Republika Srpska and the Republic of Serbia that is identical to the Confederation Agreement between the Republic of Croatia and the Federation of Bosnia and Herzegovina. But the conclusion of such a Confederation Agreement between Republika Srpska and the Republic of Serbia will be tantamount to a de facto, but not de jure, absorption of Republika Srpska by the Republic of Serbia. In other words, you will have a de facto, but not de jure, Greater Serbia that would include 49% of the territory of the Republic of Bosnia and Herzegovina.

55. It is also clear that the Constitutional Court has no authority to interfere when the Pale Serbs absent themselves so as to prevent the establishment of a quorum in the House of Peoples. Thus, there is no way the Constitutional Court can force the House of Peoples and therefore the Parliamentary Assembly to function and operate against the wishes of the Pale Serbs.

Article VII. The Central Bank

56. This provision provides that the Central Bank's responsibility "will be determined by the Parliamentary Assembly." But since the Pale Serbs have a veto power over the operations of the Parliamentary Assembly, this Central Bank will never be able to do anything effectively. That is made clear by the next sentence which makes it clear that the Central Bank cannot for a period of six years "extend credit by creating money." And it can only get that authority when expressly

granted by the Parliamentary Assembly, which will never occur because of the Pale Serb veto power. Thus, there will be a Central Bank in name only.

Article VIII. Finances

Basically, the Parliamentary Assembly will have no effective authority to raise revenue against the wishes of the Pale Serbs. Likewise, the Pale Serbs will simply refuse to provide the required one-third of the revenue of the Parliamentary Assembly. The fact that the Parliamentary Assembly must rely upon the Federation and Republic Srpska for its revenue is a fatal defect here. Once again, it is similar to the arrangement under the American Articles of Confederation whereby the Central Government had to rely on the States to provide revenues to it. They never did it, which is why the Articles were replaced by the US. Constitution.

Article XII. Entry Into Force

58. "1. This Constitution shall enter into force upon signature of the general Framework Agreement as a constitutional act amending and superseding the Constitution of the Republic of Bosnia and Herzegovina." This procedure is obviously unconstitutional under the current Constitution of the Republic of Bosnia and Herzegovina. Indeed, this new Constitution is not even required to be submitted to the Parliament of the Republic of Bosnia and Herzegovina. For all intents and purposes, this new Constitution has come into effect immediately in accordance with its terms without the approval of the Parliament of the Republic of Bosnia and Herzegovina and without following the amendment procedure in the current Constitution of the Republic of Bosnia and Herzegovina. In other words, under the terms of this Constitution, the Republic of Bosnia and Herzegovina, its Parliament, and all its institutions have basically gone out of existence as of November 22, 1995. That is the reason why they got rid of the name "Republic of Bosnia and Herzegovina" in Article I.

Annex II. Transitional Arrangements

1. Joint Interim Commission

Notice here that the "Parties" established the Joint Interim Commission to implement the Constitution of Bosnia and Herzegovina. But the Parties are the Republic of Bosnia and Herzegovina, the Republic of Croatia, and the Federal Republic of Yugoslavia. Why should Croatia and the rump Yugoslavia have anything to say about the implementation of the Constitution for Bosnia and Herzegovina?

4. Offices

60. It appears that this language allows for the continuation of "governmental offices, institutions, and other bodies of Bosnia and Herzegovina" to operate "in accordance with applicable law" until superseded. Notice, however, that these offices and institutions are no longer operating in accordance with the Constitution of the Republic of Bosnia and Herzegovina. Also, it is not clear that this transitional provision would apply to the Parliament of the Republic of Bosnia and Herzegovina. The title "offices" would not seem to include Parliament itself.

Annex 5. Agreement on Arbitration

61. Basically, this Agreement requires arbitration between the Federation of Bosnia and Herzegovina and the Republika Srpska. The Republic of Bosnia and Herzegovina has nothing to do with it. Therefore, pursuant to this Agreement, the Federation, and Srpska is being treated as if they were de facto independent states.

Annex 6. Agreement on Human Rights

62. Article I treats the Federation of Bosnia and Herzegovina and Republika Srpska as if they were de facto independent states with obligations under international human rights treaties.

63. Article III(2): "The salaries and expenses of the Commission and its staff shall be determined jointly by the parties and shall be borne by Bosnia and Herzegovina." In other words, the Pale Serbs have a veto power over the operation of the Commission. Hence, I doubt very seriously that this Commission will ever come into existence. Moreover, it is clear that the salaries and expenses will not be paid for by the Federation of Bosnia and Herzegovina and Republika Srpska. Rather, it says they will be paid for by "Bosnia and Herzegovina," which cannot generate its own revenue. If they were serious about the Commission, they would require the expenses to be paid for by the Federation and Republika Srpska.

64. So this entire Annex on Human Rights Implementation and Machinery looks fine on paper. But since there is no provision for effective financing, I doubt very seriously that it will ever come into effective and meaningful operation.

Annex 7. Agreement on Refugees and Displaced Persons

65. Article I. This says nothing at all about who will be responsible for paying compensation to refugees for "any property that cannot be restored to them."

Commission for Displaced Persons and Refugees

66. "2. The salaries and expenses of the Commission and its staff shall be determined jointly by the Parties and shall be borne equally by the Parties." So here it is required that the Federation and Republika Srpska pay the expenses, as opposed to "Bosnia and Herzegovina" which is the case for the Human Rights Commission. Nevertheless, these matters must be "determined jointly by the Parties." In other words, the Pale Serbs have been given a veto power over the establishment and operation of the Commission. Hence, I doubt very seriously that it will ever be able to operate effectively.

67. Article XII(2). The Commission has the power to award "just compensation as determined by the Commission." But there is no effective mechanism here for this compensation to be paid. For example, there is no requirement that the Federation or especially Republika Srpska pay such compensation. If this provision were to have any meaning, clearly Republika Srpska would be required to pay "just compensation" for all the property it has destroyed.

68. Paragraph 6. This language about compensation bonds means nothing. There is no obligation here by anyone to honor these compensation bonds.

69. Article IV. Property Fund. Once again, there is no fixed capital contribution for this Fund. So I doubt very seriously that anything will come of it, let alone the so-called compensation bonds.

70. Basically, this Fund will depend on grants from the international community.

Annex 8. Agreement on Commission to Preserve National Monuments

71. Article III: "The salaries and expenses of the Commission and its staff shall be determined jointly by the Entities and shall be borne equally by them." In other words, once again the Pale Serbs have a veto power over the function of this Commission. So it probably will never get off the ground.

72. This is a joke and a half that Republika Srpska has agreed to protect national monuments when in fact it has done everything possible to destroy them throughout Bosnia. This Annex is the height of hypocrisy and absurdity.

Annex 9. Agreement on Establishment of Bosnia and Herzegovina Public Corporations

73. In the Preamble, notice that the Republic of Bosnia and Herzegovina is no longer even mentioned. Under the new regime, the Republic of Bosnia and Herzegovina will disappear. Hence, the Federation and Republika Srpska are being treated as if they were de facto independent states here.

74. Article II(5). "Within 30 days after this Agreement enters into force, the Parties shall agree on sums of money to be contributed to the Transportation Corporation for its initial budget. ..." In other words, once again, the Pale Serbs have a veto power over the operation of this Transportation Corporation, which means that it will probably never come into effective operation. This is nothing more than a mere paper corporation.

75. Article III. Other Public Corporations. This Article is the height of cynicism. Effectively it recognizes that the only public corporation set up was the transportation corporation, which is only on paper. There is not even an obligation to set up any other types of public corporations to deal with utilities, energy, post and communications. The establishment of these public corporations is subject to the veto power of the Pale Serbs, so they will never be set up.

Annex 10. Agreement on Civilian Implementation of the Peace Settlement

Article V. Final Authority to Interpret. "The High Representative is the final authority in the theater regarding interpretation of this Agreement on the civilian implementation of the peace settlement." In other words, the High Representative will basically run Bosnia and Herzegovina as he or she sees fit with respect to non-military matters. IFOR will have the power and authority to do whatever it wants with respect to military matters. Hence, there will be no real sovereign authority or control left to the Federation of Bosnia and Herzegovina or any of the Central Authorities for "Bosnia and Herzegovina." The President, the Presidency, the Government, and the Parliament will constitute merely a puppet regime devoid of any real independence from NATO.

Annex 11. Agreement on International Police Task Force

77. Under this Annex, it appears that the United Nations Organization is basically going to take over and assume supervisory jurisdiction for all domestic law enforcement activities within Bosnia. Therefore, the Bosnian government will basically lose control over this attribute of State sovereignty as well.

Agreement on Initialing the General Framework Agreement for Peace in Bosnia

Letter by Granic to Kinkel, November 21, 1995

78. Notice that in this letter the Republic of Bosnia and Herzegovina no longer exists. Granic for Croatia does not agree to respect "the sovereignty, territorial integrity and political independence of" the Republic of Bosnia and Herzegovina. The same applies to the other letters by him.

Letter by Milutinović to Kinkel of 21 November 1995:

79. Notice that the Federal Republic of Yugoslavia does not agree to respect "the sovereignty, territorial integrity and political independence of" the Republic of Bosnia and Herzegovina. The same applies to the other letters by him.

81. Concerning the letter by Granic to Boutros Ghali of 21 November 1995, I doubt very seriously that the Republic of Croatia "shall strictly refrain from introducing into or otherwise maintaining in Bosnia and Herzegovina any armed forces or other personnel with military capability." The undoubted violation of this Agreement would arguably create a material breach of the Dayton Agreement that the Republic of Bosnia and Herzegovina could rely upon to pull out of the Dayton Agreement. The same argument applies to Granic's other letters to the same effect.

82. Concerning the letter by Milutinović to Boutros Ghali of 21 November 1995, I doubt very seriously that "the Federal Republic of Yugoslavia shall strictly refrain from introducing into or otherwise maintaining in Bosnia and Herzegovina any armed forces or other personnel with military capability." Arguably, the breach of this commitment, which undoubtedly will occur, will be a material breach of the entire Dayton Agreement that would give justification to the Republic of Bosnia and Herzegovina for pulling out of this Agreement. The same rationale would apply to the other letters by Milutinović to that effect.

Letter by Izetbegović to Christopher, November 21, 1995, on Confidence Building Measures

83. Notice that the Republic of Bosnia and Herzegovina no longer exists.

Milošević Letter to Christopher of November 21, 1995,

84. Notice that he does not undertake any obligation to develop confidence-building measures between the Federal Republic of Yugoslavia and the Republic of Bosnia and Herzegovina.

85. Notice also that the establishment of formal diplomatic relations is not called for by this Agreement, which would require the exchange of Ambassadors between the Federal Republic of Yugoslavia and the Republic of Bosnia and Herzegovina. Indeed, this Agreement does not even call for the exchange of Ambassadors between the Federal Republic of Yugoslavia and "Bosnia and Herzegovina." So in other words, Milošević has not even recognized "Bosnia and Herzegovina," let alone the Republic of Bosnia and Herzegovina. Indeed, there is no good reason for him to do so since the Republic of Bosnia and Herzegovina will go out of legal existence and Bosnia and Herzegovina will no longer function as a unified State. So why should he recognize them? He has gotten what he wanted, including half of Bosnia.

Security Council Resolution 1021 (1995)

86. Notice that in the second preambular clause there is no longer any reference to preserving the territorial integrity and political independence of the Republic of Bosnia and Herzegovina.

87. Notice also that in the third preambular clause it refers directly to "the Federal Republic of Yugoslavia" instead of to "the Federal Republic of Yugoslavia (Serbia and Montenegro)."

88. The phraseology of these two preambular paragraphs is significant victories for the rump Yugoslavia. In other words, the Republic of Bosnia and Herzegovina disappears, and the Federal Republic of Yugoslavia becomes the successor-in-law to the former Yugoslavia. Notice that under paragraph 1(b) the embargo on the delivery of heavy weapons, ammunition therefor, mines, military aircraft and helicopters "shall continue to be prohibited until the arms control agreement referred to in Annex 1b has taken effect..." In other words, the delivery of heavy weapons to the Bosnian government will still be prohibited indefinitely. So the

real thrust of the arms embargo against the Bosnian government will continue into force. So the Bosnian Army still cannot obtain the heavy weapons it needs to defend its People and their Land.

90. Sub-paragraph (c) is so loaded with conditions that I doubt very seriously that the heavy arms embargo against the Bosnian government will ever terminate. It is completely meaningless. So under this resolution, the arms embargo on heavy weapons against the Bosnian government will stay in effect indefinitely. There is no commitment to a date certain that arms embargo against heavy weapons will ever terminate.

Security Council Resolution 1022 (1995)

92. Notice that in the second preambular paragraph, the traditional reference to preserving the territorial integrity and political independence of the Republic of Bosnia and Herzegovina has disappeared.

93. Notice that in the fourth preambular paragraph, there is no longer a reference to "the Federal Republic of Yugoslavia (Serbia and Montenegro)," but rather simply to "the Federal Republic of Yugoslavia." In other words, the Federal Republic of Yugoslavia is being treated as if it were the successor-in-law to the former Yugoslavia despite the General Assembly resolution and action to the contrary.

94. Once again, these language changes are significant victories for Milošević. In other words, Milošević got his way at the Security Council as well as at Dayton.

95. Under paragraph 1, therefore, the economic sanctions against the rump Yugoslavia "are suspended indefinitely with immediate effect..." Thus, whereas the arms embargo against the Bosnian government with respect to heavy weapons continues into effect indefinitely, the rump Yugoslavia gets economic sanctions against it suspended immediately on an indefinite basis, though subject to provisions "of paragraphs 2 to 5 below." So in other words, Milošević gets everything he wants and the Bosnians get nothing but a promise in the future. This is a real piece of dirty work by the Security Council.

96. The provisions keeping sanctions on the Bosnian Serbs mean nothing since the whole source of leverage was over Milošević and Serbia.

97. Paragraph 5 of the resolution basically frees up the frozen Serb assets held around the world for Milošević to go after.

Conclusion:

98. The above comments speak for themselves and require no further elaboration from me. It is for you to decide where to go from here, whether to accept the Dayton Agreement or reject it. In the event you decide to reject the Dayton Agreement, then I am fully prepared to return to the World Court immediately for the purpose of obtaining an official order against this carve-up of the Republic of Bosnia and Herzegovina and for the purpose of breaking the heavy weapons arms embargo against the Bosnian Army that will still continue in effect for quite some time. I cannot decide this matter for you. It is your future that is at stake. It is your State. It is your Destiny. It will be your Children and Grandchildren who will have to live with this decision.

May God always be with you.

Your friend,
Francis A. Boyle
Professor of International Law

14

The USA's Role in the Partition of Bosnia

14.1 Clinton's Bosnian Storm

By Musadik Borogovac
Tuesday, 11 June 1996

If you are concerned about the US soldiers in Bosnia, do not blame Bosnia. US soldiers will stay in Bosnia as long as Milošević needs them to ensure that Bosnian refugees who want to go back home will not be able to do so. Why? Please note that, by the Dayton agreement, US soldiers are guarding the borders of the Serb Republic (the graveyard state created by methods of genocide and war crimes) and not the state borders that the American people recognized on April 7, 1992.

If you think that Clinton's Bosnia envoy Richard Holbrooke is a good businessman, you are right, since he sold Milošević's plan for (first illegal, then legal) carving Bosnia to the world as the US plan from Dayton. While speaking about the necessity of Bosnian elections, against the wishes of the Bosnian people and their ability to vote, he was selling out some basic principles of the American people and US troops in Bosnia, too.

If you think the NATO exercise against Serbian military positions in Bosnia (summer 1995) brought peace to Bosnia, you are right. The NATO bombs destroyed a few of Serb warehouses, but gave them what they could never get by legal means or by war—Dayton papers (November 1995) upholding the creation of a new state, on half of Bosnian land, protected and guaranteed by the US military. But now the Administration is planning to rebuild those warehouses with promises of financial credit, and is also insisting on elections that will nullify Bosnia's pre-war Constitution and make the final rendering of the Republic of Bosnia-Herzegovina irreversible forever.

If you believe the isolation of Karadžić is important for the implementation of Clinton's Dayton agreement, you are right, since the US Administration does not wish to jeopardize Karadžić's project of creating "Three Bosnias" with his notorious reputation as a war criminal. Still, the Dayton Plan for Bosnia is nothing but Karadžić's Plan for "Three Bosnias" minus Karadžić. It is designed to deceive not only the Bosnians but also the Americans who asked for several years that something be done *for* Bosnia—not *against* Bosnia.

If you believe the Administration is representing US interests in Bosnia, you are wrong, since Greater Serbia interests are not necessarily American interests. De jure, a few Russians are under NATO command, but de facto, all US soldiers are under Milošević's or Karadžić's command. The most recent example was an immediate extradition of seven Bosnian survivors from Srebrenica to Karadžić's militia because they were in uniform. An American officer delivered those Bosnians to Karadžić's Serb "authorities" because, for the US, Bosnian sovereignty is now a matter of the past after the Dayton agreement took effect.

If you think the Administration allowed Iranian arms to supply Bosnia, you are wrong. The majority of those supplies for Bosnia were for, and ended up in, Croatia (as that country became the new player against Bosnia; a shift that happened when it was clear that Serbia alone was not powerful enough to render Bosnia).

If you think NATO stopped Karadžić's Serbs, you are wrong. NATO bombed some infrastructure only (not tanks or infantry), in eastern Bosnia; Karadžić lost western Bosnia after he lost the four-year long battle for Bihać town where Bosnians never accepted "safe havens" and "demilitarization." It was not NATO that stopped the Serbs but the fact that Karadžić's military was a war-crime machine and not a war machine built for the long run. Bosnian liberation advance was stopped in Dayton when Serbs lost more than had been negotiated. Most importantly, corridors were returned to Karadžić's "entity" and Bosnian Army Bihać Corps again circled by the Croat and Serb "entities."

If you think the siege of Sarajevo is lifted, you are wrong, since the circular noose has only expanded and Tuđman's Croats in Bosnia have again permission (now backed by the US) to join the blockade of Sarajevo institutions of still legal

Republic and blackmail Bosnians accepting (not yet legal) "entities." The Dayton Plan becomes a new Bosnian Constitution and division of Bosnia permanently, only if *any* election occurs in Bosnia regardless of the results or abilities of refugees to vote.

You are also wrong if you think the Administration plans to arm Bosnians in accordance with the Dayton agreement. The major condition for that in Dayton Plan is the compliance of Croatia and the Bosnian Croats to join in "Croat-Bosnian Federation." Why should a regime that counts on US support in annexing a part of Bosnia be committed to working on a Croat-Bosnian Federation if the arms embargo on Bosnia is to be lifted and Bosnians are eventually released of the Croatia communication blackmail? That embargo has made possible the Croatian ultra-nationalist movement within Bosnia and forced the Bosnians to accept old and new blackmails of new US allies—the Croatian/Tuđman's separatists—instead of Croats loyal to the integral Bosnia and Sarajevo Republic institutions.

If you think President Clinton stopped the atrocities in Bosnia, you are wrong, since the Bosnian army, with its local soldiers and their simple survival instinct, stopped them. Actually, in order to stop the Bosnian Army advances and Congressional initiative to lift the arms embargo on Bosnia, Clinton bombed the Serbs (i.e., their warehouses) into their acceptance of "only one-half of" Bosnia, and declared the slaughter in Srebrenica a "new opportunity for peace." However, it is easy to have peace at home (or a "successful foreign policy") if one gives the murderers what they want. Representing Serb General Mladić's genocide of the people in "UN demilitarized–safe havens" as the "Serb military victories" was a method that Administration accepted in order to hide from Americans the real military Serb inferiority on all other frontlines.

The real goal of NATO raids was hiding the truth of Serbian defeat by the Bosnians; it was a panicked measure implemented to stop Congressional decision to lift the arms embargo to Bosnians and allow the victim to win this war. Four years of Bosnian victories was sold by Clinton to his own people as his victory in his pre-election campaign.

If you think the US Administration is hiding evidence of Milošević's guilt about his connection with concentration camps and genocide in Bosnia because of concerns for the allies in Europe, you are wrong. The Administration is in direct alliance with the Milošević/Tuđman regimes as the two proved insufficient to transform Bosnia from a rational, modern, and parliamentary state, into a "Muslim state." That transformation was desirable to the Administration in order to turn your feelings against very ordinary Bosnian people who are very similar to you.

If you think Administration's terminology (such as "Muslim-led government") is insignificant, occasionally consider the consequences for the USA legal system and integrity if the term "Protestant-led government" was used for the USA. The slaughter of Muslims in Bosnia was unavoidable for such transformation to be permanent and "Serb Bosnia" to be safe.

If you think that President Clinton is not independent enough of the UN, you are wrong. This is the first time in the history of the UN that one formally armed criminal separatist movement succeeded in destroying a legal UN member state. The UN charter is thus violated and US troops and US "credibility" feature as the guarantor of the existence and safety of this illegally created "entity." The term "entity" is Holbrooke's diplomatic marketing product intended to hide from Bosnians, and Americans too, the fact that the half of the territory set up by an extreme nationalist movement has all the attributes that International law requires for a real state: legislative, judicial and executive powers. Warren Christopher is a lawyer who knows full well what that implies. So a UN fraud, a US public image crisis, and an armed minority group have led to the creation of a new illegal state. The US has taken over a leading role in making it legal.

In the Newspaper of American Croats "Zajednicar" an interesting article regarding the Dayton agreement was published on November 23, 1995, right after the agreement was signed. The following are excerpts from the much longer article.

14.2 Requiem for a Nation

By Stjepan Balog

Seeing the signing of the so-called peace agreement in Dayton was like watching a very sick friend die. Maybe it was unreasonable to expect Bosnia to survive but until those signatures, at least there was hope. I am not sure what hurt the most, the fact that Croatia played an important role in the partition of Bosnia, was it seeing some of the Bosnians in Sarajevo opening champagne bottles as if the end of Bosnia wasn't their concern or was it the fact that the Serbs have gotten away with it. But no matter whose fault it was, with those signatures in Dayton, a country ceased to exist.

Because of the excellent public relation campaign by the White House, the impression was given that Bosnia will continue to exist as a state within its traditional borders and that the 49% that the Serbs have gotten is just an administrative problem or that the 51% that the so-called Federation (of Croats and Bosnians) will exist as a single unit. None of it is true. The Serbs will retain their army, their own government and eventually they will become a confederation with Serbia proper. The reason that the Serbs never objected to the Croatian/Bosnian "Federation" was the knowledge that it gave them the legal framework to do the same (with Serbia). As far as the Croats and the Bosnians sharing the remaining 51%, that is true, sort of.

The only difference is that Croatian flag will fly over approximately one-half of that 51% and the Bosnian flag over the remaining 25% (approx.). What this agreement in Dayton means is that the Bosnian government, the one that was originally elected by the majority of Bosnians and recognized by all the international organizations will control less than 25% of what used to be Bosnia. All the other stories about one government for all of the Bosnia, a new Constitution, Supreme Court and all the other things promised is just a window dressing to make the partition of Bosnia more palatable. For example, if the true map of Bosnia was shown, with Croatian and Bosnian parts clearly visible, it would look awfully bad, so Croatian and the Bosnian parts were always shown together. Mr. Roger Cohen (the New York Times), who has been involved in reporting on Bosnia from the beginning of the war wrote the day after Dayton signing: "On paper, it is a bewildering, apparently unworkable jigsaw, establishing two distinct self-government units, a Muslim/Croat Federation and a Serbian republic...." (The New York Times, November 21, 1995)

...

But, it was the Bosnian government that has shown very poor leadership; it was the Bosnian government that ultimately signed the so-called "peace agreement." No matter what happened, no matter how much pressure was put on them (if any), the signing of the Dayton agreement is actually considered (by the true Bosnian patriots) to be an act of treason. Could anyone picture Charles DE Gaulle signing over 75% of France to the Germans even though the Germans controlled ALL of it. Could anyone picture any other world leaders signing away most of their countries to their enemies? I could see them resigning from office, I could see them losing the country in a war, but to give it away at a table is rare. Actually, I don't remember ever reading anywhere that a leader voluntarily signed over most of his country to someone else. The realities of the battlefield were such that militarily Bosnia maybe couldn't do any better than it did (especially with the arms embargo against it), but still he should have never agreed to that "peace agreement," at least not the one that gives the Serbs so much.

15

POST-DAYTON ELECTIONS

15.1 Petition against Elections in Bosnia

Boston, May 19, 1996

Bosnian Congress, USA was co-sponsoring the following petition of Bosnian refugees against the elections which took part according to Dayton agreement rules.

We, the citizens of the Republic of Bosnia-Herzegovina, who were exiled by force from our country into the USA and who understand the importance of today's events for the future of our homeland, are sending to the representatives of the government of Bosnia and Herzegovina and to the whole world the following:

PETITION

Regarding the announcement of the rules for the election of the governing officials by the Temporary Election Committee of the Organization for Security and Cooperation in Europe (OSCE), first in the city of Mostar, and shortly after in all of the Bosnia-Herzegovina, we strongly demand that the elections be postponed until the return of all Bosnian refugees to their homes is completed. If the elections go on as planned by the OSCE Temporary Election Committee and its leader Mr. Robert Frowick, we know that the result would be the destruction of Bosnia-Herzegovina as an independent country and the refugees, who were the victims of the genocide and ethnic cleansing, never would be allowed to return to their homes.

Having seen the previous performance of our government and its readiness to cave in under pressure, we are justifiably concerned about its future actions. No one, much less the highest officials of the government of Bosnia-Herzegovina, has the right to take actions which will lead to the destruction of our homeland, and your participation in these elections would mean the capitulation of our country.

We have been the victims of genocide committed by the enemies of our country, and the wounds inflicted on us are still fresh and will never fully heal. Because of the wounds inflicted on us and in honor of those Bosnians who died for our homeland, we insist that you don't hold the elections in Mostar and other parts of the country until we are allowed to participate in them personally at our HOME.

The refugees from Bosnia and Herzegovina, dispersed in 127 countries all over the world, are living through the nightmare of slaughter and genocide inflicted on them by the latest form of fascism. Your participation in the elections before refugees return to their homes would put you in the same class with those who committed genocide on our people, as you would be killing our country. Don't be participants in the genocide of your own people and country. Don't you kill us too!

If you, the top officials of the government, decide not to listen to our voice, we hope that our brothers and sisters at home, as well as any patriots of an undivided Bosnia-Herzegovina, will. By boycotting these elections, we will show the creators of the Dayton agreement, which is immoral and every day adusted to accommodate our enemies, that we are a people with dignity and that we are aware of the scheme against us.

LONG LIVE UNDIVIDED BOSNIA-HERZEGOVINA

Signatories are omitted. The long list of the supporters of the Petition can be found on the website of the Bosnian Congress: www.hdmagazine.com/bosnia

15.2 The Correspondence between European Authorities (OSCE) and Bosnian Refugees

The President of OSCE Mr. Flavio Cotti contacted the Committee of Bosnian Refugees, the organization formed by refugees who support the Petition. Mr. Cotti was concerned because Bosnian refugees in their Petition clearly sent the message to the rest of the world that they did not recognize the elections. Let us mention also that in his letter Mr. Cotti clearly stated: "... the majority of the involved authorities expressed the clear desire to have the elections held at the scheduled time." (i.e. before the return of refugees) which is a valuable testimony against Izetbegović's government. The correspondence between the Bosnian Refugees and OSCE is the following.

FEDERAL DEPARTMENT OF FOREIGN AFFAIRS
TELEFAX

Addressee:	Committee of Bosnian Refugees in Boston
	attn. Mr. Muhamed Borogovac
	Boston, USA
Addressee's fax:	001 810/828 30 69
Ref./initials:	p.B.73.-H.O.-MAH/CIA
Date:	6.09.96
Sender:	POLITICAL DIVISION I
	Federal Department of Foreign Affairs
	CH-3003 Berne, SWITZERLAND
Sender's fax:	011 41/31 324 95 55
Sender's phone number	
(M. Maurer):	011 41/31 322 31 98
	Berne, 4 September 1996

Committee of Bosnian Refugees in Boston
attn. Mr. Muhamed Borogovac
Boston, USA

Dear Sir,

I fully understand your great concern regarding the present developments in Bosnia and Herzegovina. As you certainly are aware, I have always, in my capacity as Chair-in-Office of the OSCE, also pointed out the negative developments which occurred in your home country. Even recently, on 14 August in Geneva, I voiced my deep concern about the situation in Bosnia and Herzegovina during my meeting with US Secretary of State Warren Christopher and the three Presidents Izetbegović, Tuđman, and Milošević. I thereby said clearly that liberty of movement still hasn't been secured less than one month before the elections are to take place. I furthermore indicated that the return of refugees to their hometowns is always being hindered and that no end has been set to the establishment of ethnically cleansed areas. The decision made on 27 August by the Provisional Election

Commission to put off the municipal elections because of the manipulation of refugee voter registration has, therefore, my full support.

Despite my not very positive assessment of the developments in Bosnia and Herzegovina, it is my belief that there is no alternative to the holding of all other elections. On 25 June, when I decided, as Chairman-in-Office to set the election date on 14 September, I was guided by two main reasons: the first factor was the unanimity I noted in this respect among the participating States in the Review Conference in Florence held in the middle of last June; the second factor was the impression I gathered during my five trips to Bosnia that the majority of the involved authorities expressed the clear desire to have the elections held at the scheduled time.

I still hope to rely on this majority which committed itself to free elections in Bosnia. Only with elected representatives can the common authorities provide for by the Dayton agreement be indeed set up and begin to function. To my mind an encouraging indication is the fact that more than 600 000 Bosnian refugees have registered for the elections, thereby showing their will to take part in the future of their country. In making up for approximately one-third of the voters the Bosnian refugees abroad can have considerable influence on the outcome of the elections. It is necessary to work together and to cooperate in order to bring your country out of the cycle of hatred and violence. I would, therefore, like to appeal to you to participate in the elections and give the peace process a chance of making its way in Bosnia and Herzegovina.

Yours sincerely.
THE HEAD OF THE FEDERAL
DEPARTMENT OF FOREIGN AFFAIRS
Flavio Cotti
Federal Councilor

Our response to OSCE
Committee of Bosnian Refugees
Boston, MA, USA
To: Mr. Flavio Cotti
The Head of the Federal Department of the Foreign Affairs
Switzerland

September 7, 1996

Honorable Flavio Cotti,

Thank you very much for your fax from September 6, 1996. In your capacity as Chairman-in-Office of the OSCE, you are fully responsible for the decision to hold elections on Sept. 14, 1996. Even from your letter it is obvious that the minimum conditions for free elections in Bosnia-Herzegovina have not been met as required by the UN. Charter and Dayton's agreement. You can not base your decisions on "hopes" and "commitment of the involved authorities to free and fair elections", as you are saying in your letter. Your decisions must be made in accordance to the UN. Charter, Dayton's agreement and the situation on the ground. The fact that Bosnian authorities expressed the desire to have the elections held does not make the elections free, fair, and regular. The UN. Charter and Dayton agreement are legal documents and your decisions should be based only on these two documents and not on the desire of involved politicians. The fact that 600,000 Bosnian refugees have registered in the voter registration lists, far away from their homes, does not make this election free, fair and regular. The fact is that Bosnian refugees have been denied the possibility to take part in the elections in their home cities, and this is what makes the elections completely irregular.

Please, make just and correct decision. Postpone the elections until the refugees will be given a chance to return to their homes and take part in the elections in their home cities. Otherwise, The Committee of Bosnian Refugees will ask Bosnian people to boycott the elections. The Bosnian people will never recognize the results of these elections.

COMMITTEE OF BOSNIAN REFUGEES
Dr. Muhamed Borogovac, USA
Dr. Vahid Sendijarević, USA
Dr. Zlatko Sijerćić, USA
Stjepan Balog, USA
Musadik Borogovac, USA
Jasminko Bešo, USA

Ajsa Fazlić, Canada
Osman Kerić, USA
Nihada Kadić, Croatia
Almin Muratagić, Sweden
Armin Karabegović, USA

fax. (810)828-3069 (USA)

CC: Bosnian Refugees and Bosnian People
        All American Congressmen and Senators
        News Media
        News Groups on Internet

After this Mr. Cotti writes a letter where he explains to who Refugees can officially file their complaints. That's, why the Refugees wrote the following letters to Mr. Robert Frowick, Mr. Raymund Kunz and Mr. Ed van Thijn.

From: Committee of Bosnian Refugees
            Boston, USA
            Fax #: (313) 828-3069
Date: September 12, 1996

To: Mr. Raymund Kunz
            Ambassador
            Head of the OSCE Coordination Unit
            Federal Department of Foreign Affairs
            3003 Berne, Switzerland
            Fax #: 011 41 31 324 1289
            Tel.: 011 41 31 322-3023
            Total number of pages including this one: 5

Honorable Raymund Kunz,

Please find enclosed copies of letters addressed by the Committee of Bosnian Refugees to the Chairman of the Provisional Election Commission, Ambassador

Robert Frowick and the Chairman of the Election Monitoring Group, Mr. Ed van Thijn. Please transmit the letters to both gentlemen and the federal Councilor Flavio Cotti.

Sincerely yours,
FOR COMMITTEE OF BOSNIAN REFUGEES
Dr. Vahid Sendijarević

LETTER TO MR. FROWICK AND MR. ED VAN THIJN.

From: Committee of Bosnian Refugees
            Boston, USA
            Fax #: (313) 828-3069
Date: September 12, 1996

To: Robert Frowick
            Ambassador
            Chairman of the Provisional Election Commission in BH

RE: Certification of elections in Bosnia and Herzegovina

Honorable Robert Frowick,

There are many facts which confirm that the elections in the Republic of Bosnia and Herzegovina on September 14, 1996, can not be fair, free, or regular. The following is a list of some irregularities which directly affect the refugees whom we are representing, as well as the Bosnian people:

1. The refugees, who are the victim of genocide and ethnic cleansing, have been denied the right to vote in their own hometowns.

2. The refugees have been denied the right to participate in election campaigning in their hometowns. The fact is, they have been forced to stay hundreds, even thousands, of kilometers away from the place where election process is occurring.

3. Most refugees are forced to live in foreign countries incomplete information isolation because most of them are not able to comprehend even the TV news which is broadcast in a foreign language.

4. Practically all refugees in countries far away from Bosnia have been denied the right to participate as candidates in the elections, which goes against the basic principles of free and fair elections.

5. Over 200,000 Bosnians have been killed and 2,000,000 have been forced from their homes in order to change the ethnic structure of Republic of Bosnia and Herzegovina. The method by which the elections have been conducted is directly legalizing the results of the genocide and ethnic cleansing.

6. The elections for local municipal governments were postponed because minimum conditions for free, fair and regular election were not fulfilled. Why is it that elections for state officials are being held when the conditions for local elections were not met.

We expect that you as the Chairman of the Provisional Election Commission will pronounce the elections, which will be held on September 14, 1996, irregular. Otherwise, you will further the injustices already done to the Bosnian people. Bosnian refugees do not accept the explanation that "elections are regular, Balkan style", which is a discriminatory statement. Bosnian refugees do not accept the results of elections which are not free, fair, or regular. They do not accept the treatment as people of less value.

The fact that Bosnian authorities expressed the desire to hold the elections does not make the elections free, fair and regular. The UN. Charter and Dayton's agreement are legal documents and your decisions should be based on these two documents and not on the wishes of involved politicians, some of whom committed crimes against humanity.

Please, make a just and correct decision to proclaim the elections irregular.

Sincerely yours,
FOR COMMITTEE OF BOSNIAN REFUGEES
Dr. Vahid Sendijarević

CC: Federal Councilor Flavio Cotti, the Chairman-in-Office of the O.S.C.E.,
        Mr. Ed van Thijn, Chairman of the Election Monitoring Group
        Bosnian refugees and people

Bosnian government
All American Congressmen and Senators
News Media
News Groups on Internet

From: Committee of Bosnian refugees

                    Boston, USA

                    FAX#: (313) 828-3069

Date: January 3, 1997

To: Robert Frowick, Ambassador

                    Chairman of the Provisional Election Commission in Bosnia and Herzegovina

Re: Preparations for local elections in Republic of Bosnia and Herzegovina

The Honorable Robert Frowick,

As the Chairman of the Provisional Election Commission in Bosnia and Herzegovina, we believe that you are not acting in the best interests of the Bosnian refugees. In particular, we are opposed to your plans to legalize P2 forms in Bosnia and Herzegovina so that Serbs from Croatia can get the right to vote in local elections and to hold local elections before the Bosnian refugees can return to their homes.

According to a TWRA report on December 14, 1996, you spoke at a press conference in Sarajevo about the preparations for local elections in Bosnia and Herzegovina that should be held in six months. It was reported that you met with Biljana Plavšić and other Serb leaders in Banja Luka on November 30, 1996 and that you signed an agreement according to which the Serbs permit extension of the OSCE Mission mandate and the role of the OSCE in the preparation, implementation, and supervision of local elections. In return, the P2 form will become valid so that Serbs from Croatia get the right to vote in local elections if they live in Bosnia at the moment.

At the same time, the Bosnian refugees, who were victims of genocide and ethnic cleansing, have been denied the right to return to their homes and vote in their own hometowns. When the general elections were held in September 1996, the Bosnian refugees were forced to stay hundreds, even thousands, of kilometers away from their home towns while the elections were taking place.

Those elections were completely irregular. Even before the elections, the president of OSCE, Mr. Flavio Cotti, claimed that the elections could not be regular under conditions where half of the Bosnian population was not allowed to vote in their hometowns. Therefore, the local elections were postponed. Let us remind you that many more voters took part in the general elections than was theoretically possible. Let us also remind you that the independent international controllers found 30,000 irregular votes in Sarajevo alone (all for Alija Izetbegović, which makes him the illegally elected president). You should also remember that only a handful of Bosnians were allowed to cross the borders of the Serbian Republic (Republika Srpska) to vote and still there were much more votes than the number of registered voters before the war. We remember very well your statement that the elections were fair-Balkan style. This is a very sad and discriminatory statement. Bosnian refugees all over the world proclaimed the general elections and all results of those elections null and void.

Please, make a just decision and do not legalize P2 forms in Bosnia and Herzegovina or allow local elections to take place before the refugees can return to their homes to exercise their basic human right to vote. If these elections occur without the full and unhindered participation of all Bosnian citizens, you will be responsible for legalizing the results of the ethnic cleansing and genocide which occurred in Bosnia and Herzegovina.

Sincerely yours,
For Committee of Bosnian Refugees
Dr. Vahid Sendijarević

CC: Commission on Security and Cooperation in Europe,
       Washington, DC; E-mail: CSCE@HR.HOUSE.GOV
       The USA Congress and Senate
       Bosnian Government
       News media and Newsgroups on The Internet

Committee of Bosnian Refugees
Dr. Muhamed Borogovac
Dr. Vahid Sendijarević

Dr. Zlatko Sijerćić
Stjepan Balog
Musadik Borogovac
Jasminko Bešo
Ajsa Fazlić
Osman Kerić
Bedrudin Gusic
Nihada Kadić
Armin Karabegović
Mr. Kenan Saracević

16

His Holiness, the Pope in Bosnia

Bosnian Congress, USA
Boston, April 10, 1997

The whole world is familiar with the fact that His Holiness, John Paul II, sided with Bosnia-Herzegovina during the entire war. In addition to the Vatican recognizing the Republic of Bosnia-Herzegovina as an independent and a sovereign state, during some of the most critical moments of the war, the Pope offered the most valuable help possible, moral and political support. Let's just consider the fact that during the fighting between the HVO and the Bosnian Army, the Pope made a decision of the need for Bosnia to have its own Cardinal. That was a tremendous boost for the unity of the Bosnian Nation and a clear signal to the Bosnia-Herzegovina Catholics that their Capital is in Sarajevo, and not in Zagreb. The Pope strongly opposes the policy of the BH Croat leadership who works for the destruction of Bosnia-Herzegovina since the very beginning. The visit by His Holiness the Pope is again serving as a symbol of His support for the independent and the sovereign state of Bosnia-Herzegovina.

However, the enemies of Bosnia-Herzegovina that have infiltrated the Government and also the Islamic community in BH are using the Pope's visit to Sarajevo as another attempt to further destabilize the B&H state. The Bosnian national anthem will not be played, and there will not be a Bosnian Army Honor Guard. Even worse, there will not be any representatives from the B&H Islamic leadership to welcome the Pope. In the name of God, why not?

We all know that the current leadership of the Islamic community is just an extension of Alija Izetbegović's power and that Alija Izetbegović removed the legally elected Reis ul Ulema - H. Jakub ef. Selimoski (the highest Islamic leader in that region) and that he appointed his own man, Mustafa ef. Cerić to that position. We are all aware of the fact that Izetbegović's government and the leaders of the Islamic community had no problem meeting numerous times with the people who committed Genocide against the Bosnian people. Alija Izetbegović didn't suspend the negotiations and other contacts with the Bosnian enemies even when they murdered the president of his Government, Dr. Hakija Turajlić and massacred people from the "safe havens" Srebrenica and Žepa. Why is it that this government that hasn't shown even a trace of dignity and revulsion when dealing with our greatest enemy, are now boycotting the Pope's visit?

The answers are the following:

Alija Izetbegović is an enemy of Bosnia-Herzegovina and he was promoted to the leadership of our homeland in order to destroy it. Izetbegović and his lackeys are boycotting the Pope because The Pope is a supporter and a friend of a unified B&H, meaning a threat to Izetbegović's goal, the division and destruction of B&H.

The boycotting of the Pope's arrival by the "leaders" of the BH Muslims shows how far Alija Izetbegović (the man who in his youth declared himself as a Serb) would go in order to eliminate the B&H Muslims. The Vatican measures time by centuries and such an insult will create antagonism towards the B&H Muslims throughout the world for centuries. Such an act of insensitivity could only be perpetrated by someone whose wish is B&H total demise. But despite his behind-the-scenes maneuverings and the organizing of the anti-Papal boycott, Alija Izetbegović has reserved a place for himself as the appearance of a democrat who will receive the Pope. The appearance will be that the Muslim people of B&H are too primitive and apathetic and who without any valid reason are boycotting the Pope, while Izetbegović will appear as the only one among them tolerant and understanding enough to be able to talk to.

BH Muslims are in ever larger numbers becoming aware of who Alija Izetbegović really is when he signed the agreements that have divided B&H just as the Bosnian Army started to liberate its homeland. The Bosnian tragedy lies in the fact that the Government of Alija Izetbegović consists of people that are supported by the powerful enemies of B&H.

That is why we Bosnian patriots are using this opportunity to advise His Holiness the Pope and the Vatican that this insult brought against the Holy Father, is not the action of the B&H Muslims, but rather that of Bosnia's enemies who, thanks to some political maneuvers, have infiltrated our government.

We, the Bosnian Congress, salute His Holiness, John Paul II and we support him with all our best wishes. We beg him to continue His support for B&H, because by that action, our and His enemies' job of destroying BH will be much more difficult. We condemn most severely the actions by Izetbegović's stooges and the Serbian agents, who have assumed total power in our homeland.

The presidency of the Bosnian Congress,
Dr. Muhamed Borogovac
Dr. Vahid Sendijarević
Stjepan Balog
Musadik Borogovac
Ajsa Fazlić
Fax: (810) 828-3069

17

Legal Suit against
Dayton Agreement

To the Constitutional Court of the Republic of Bosnia and Herzegovina
Address: Omladinska br. 9, Sarajevo, RBiH
Plaintiff: Committee for Refugees of the Republic of Bosnia-Herzegovina
Telephone: (617) 783-xxxx, (810) 828-xxxx
Fax: (810) 828-xxxx

LEGAL SUIT

Declaring the "General Frame of Agreement for Peace in Bosnia-Herzegovina,"
signed in Paris on December 14, 1995, null and void because it leads to a dissolution
of the Republic of Bosnia-Herzegovina (hereafter "R B&H").

In Paris, France on December 14, 1995, the "General Frame of Agreement for
Peace in Bosnia-Herzegovina," also known as the Dayton Agreement (hereafter
the "AGREEMENT"), was signed. The AGREEMENT divides Bosnia-
Herzegovina (hereafter "BH") into two so-called "entities": Federation B&H
and the Serb Republic (Annex 2). These "entities" are entitled to from legitimate
international relations with other states (Annex 4), including formations such
as a confederation. Citizens of BH can have dual citizenship. The authority of
what is named "Bosnia-Herzegovina" is merely symbolic, while true power,
including military power, falls within the jurisdiction of the so-called "entities."
The borders of the two "entities" have been drawn in such a way as to surrender
to the Serb Republic regions (municipalities) in which members of the Bosnian

nation (original: Bosniak) and Croatian nation (prior to 1992) jointly constituted an absolute majority, and in which the Bosnians and Croatians owned the majority of private property and land.

The AGREEMENT was signed by Mr. Alija Izetbegović, acting as the President of the Presidency of the RBH, and was later approved by the so-called "Parliament of the RBH" in an attempt to give a semblance of legality to said AGREEMENT and unfairly impose obligations upon all citizens in BH.

CLAIM 1

The Agreement is a legal international document and as such acquires the status of a law according to the hierarchy of legal documents. In turn, as law, it must be in accordance with the Constitution of the RBH. However, the Agreement strongly VIOLATES fundamental points of the Constitution of the RBH.

EVIDENCE

According to Article 3 of the Constitution of the R B&H, equality is granted to all nations and ethnic groups on all R B&H territory. However, the Serb Republic has become a homeland to the Serbian people. As per the AGREEMENT, these Serbs are recognized as a "constitutional" nation, thereby relegating Bosniaks and Bosnian Croats in this territory to the inferior status of second-class citizens in relation to these Serbs. For equality to exist among the citizenry, all citizens must have the same legal status, a status guaranteed by the RBH Constitution but not by the AGREEMENT. Therefore, the AGREEMENT is in direct violation of the Article 3 of the Constitution of the R B&H.

According to Article 5 of the Constitution of the R B&H, territory and borders of the Republic, and its regions, counties and municipalities, can be changed by a decree of the Parliament of the R B&H, but only in accordance with the expressed will of the population of the relevant region (those of a certain region whose borders or county limits are proposed to be changed) and in the general interests of the Republic.

Although the citizens of the Republic on March 1, 1992, voted on a referendum, which passed with the qualifying two-thirds' majority of votes, calling for their state to remain the unified and indivisible Republic B&H, The AGREEMENT divides the Republic B&H into two states along the lines of legislative, executive and judicial power, and along the lines of military and police organization. Neither the Bosnian nationals in the Drina river valley and Podrinje (East Bosnia), nor the

Bosnian Croats and Bosniaks in the Bosnian Posavina (North Bosnia), who jointly constitute an absolute majority in these two large regions, never declared their will to be incorporated into the Serb Republic. To the contrary, they launched a heroic struggle to prevent themselves and their homesteads from being forcefully annexed to the Serb Republic.

In addition, Mr. Krešimir Zubak, the legitimate representative of the Croatian people in B&H, refused to sign the AGREEMENT. That is why the AGREEMENT runs contrary to the declared will of the absolute majority of the residents of Podrinje and Bosnian Posavina regions. The AGREEMENT is also contrary to the general interests of the Republic of B&H and is thus a blatant violation of the Article 5 of the Constitution of the RBH.

CLAIM 2

According to Article 352 of the Constitution of the RBH, the office of the Presidency of the RBH is held by an official for a period of four years who is elected by the Parliament of the RBH. After four years, both the Presidency and the Parliament are relieved of their mandate to rule, conduct affairs in the name of the RBH, and make any binding agreements in the name of the Republic. The legal mandates for both Mr. Alija Izetbegović and the "Parliament" of the RBH, however, had long expired when Mr. Izetbegović signed, and Parliament later approved, said AGREEMENT.

EVIDENCE

We point out strongly that the AGREEMENT signed on December 14, 1995, was not signed by legitimately authorized representatives of the Republic of Bosnia-Herzegovina. That is why said AGREEMENT is in violation of Articles 144 and 352 of the Constitution of the RBH. As such, it is thus null and void.

CLAIM 3

It is very likely that some members of said Parliament and the office of the Presidency might have been misled and/or acted in error when the AGREEMENT was signed. This is because they were not made fully aware of all of the consequences such a historical document could have towards changing or conflicting with the Constitution of the R B&H, an internationally recognized state since Bosnian language translations of two memoranda from Professor Francis Boyle were not made available to them. The first memorandum was sent to the Parliament on March 24, 1994, and the second memorandum was sent on September 11, 1995.

EVIDENCE

The memoranda of Professor Francis Boyle were delivered in time to the highest officials of the Republic, but in minutes of the meeting about the AGREEMENT of the Presidency of the R B&H there is no record of any discussion taking place regarding the contents of Professor Boyle's two memoranda, despite the fact that Professor Boyle is an international and constitutional law expert and advisor to the aforementioned bodies of the Republic. Due to the lack of discussion regarding Professor Boyle's advice then, those who signed the AGREEMENT on behalf of RBH apparently did so with little thought to the constitutional consequences of such a document.

CLAIM 4

The division of the land in BH into so-called "entities" represents the legalization of aggression against the sovereign and internationally recognized (1992) Republic of Bosnia-Herzegovina. It also represents legalization of the genocide against Bosnian and Croatian people. For this reason, the AGREEMENT is a most flagrant violation of International Law.

EVIDENCE

Beyond the shadow of a doubt, the dissolution of the RBH resulting from the AGREEMENT is proof enough of its divisive effects.

CONCLUSION

The AGREEMENT stands in complete opposition to the Constitution of the Republic of Bosnia and Herzegovina, according to which the RBH first received full international recognition in November 1943 within the borders set up by the AVNOJ (Anti-Fascist Council of Liberation of Peoples of Yugoslavia), because it violates Articles 3, 5, 144 and 352 of the Constitution of the RBH and International Law. Therefore we suggest that in accordance with Article 398 of the Constitution of the Republic of Bosnia and Herzegovina, a procedure is initiated to examine the constitutionality of the AGREEMENT, and also that the following sentence is passed:

SENTENCE

It has been established that the "General Frame of Agreement for Peace in Bosnia-Herzegovina" signed in Paris, France, on December 14, 1995, is in violation of International Law and Articles 3, 5, 144 and 352 of the internationally recognized Constitution of the Republic of Bosnia-Herzegovina, and is therefore null, void, and non-binding for the Republic of Bosnia-Herzegovina.

Date: May 14, 1995

Attached: A photocopy of Memorandum of Prof. Dr. Francis Boyle, sent to the Parliament of the Republic of Bosnia and Herzegovina.

PLAINTIFF: Committee of Refugees of Bosnia-Herzegovina, represented by executive members:

Prof. Dr. Vahid Sendijarević,
Docent. Dr. Muhamed Borogovac,
Osman Kerić, dipl. oecc,
Ajsa Fazlić, Prof.,
Mr. Kenan Saracević, dipl. Eng,
Asmir Skokić

Epilogue

How did this case end? The Constitutional Court of The Republic of Bosnia-Herzegovina did not take the case into consideration until it was too late, i.e. until the new Constitutional Court was formed. As the Committee of Bosnian Refugees does not recognize the Dayton Constitution, they forbade to the Dayton Constitutional Court do discuss the case. They filed the following complaint:

1. The Dayton Agreement is in violation of the Constitution of the Republic of Bosnia and Herzegovina and this is why a legal suit against the Dayton Agreement has been filed with the Supreme Court (Constitutional Court) of the Republic of Bosnia-Herzegovina in Sarajevo. Only the Constitutional Court of the Republic of Bosnia and Herzegovina has the constitutional (legal) authority to decide on the constitutionality of Dayton Agreement.

Refugees and we the people of the Republic of Bosnia and Herzegovina do not recognize any institution which has resulted and will result from the Dayton Agreement including the "Dayton Constitution" and the "Dayton Constitutional Court". The "Dayton Constitutional Court" is not authorized to make any decision about the legality of the "Dayton Agreement".

18

LEGAL SUIT AGAINST
YUGOSLAVIA FOR GENOCIDE

On 23 July 1997, the Serb government have filed its Counter-Memorial at the International Court of Justice in The Hague in response to the Memorial already filed by the Government of the Republic of Bosnia and Herzegovina in Bosnia's pending World Court lawsuit against the rump Yugoslavia for genocide against the Bosnian People. The best description of that lawsuit is given in the following letter of Prof. Francis Boyle to Bosnian patriots.

From:
Francis A. Boyle
Law Building
504 E. Pennsylvania Ave.
Champaign, Ill. 61820
Phone: 217-333-7954
Fax: 217-244-1478
Email: FBOYLE@LAW.UIUC.EDU
To: "'M. B.'"<azra@tiac.net>

Dear Friend:

They (Bosnian Weekly magazine "Most") are free to publish this if they wish, just let me know. Also, I am prepared to answer their questions on it over the phone.

Yours truly,
Francis Boyle.

The Next Stage in Bosnia's World Court Lawsuit Against Serbia for Genocide

Dear Friends:

Many of you have asked me to explain to you in simple terms what will be the next stage in the development of Bosnia's World Court Lawsuit against Serbia for inflicting genocide against the People and the Republic of Bosnia and Herzegovina. Serbia timely filed its Counter-Memorial with the World Court on 23 July 1997. The next stage in these proceedings is governed by Article 45 and Article 54 of the Rules of Procedure of the International Court of Justice.

Article 45 provides as follows:

Article 45

1. The pleadings in a case begun by means of an application shall consist, in the following order, of a Memorial by the applicant; a Counter-Memorial by the respondent.
2. The Court may authorize or direct that there shall be a Reply by the applicant and a Rejoinder by the respondent if the parties are so agreed, or if the Court decides, proprio motu or at the request of one of the parties, that these pleadings are necessary.

Serbia has attempted to stall, delay, and draw out these World Court proceedings as long as possible in the hope and expectation that the Bosnian government can be forced to drop this lawsuit against it because Serbia knows full well that Bosnia will win the lawsuit at the end of the day. Therefore, I suspect that Serbia will request the World Court to order Bosnia to file a Reply to its Counter-Memorial. Of course, Bosnia must vigorously oppose this request and demand that this case is set for a hearing and a trial by the World Court as soon as possible. As I repeatedly told the World Court in this case: Time is of the essence for the People and the Republic of Bosnia and Herzegovina!

Assuming that the World Court rejects Serbia's request for further delay in this case, then Article 54 of the Court's Rules of Procedure governs the next stage of the proceedings:

Article 54

1. Upon the closure of the written proceedings, the case is ready for hearing. The date for the opening of the oral proceedings shall be fixed by the Court, which

may also decide, if occasion should arise, that the opening or the continuance of the oral proceedings be postponed.

2. When fixing the date for, or postponing, the opening of the oral proceedings the Court shall have regard to the priority required by Article 74 of these Rules and to any other special circumstances, including the urgency of a particular case.

3. When the Court is not sitting, its powers under this Article shall be exercised by the President.

You will note that Article 54, paragraph 2, expressly provides that when the World Court fixes the date for the oral proceedings in this case "the Court shall have regard...to any other special circumstances, including the urgency of a particular case." The Bosnian Government must make it very clear to the World Court that both the "special circumstances" and the "urgency" of this case involving genocide against the People and the Republic of Bosnia and Herzegovina require it to be scheduled for a hearing as soon as possible. This is the first and the only case every filed with the International Court of Justice on the basis of the 1948 Genocide Convention. The World Court must act as expeditiously as humanly possible in order to hear the next stage in Bosnia's complaint about genocide against Serbia.

Bosnia has already won what is tantamount to two pre-judgments on the merits of this case in the World Court's Order of 8 April 1993 and the World Court's Order of 13 September 1993, as conceded by the late Judge Tarassov in his Declaration attached to the first Order, and in his Dissenting Opinion attached to the second Order. In other words, under the leadership of Slobodan Milošević, Serbia has indeed committed genocide against the People and the Republic of Bosnia and Herzegovina, both directly and indirectly by means of its surrogate army under the command of two individuals already indicted for international crimes in Bosnia: Radovan Karadžić and Ratko Mladić. Nevertheless, for almost four years the entire international community refused to discharge their solemn obligation under Article 1 of the Genocide Convention "to prevent" this ongoing genocide against the Bosnian People that was so blatantly taking place in the Republic of Bosnia-Herzegovina.

The Bosnian People and Government must stand up as ONE and make it absolutely clear to the great powers of the world, and especially o the United States and to Europe, that under no circumstances will they withdraw their lawsuit against Serbia for genocide. This World Court lawsuit is the only justice that the Bosnian People will ever get from anyone in the entire world on this or any other issue!

If this lawsuit is withdrawn, then Serbia and its supporters around the world, together with the United States, the United Nations, the European Union and its member states, will be able to rewrite history by arguing that genocide never occurred against the People and the Republic of Bosnia and Herzegovina. All the great powers and these international institutions will then argue that the reason why Bosnia dropped its lawsuit for genocide against Serbia was because Bosnia was afraid of losing its World Court lawsuit. In this manner these great powers together with the United Nations and the European Union will be able to justify their refusal to prevent the ongoing genocide against the People and the Republic of Bosnia and Herzegovina for almost four years despite the obvious requirements of the 1948 Genocide Convention, the 1945 United Nations Charter, and the two World Court Orders of 8 April 1993 and 13 September 1993.

Bosnia has already won this World Court lawsuit. All that Bosnia must do now is to see this lawsuit through to its ultimate and successful conclusion. It is inevitable that the World Court will definitively rule that Serbia and its surrogate Bosnian Serb armed forces committed genocide against the People and the Republic of Bosnia and Herzegovina. At that time, the claims of the Bosnian People for genocide will be vindicated for the entire world to see and for all of history to know. After all that they have suffered, and endured, and accomplished, the Bosnian People owe it to themselves and to their children and to their children's children, as well as to all the other Peoples of the world and to their children and to their children's children, to prosecute this World Court lawsuit through to its successful conclusion. Save Bosnia's World Court lawsuit against Serbia!

Epilogue

The International Court of Justice, on February 26, 2007, in its legally binding judgment in the case of Bosnia and Herzegovina v. Serbia and Montenegro „Finds that Serbia has violated the obligation to prevent genocide, under the Convention on the Prevention and Punishment of the Crime of Genocide, in respect of the genocide that occurred in Srebrenica in July 1995." The Court ruled that the genocide was committed by the government and institutions of "Republika Srpska" and specifically the Army (VRS) and Police (MUP) of "Republika Srpska" and that Serbia had an obligation to prevent the genocide.

19

BOSNIAN DECLARATION

OF INDEPENDENCE

COMMITTEE OF REFUGEES OF THE REPUBLIC OF
BOSNIA-HERZEGOVINA
P.O. BOX 986
Troy, MI 48099-0986
U.S.A.
Tel.#: (248) 828-3193
Fax. #: (248) 828-3069
Bosanski_kongres@nkrbih.com

DECLARATION OF INDEPENDENCE
December 6, 1997

1. The Dayton Agreement is in violation of the Constitution of the Republic of Bosnia and Herzegovina and this is why a legal suit against the Dayton Agreement has been filed with the Supreme Court (Constitutional Court) of the Republic of Bosnia-Herzegovina in Sarajevo. Only the Constitutional Court of the Republic of Bosnia and Herzegovina has the constitutional (legal) authority to decide on the constitutionality of Dayton Agreement. Refugees and we the people of the Republic of Bosnia and Herzegovina do not recognize any institution which has resulted and will result from the Dayton Agreement including the "Dayton Constitution" and the "Dayton Constitutional Court". The "Dayton Constitutional Court" is not authorized to make any decision about the legality of the "Dayton Agreement".

164

2. The "Dayton Constitution" was negotiated between enemies of our homeland against the interests of the Bosnian people and our country. The "Dayton Constitution" was not adapted according to procedures required by the Constitution of the Republic of Bosnia-Herzegovina and as such is not valid.

3. The "Dayton Constitution" annuls the freely expressed will of the citizens of the Republic of Bosnia-Herzegovina at the referendum on Bosnian independence held on March 1, 1992. The "Dayton Constitution" artificially creates new "entities", the "Federation of Bosnia-Herzegovina" and the "Serb Republic" on the territory of the Republic of Bosnia-Herzegovina.

4. Even if the constitutionality of the Dayton Agreement were conceded, up to now, many provisions of the Dayton Agreement did not comply with, such as a free return of refugees to their homes and, therefore, it is obvious that the Dayton Agreement has annulled itself.

5. For all the above reasons, we, the people of the Republic of Bosnia-Herzegovina do not recognize the Dayton Agreement. We, the Bosnian people, pursuant to the Constitution of the Republic of Bosnia-Herzegovina and the results of the referendum for independence have the right to liberate our homeland from both aggressor countries, Croatia and Yugoslavia, and to implement the power of the Constitution of the Republic of Bosnia-Herzegovina on every square millimeter of our homeland.

6. General elections in September 1996 and local elections in September 1997 were held according to the "Dayton Constitution" and are not in compliance with the Constitution of the Republic of Bosnia-Herzegovina. The elections were a farce and an exercise in absurdity. Both elections had a major goal of putting on a "democratic face" to the illegitimate change of the Constitution of the Republic of Bosnia-Herzegovina, and thus "legitimize" the situation created by genocide, and aggression.

7. As already mentioned, even the conditions required by the Dayton Agreement were not met in those elections. The refugees were denied the right to return to their homes and to take part in the elections in their hometowns. Even according to the provisions of the Dayton Agreement elections were not valid.

8. Because of all the foregoing facts, we, the people of the Republic of Bosnia-Herzegovina do not recognize these elections and any future elections until the entire territory of the Republic of Bosnia-Herzegovina is liberated and the legitimate Constitution is implemented in the entire territory of our homeland.

The Committee of the Refugees of the Republic of Bosnia-Herzegovina
Dr. Vahid Sendijarević <sendijv@udmercy.edu>
Dr. Muhamed Borogovac <Bosanski_kongres@nkrbih.com>
Dr. Zlatko Sijerčić <sijercic@slb.com>

Stjepan Balog <stjepan@flash.net>

Musadik Borogovac, dipl. oecc. <musadik@hdmagazine.com>

Jasminko Bešo, dipl. oecc. <jbeso@earthlink.net>

Ajsa Fazlić, prof. tel. (613) 733-3118 (Canada)

Osman Kerić, dipl. oecc. <okeric@prairie.nodak.edu>

Nihada Kadić <zenskagr@alc.tel.hr>

Mr. Kenan Saracević, dipl. eng, tel.(617) 322-8173 (USA)

Asmir Skokić, tel. (248) 828-3193

20

THE DECLARATION OF THE REPUBLIC OF BOSNIA-HERZEGOVINA

The following is the document that Bosnian victims of genocideissued after the 2007 verdict of the Internationa Court of Justice in the caseof genocide in Bosnia as it was published by the prestigeous Henry Jacson society. That document is the best legal sumarry about what was done in *Bosnia https://henryjacksonsociety. org/2010/10/29/the-declaration-of-the-republic-of-bosnia-herzegovina/*.

Henry Jackson Society EXECUTIVE SUMMARY:

1. The International Court of Justice and International Criminal Tribunal for the former Yugoslavia have ruled that the Bosnian Serb entity 'Republika Srpska' is guilty of genocide, and that Serbia is guilty of failure to prevent and punish genocide.
2. These rulings provide a legal basis for the abolition of the regime established by the 1995 Dayton settlement, which was illegitimately derived from this genocide.
3. To uphold the Dayton regime is to recognize the precedent, that a legitimate constitutional order may be overthrown by aggression and genocide.
4. The international community should work with the citizens of Bosnia-Herzegovina to restore the legitimate constitutional order of the Republic of Bosnia-Herzegovina.

Based on the binding judgment of the International Court of Justice (ICJ) of February 26, 2007 in the case of Bosnia and Herzegovina v. Serbia and Montenegro, We, the people of Bosnia and Herzegovina, who are decisively against any form of discrimination, committed to the rule of law and the justice for the victims of aggression and genocide, obeying the Convention on the Prevention and Punishment of the Crime of Genocide, obeying the European Charter of Local Self-Government, obeying the Charter of the United Nations, have decided by means of this Declaration to implement the judgments of the International Criminal Tribunal for the Former Yugoslavia (ICTY) and the judgment of the International Court of Justice (ICJ) of February 26, 2007 in the case of Bosnia and Herzegovina v. Serbia and Montenegro, on this 24th day of September, 2010, adopt

The Declaration of the Republic of Bosnia and Herzegovina

The International Court of Justice, on February 26, 2007, in its legally binding judgment in the case of Bosnia and Herzegovina v. Serbia and Montenegro „Finds that Serbia has violated the obligation to prevent genocide, under the Convention on the Prevention and Punishment of the Crime of Genocide, in respect of the genocide that occurred in Srebrenica in July 1995." The Court ruled that the genocide was committed by the government and institutions of "Republika Srpska" and specifically the Army (VRS) and Police (MUP) of "Republika Srpska" and that Serbia had an obligation to prevent the genocide. Filing the lawsuit for genocide in 1993 preceded all subsequent constitutional and legal arrangements for Bosnia and Herzegovina. The final judgment of the International Court of Justice supersedes all constitutional arrangements that are offered today to the victims of aggression and genocide including Annex 4 to the Dayton Agreement.

Therefore, We, the people of Bosnia and Herzegovina, the victims of aggression and genocide, based on the binding judgment of the International Court of Justice and applying the legal right to RESTITUTION IN INTEGRUM (restoration of the original condition) based on the peremptory norms of International law JUS COGENS, adopt The Declaration that We will exclusively obey the constitution of the Republic of Bosnia and Herzegovina and that we will fight to restore the institutions of the nation as they were before the aggression and genocide, and We declare null and void the Dayton Constitution and institutions created under the Dayton Constitution.

The constitution of the Republic of Bosnia and Herzegovina is the only legally binding document on the basis of which the independence of Bosnia and Herzegovina has been recognized. This constitution ended communism and provided for free multiparty elections in Bosnia and Herzegovina in 1990 and provided for a free referendum of its independence in 1992. Under this constitution, Republic of Bosnia and Herzegovina became a UN member nation.

This constitution provides that each individual is sovereign on the entire territory of Bosnia and Herzegovina irrelevant on ethnicity or religion.

Article 154 of the Constitution of Republic of Bosnia and Herzegovina: "It is a sacred and inalienable right and duty of citizens, all members of all ethnic groups living in Bosnia and Herzegovina to protect and defend the liberty, independence, sovereignty, territorial integrity and unity, and the organization of the Republic defined by the Constitution."

Article 154 of the Constitution of Republic of Bosnia and Herzegovina: "No person has the right to recognize or to sign the capitulation, or to accept or recognize occupation of the Republic of Bosnia and Herzegovina or any single part of it. No person has the right to prevent the citizens of the Republic of Bosnia and Herzegovina from fighting any aggressor against the Republic. Such acts are unconstitutional and they are punishable as treason against the Republic. Treason against the Republic is the heaviest offense against the people, and is treated as a criminal act of the highest degree."

The international community acknowledged the will of people of Bosnia and Herzegovina, as expressed in a referendum on March 1, 1992, and recognized the Republic of Bosnia and Herzegovina as a sovereign nation.

The rump-Yugoslavia (Serbia and Montenegro today) and the Yugoslav People's Army (JNA) have waged a war of aggression in 1992 against the Republic of Bosnia and Herzegovina in order to create an ethnically pure greater Serbia that led to the killing, genocide and suffering unseen in Europe since World War II. In legally binding Resolutions 752 and 757 from 1992, the UN Security Council adopted economic sanctions and political isolation to Serbia and Montenegro as punishment for their aggression against the Republic of Bosnia and Herzegovina.

In the provisional measures of the International Court of Justice on September 13, 1993, "the Court recorded that, since its Order [to Serbia and Montenegro] of April 8, 1993, and despite it and many resolutions of the United Nations Security Council, "great suffering and loss of life has been sustained by the population of Bosnia-Herzegovina in circumstances which shock the conscience of mankind and flagrantly conflict with moral law ..."

After the aggression and genocide, the constitution of Republic of Bosnia and Herzegovina was illegally (with genocide) suspended and illegally replaced by the Dayton Constitution. There are no legal provisions under the international law nor customary laws that can be used as bases to replace constitution and political system of a sovereign nation by aggression and genocide. People of Bosnia and Herzegovina were deprived of their will through aggression and genocide. This is why we are obliged to return the state of Bosnia and Herzegovina to the constitutional, legal and territorial status that the state of Bosnia and Herzegovina had before the aggression and genocide.

The goal of the aggression and genocide against the people of Republic of Bosnia and Herzegovina was to create an ethnically pure greater Serbia at the expense of territory of the Republic of Bosnia and Herzegovina. The lawfulness and justice in the case of Bosnia and Herzegovina will be accomplished only after the goal of the aggression and genocide is denied to the perpetrators of the aggression and genocide. According to International law, and domestic laws, anything that was achieved unlawfully cannot be recognized as lawful.

The Dayton Agreement signed in Paris on December 1995 has rewarded the aggression and the genocide by imposing an illegal and unjust division on the Republic of Bosnia and Herzegovina into two "entities": "Federation of Bosnia and Herzegovina" and "Republika Srpska", and by constructing unjust and self-paralyzing constitutional system that resulted in ineffective government structures.

The aggression and genocide were the foundation on which the Dayton Agreement and Dayton Constitution was forced on the victim nation, Republic of Bosnia and Herzegovina. According to the Convention on the Prevention and Punishment for the Crime of Genocide, nothing can justify the subjugation of the people of Bosnia and Herzegovina under the jurisdiction of the constitutional, legal, and political arrangement of the Dayton Bosnia and Herzegovina.

By the UN Charter, the United Nations were obligated to protect its member state, the Republic of Bosnia and Herzegovina, from aggression and genocide, and not to reward the perpetrators of aggression and genocide with the territory of the victim state.

The Dayton Constitution of Bosnia and Herzegovina (Annex IV of the General Framework of the Dayton Agreement) was imposed by aggression and genocide, and it was never properly adapted in accordance with the procedures for the amendment of the Constitution of the Republic of Bosnia and Herzegovina. Therefore, we will never recognize the Dayton Constitution nor any constitution or constitutional changes that might be adapted by institutions of the Dayton Bosnia and Herzegovina.

If not nullified, the Dayton Constitution could become a LEGAL AND POLITICAL PRECEDENT that a constitution of a sovereign nation can be changed by foreign aggression and more so by aggression and genocide. The Dayton Constitution is a result of aggression and genocide and to build a future of Bosnia and Herzegovina on a base of the Dayton Constitution amounts to complicity in genocide. The Dayton constitution is the constitution of aggression and genocide against people of Republic of Bosnia and Herzegovina by other means.

Under the Dayton Agreement, the unlawful governing power over the victims of aggression and genocide in the state of Bosnia and Herzegovina was put into the hands of those who committed the genocide and those who were complicit in the genocide. The people of State of Bosnia and Herzegovina take the legitimate position that the current situation is unacceptable because it implies that the victims of aggression and genocide are themselves legalizing the aggression and genocide.

Any pressure or attempt to force the victims of aggression and genocide to get used to and accept the situation created by the genocide, is an act of genocide itself.

The present situation in the state of Bosnia and Herzegovina is nothing more than an illegal attempt that started with aggression in 1992 to legalize the aggression and genocide which now is confirmed by the Judgment of the International Court of Justice.

Therefore, this Declaration makes null and void the illegal Dayton constitution of Bosnia and Herzegovina, which if not nullified could become a LEGAL AND POLITICAL PRECEDENT that a constitution of a sovereign nation can be changed by foreign aggression and more so by aggression and genocide.

This Declaration declares that both "entities," "Federation of Bosnia and Herzegovina" and "Republika Srpska" are illegal and illegitimate, as they were the products of the aggression, genocide, and illegal and illegitimate Dayton "Constitution".

With this Declaration, the people of the state of Bosnia and Herzegovina are invited to fight by all legal means to restore the Republic of Bosnia and Herzegovina, flying the flag and using the symbols of the Republic of Bosnia and Herzegovina.

Any changes in the constitution can be enacted only according to the procedures defined by the Constitution of Republic of Bosnia and Herzegovina and the legal principle that supersede national laws, such as the Charter of the United Nations and corresponding Human Rights Conventions, but under no circumstances will they be based on the decisions of parallel, negotiated, war and other ad-hoc institutions and individuals with disputed legal authority.

In order to exercise its rights, based on the peremptory norms of International law (JUS COGENS), the people of the State of Bosnia and Herzegovina do not need an approval from the institutions that were condemned for the aggression and genocide nor from other institutions whose mandate originates from any agreement including the Dayton Agreement.

Below we set our signatures as a physical expression of our belief in the right of our people to determine our own future in a manner that respects the law and sovereignty of the individual citizen.

- Ibran Mustafić, President of the Executive Board of Association "Mothers of Srebrenica and Podrinje," Potocari – Srebrenica, Bosnia and Herzegovina
- Professor Francis A. Boyle, General Agent for the Republic of Bosnia and Herzegovina with Extraordinary and Plenipotentiary Powers before the International Court of Justice (1993-1994), Champaign, Illinois, USA
- Zineta Mujic, President of Association "Mothers of Srebrenica and Podrinje," Potocari – Srebrenica, Bosnia and Herzegovina

Literature

Alibabic, Munir. "Bosna u kandzama KOS-a" (Bosnia in the claws of the Serbian Intelligence Service), Behar, Sarajevo, 1996.

Boyle, Francis. "Dayton Agreement," *http://instituteforgenocide.org/?p=8926*.

Boyle, Francis. "The Bosnian People Charge Genocide: Proceedings at the International Court of Justice Concerning Bosnia V. Serbia on the Prevention and Punishment of the Crime of Genocide, Paperback – July, 1996.

Congress of the USA. *http://thomas.loc.gov/bss/d104query.html*

Djilas, Milovan and Gace, Nadezda. "Bosniak Adil Zulfikarpašić." Bosniaken Institut, Zurich, 1995.

Gutman, Roy. "Witness of Genocide", MacMillan Publishing Company (NY), September 20th, 1993.

Halilović, Sefer. "Lukava Strategija" (Devious Strategy), Marsal d.o.o. PJ "Matica Sandzaka", Sarajevo 1997.

Izetbegović, Alija. "Islamic Declaration", Srpska rec (Serbian Word), Belgrade 1973

Silber, Laura and Allan Little. "Yugoslavia: Death of a Nation." TV Books, Inc, Distributed by Penguin USA.

Snowe, Olympia. "Bosnia And Herzegovina Self-defense Act Of 1995," Senate Session, Jul19, 1995, U.S. Senator, [R] Maine, United States, *http://www.c-span.org/video/?66260-1/senate-session&start=12244*

The Henry Jackson Society, *http://henryjacksonsociety.org/2010/10/29/the-declaration-of-the-republic-of-bosnia-herzegovina/*.

Walker, Stephen & Harris, Marshall: Dayton Not a peace Plan: *www.barnsdle.demon.co.uk/bosnia/dayton.html*.

Index

A

Abdić, Fikret, xv, xxi, 21, 25
Agrokomerc Affair, xxi, 15, 17–18, 21–22
Ajanović, Irfan, 32
Akashi, Yasushi, xv, 62
Albanians, xxi, 6, 12–13, 19, 27
Alkalaj, Sven, 102
America. *See* USA
American Congress, 97–98, 100–101, 107
Americans, xvi, xxi, 37, 60, 75, 100–102, 107, 109, 135–38
Andrić, Ivo, xv, 6, 37, 83
anti-bureaucratic revolution, xvi, xix, 22
Arafat, Yasser, 62–63
Arkanovci, 45
Armenians, 5
Article III, 118, 120, 123–24, 128–30
Article IV, 123–24, 129
Austrians, 7
autonomous regions, 27, 30, 38
AVNOJ (Antifascist Council of the People's Liberation of Yugoslavia), xiii–xiv, 36–38, 157

B

Badinter, Robert, xvi
Bajramović, Sejdo, xvi
Bajrić, Meša, 44–45
Balkans, 11, 46, 100, 123
Balog, Stjepan, 84–85, 87–89, 94, 138, 144, 150, 153, 166
Banja Luka, xi, 5, 58, 61, 69, 74, 91, 110, 112

Basques, 68
Becković, Matija, 20
Belgrade, xxii, 5, 15, 21, 26, 37, 46–47, 77, 88, 91, 173
Bešlagić, Selim, 45–46, 48, 50, 57, 59
Bešo, Jasminko, 144, 150, 166
B&H (Bosrnia and Herzegovina), xiii, xv, xx, xxvii, 29, 31–33, 41, 46–47, 49, 54, 59, 61–71, 74–76, 78–82, 84, 90–91, 96, 103–4, 106–7, 152–57
  division of, 51–52, 63, 82, 91
  unified, 61, 75, 81, 152
B&H Army, 33, 41, 43–44, 54, 58, 66, 74–75, 92, 105
B&H Constitution, 29, 34, 63, 65, 69, 72
B&H Croats, xix, 49
B&H Muslims, 70, 152
Biden, Joseph "Joe," 70–71
Bihać, 5, 52, 69, 103–5, 108
Bijedić, Džemal, xvi
Bijeljina, xxi, 5, 41–44
  Bosniaks of, 43
Boban, Mate, xvi, xviii, 9, 49, 61, 67, 92
Bogdanović, Dimitrije, 20
Borogovac, Muhamed, xxvii, 4, 6, 8, 10, 12, 14, 16, 18, 20, 22, 24, 26, 94, 142, 144, 148–50, 152–53, 158, 165–66
Borogovac, Musadik, 135, 144, 150, 153, 166
Bosnia, xi, xv–xxi, xxiii–xxvii, 3–5, 7–9, 11–15, 17–26, 29, 33, 45–47, 51–54, 57–69, 71, 73–77, 79, 81–113, 115–43, 145–49, 157–65, 167–73

conquered, 11
  destruction of, 85, 93
  division of, xvii–xviii, 8, 13–14, 18,
    38, 52, 58, 62, 71, 81, 84, 111,
    115, 137
  liberation of, xix, 59
  occupied, xxi
  partition of, 71, 135, 138–39
  preservation of, 85, 88
  unified, xvii–xix, 14, 83, 87–88
  united, 86
  Western, 52, 110, 136
Bosnia and Herzegovina, xxvii, 8–13, 15–
    21, 23–24, 26–29, 44–45, 70, 77–79,
    90–94, 99, 101–2, 108–12, 115–22,
    124–32, 140–44, 151–52, 154, 156–
    58, 162–65, 167–72
  destruction of, 140, 151
  division of, xxi, xxvii, 8, 18, 38, 92,
    94, 109, 112
  partition of, 17, 24
  state of, 170–71
Bosnia-Herzegovina
  Catholics of, 151
  Communist Party of, 12
  enemies of, 112, 151
  government of, 70, 141
  territory of, 18, 93, 111
Bosnia-Herzegovina Constitution, 60, 70
Bosniak Assembly, xviii
Bosniak Institute, 10, 20
Bosniaks, xiii, xv–xviii, xx–xxi, 4–14,
    16–19, 21, 23–25, 34–35, 42–43,
    45, 47–50, 52, 54–56, 58, 60–63,
    67–68, 71–72, 79–82, 88–89, 94–95
Bosnian Army, xi, xviii, xxi, xxiv, 5, 35,
    44, 52, 58, 63, 67, 69, 91–92, 98, 101,
    103–5, 109–13, 133–34, 137, 151–52
Bosnian Army Bihac Corps, 136
Bosnian Army Honor Guard, 151
Bosnian Assembly, xx, 62, 74
Bosnian Church, 11–12
Bosnian Communist Party, 16
Bosnian Congress, 84, 89–90, 94, 96–97,
    101–2, 109, 140–41, 151, 153

Bosnian Constitution, xvii–xviii, xx–xxi,
    12, 17, 22, 57–58, 66, 70, 93, 137
Bosnian Croats, xviii, 9, 13, 47, 51, 63, 67,
    81, 83, 137, 155
Bosnian Declaration of Independence, 164
Bosnian Eastern Orthodox, 12
Bosnian enemies, 33, 152
Bosnian government, xix, xxii, 17, 22,
    26, 29, 51, 61, 63, 65, 68, 71, 82,
    90, 100–102, 109–10, 131–33, 139,
    148–49, 161–62
Bosnian independence, 17, 165
Bosnian Krajina, 110
Bosnian leaders, xxi, 21, 101
Bosnian leadership, 17, 19, 101
Bosnian Muslim Communists, 17
Bosnian Muslims, xv–xvi, xxii, 8, 10–12,
    17–18, 21–22, 25, 67, 95
Bosnian Parliament, xix, 116
Bosnian Posavina, 156
Bosnian Refugees, 110, 135, 140–41, 143–
    44, 147–49
Bosnian Serb Army, xx, 65
Bosnian Serbian Republic, 109
Bosnian Serbs, xx, 13, 67, 77, 82, 103, 110,
    133, 167
Bosnian territory, 91, 101, 108–9, 121
Bosnian War, xvii, xxv, 67, 71, 92, 102
Bosnia's independence, 24, 34, 44, 91
Bosnia's Socialist Party, xvii
Boston, xxvii, 22, 102, 140, 142, 144–46,
    148, 151
Boyle, Francis, 116–17, 156–58, 160, 172
Bratunac, 29, 50
Brčko, 45, 48, 50, 69, 80, 103, 109
Brkić, Miljenko, 9
Bush, George Washington, xviii, 39–40,
    65–66, 74–75, 78

C

Catholics, 11–12, 27, 40, 47
Čengić, Hasan, 17, 24–25
Central Bank, 126–27
Cerić, Mustafa, 81, 152
Cerska, 54
Chetniks, xi, xvii, 16, 18, 42–43, 50

Christopher, Warren, xvii, 70–71, 74, 101, 132, 138, 142
civil war, 67, 92
Clinton, William "Bill," 40, 70, 74–76, 99–101, 107, 121, 123, 137–38
Committee of Bosnian Refugees, 141–42, 144–47, 149, 158
communist rule, 12, 15, 17, 23
communists, xiv, 17, 23, 40, 45, 55, 69, 95
Confederation Agreement, 126
congress, 22, 25, 97–99, 172
Constitution of Yugoslavia, 22
Ćosić, Dobrica, 21
Cotti, Flavio, 141, 143–45, 149
creation, xviii, xxvi, 11, 23, 36, 38, 71, 82, 88, 91, 93, 107, 135, 138
Croat-Bosnian Federation, 137
Croat Federation, 91
Croatia, xvi, xix, xxi, xxv–xxvi, 5, 7–8, 26–28, 30–33, 36, 38, 42, 47, 49, 51–53, 83–85, 87–88, 91, 107–8, 136–38, 148
Croatia, Republic of, 118, 120, 122–23, 126–27, 131
Croatian Army, 52
Croatian Communists, xxi, 37
Croatian Democratic Union, xxii, 36
Croatians, 4, 8, 11, 22, 34, 36–37, 52, 58, 61, 83, 108, 139, 155–57
Croatian war, 29
Croats, xvii, xx, xxii, 4–13, 17–19, 23, 25, 27, 31, 34, 36, 38, 47, 51–52, 61, 63, 67–68, 82–83, 85–89, 139
Cvetković, 38
Cvetković/Maček, 8
Cyprus, 92, 118

D

Dayton, xiii, xviii, 111, 115, 118, 133, 135–36, 138–39, 173
Dayton Agreement, xxiii, xxv–xxvi, 117–19, 123, 131, 134–39, 141, 143–44, 147, 154, 158–59, 164–65, 168, 170–72
Dayton Constitution, 158–59, 164–65, 168–71

Dayton Plan, 137
Delić, 112
Delimustafić, Alija, xvii, 96, 112, 173
Dizdarević, Raif, xvii, 22
Djilas, Milovan, 31
Doboj, 52, 74, 109
Doko, Jerko, xvii
Dragon of Bosnia, 57
Dreković, Ramiz, 112
Drnovšek, Janez, xvii, 30
Dudaković, Atif, 105, 110
Duraković, Nijaz, xvii, 23, 37, 77, 96
Džemal Bijedić, 8, 12, 15–16

E

Eagleburger, Lawrence, xvii, 68
EC (European Community), xiii, 31, 34
Election Monitoring Group, 146–47
ethnic cleansing, xxvii, 66, 77, 81–82, 87–88, 140, 146–47, 149
ethnic groups, xvi–xvii, 4, 6, 8, 12, 17, 34, 37, 48, 155, 169
EU (European Union), xiii–xiv, xvi, xxvi, 162–63
Europe, 7, 34, 39, 87, 137, 162, 169

F

Fazlić, Ajsa, 41, 145, 150, 153, 158, 166
Fazlić, Muhamed, 41
Federal Executive Council, 16
Federal House, 30
Federation and Republika Srpska, 128–30
Federation of Bosnia and Herzegovina, 120–22, 126, 128, 130, 170–71
Festić, Ibrahim, xvii, xxi, 20
Filipović, Muhamed, xviii, xx, 32, 62–63, 102
Frowick, Robert, 140, 145–46, 148

G

Gace, Nada, 31
Gacko, 25
Gams, Andrija, 21
Ganić, Ejub, xviii, 24–25, 71, 83, 102
Geneva, xx–xxi, 18, 57, 61–63, 68, 70–71, 100–101, 106–7, 109, 142

genocide, xx, xxv–xxvii, 3, 5–6, 13, 19,
40, 66, 78, 82, 87–88, 98–99, 101,
105, 107–8, 135, 140–41, 146–47,
160–63, 167–72
committing, 7
Serbian, 13
victims of, xxvii, 45, 141, 149
Genocide Convention, 162–63
Georgia, xxvi
Germans, 6, 27, 61, 139
Germany, 13, 33, 79
Ghali, Boutros, xvi, 51, 131
Gligorov, Kiro, xviii, 28, 32, 37
God, 11, 48, 80, 134, 151
Goražde, xi, 69, 74–75, 92, 103, 109–10, 112
Gorski Vijenac (Njegos), 6
Granic, Mate, 131
Grbo, Ismet, 102
Greece, 34, 118
Gypsies, 5

H

Hadžihafizbegović, Emir, 57
Hajrulahović-Talijan, Mustafa, 111
Halil, 41
Halilovic, Sefer, 41, 96, 111–12
HDZ, xiii, xxii, 8, 11, 22, 36, 44, 49
Herzegovina, ix, xiii–xiv, xvi, xxiii–xxv, 9,
29, 33, 49, 57–58, 65, 90–91, 97–99,
101–2, 118–22, 124–28, 130–34,
140–43, 146–49, 157–64, 167–72
Hill, Mojmilo, 111
Hodžić, Mehdin, 42–43
Holbrooke, Richard, xviii, 119, 124, 135,
138
House of Republics, 30
Hungarians, 6–7, 11, 27
HVO, xi, xiii, 49, 51–53, 61, 63, 83, 126, 151

I

IFOR, 120–21, 130
Imamović, Jasmin, 57
Indians, 88
Islam, 9, 11–12, 67, 95
Islamic Declaration, 18, 24, 77–78, 173
Israel, 39

Ištuk, Hrvoje, 9
Izetbegović, Alija, xiv, xvii, 10, 12, 17–18,
22–23, 28–29, 35, 62–63, 65–67,
69–70, 78–79, 81–82, 87, 89–93,
95–96, 100, 104–5, 151–52, 155–56

J

Janja, 5
Janković, Ivan, 21
Jelena, Queen of Croatia, 107–8
Jergović, Miljenko, 9
Jews, 5, 78
JNA (Yugoslav People's Army), xiii, xix–
xxi, 16, 28–29, 35, 41, 43–48, 50, 58,
64–65, 111, 169
Jovanov, Neca, 21

K

Kadić, Nihada, 145, 150, 166
Kamenica, 54
Karabegović, Armin, 145, 150
Karadžić, Radovan, xviii, xx, 23, 32, 38,
48, 58, 61, 66–69, 77–78, 81, 92,
104, 111, 126, 136, 162
Kecmanović, Nenad, 19
Kemo, 41
Kerić, Osman, 145, 150, 158, 166
Kljuić, Stjepan, xviii–xix
Koljević, Nikola, xix, 109, 112
Komšić, Ivo, xix, 9, 83
Konjevića, 54
KOS, xiii, 16, 37, 96
Kosovo, xvi, xxi, xxvi, 27, 30
Kravić, Edib, 57
Krunić, Boško, xix, 30
Kučan, Milan, xix, 37
Kukanjac, Milutin, xix
Kulenović, Salih, 24, 45–46
Kunz, Raymund, 145

L

Lagumdžija, Zlatko, xix
Lazar of Serbia, 4
leaders, xviii, xx–xxi, xxvi, 9, 14, 18–20,
23–25, 48–49, 57, 59–60, 63, 67–68,
70–71, 80, 89, 139–40, 152

Ljiljan, 96
Lord Owen. *See* Owen, David
Lučarević, Kerim, 111

M

Macedonia, xvi, 20, 27–28, 31–32, 34, 65
Maček, 38
Mahmutčehajić, Rusmir, xix, 102
Manolić, Josip, xix, 83
Marković, Mihajlo, 21
massacres, 20, 42, 75, 106, 108
McKenzie, Lewis, xix
Mesić, Stipe, xix, 83
Mihajlović, Dragoslav, 21
Mihajlović-Mihiz, Borislav, 21
Mikulić, Branko, xx, 9, 15
Milošević, Nikola, 21
Milošević, Slobodan, xvi, xviii, xx, xxii, 3, 7, 19, 30–31, 36, 38, 42, 52, 68, 106, 119, 132–33, 135–36, 142, 162
Mirza, 48
Mišić, Ivica, 63, 102
Mladenović, Tanasije, 21
Mladić, Ratko, xx, 126
Momčilo, Krajišnik, xix
Montenegro, xvi, 6, 27, 31, 64–67
Most, 160
Mostar, 52, 58, 112, 140–41
Mothers of Srebrenica and Podrinje, 172
Muhić, Fuad, xx, 12, 15, 17, 22, 55
Muratagić, Almin, 145
Muslims, xxii, 6, 8, 10–13, 17–18, 23–24, 29, 31, 40, 43, 50, 55, 58, 61, 67, 72, 77–78, 89, 91, 95
Mustafić, Ibran, 172
mythology, Serbian, 6, 36

N

nationalism, Serbian, xxvii, 4–6
NATO (North Atlantic Treaty Organization), 39, 75, 117–19, 121–22, 130, 136
Neimarlija, Hilmo, 102
Neretva River, 52
New York Times, The, 84, 110, 139
Nikoliš, Gojko, 21

NWO (New World Order), 34, 39–40, 66

O

Omersoftić, Amila, 24–25
Orić, Naser, xx, 105, 112
OSCE (Organization for Security and Cooperation in Europe), 140–42, 144, 148–49
Ottoman Empire, 4–5, 7, 9, 11
Ottomans, 5, 11
Owen, David, xx, 49, 61–63, 69, 71, 74, 79, 94, 124

P

Palavestra, Predrag, 21
Paraga, Dobroslav, xx, 37
Paris, 115, 154, 158, 170
Parliament, 27, 30, 44, 117, 119, 121, 127–28, 130, 155–58
Pašalić, Arif, 111
Pašalić, Ivić, 49
Patriotic League in Tuzla, 41
Perinović, Davorin, 9
PL (Patriotic League), xiii, 41–45, 55, 111
Plavšić, Biljana, xxi, 148
pope, 151–52
Popović, Misa, 21
Posavina, 38, 51–53, 109
Pozderac, Hakija, 21–22
Pozderac, Hamdija, xxi, 12, 15–18, 21–22, 96
Prijedor, 5, 69, 80, 109
Provisional Election Commission, 123, 142, 145, 147

R

Račan, Ivica, xxi, 37
Ravno, 78
Ražnjatović, xxi
R B&H (Republic of Bosnia and Herzegovina), xiii, xx, xxvii, 28–29, 31, 33–35, 37–38, 40, 42, 46–47, 59, 62, 65, 67–68, 154–57
Republika Srpska, xiii, xviii, xx, 18, 68, 109–10, 112, 118, 120–30, 149, 163, 167–68, 170–71

RS (Serbian Republic), xiii
RSK (Republika Srpska Krajina), 103
Rugova, Ibrahim, xxi, 20
Russia, 40, 66, 107
Russians, 40, 66, 74, 88, 110
Rustempašić, Sven, 94

S

Šaćirbey, Muhamed, xxi, 18, 94
Šaćirbey, Nadžib, 95–96
Šaćirbey, Nedžib, 94, 102, 110
Šaćirbey, Omar, 110
Sadić, Hazim, 111
Samarđic, Radovan, 21
SANU (Sciences and Arts), 20, 38
Sapunxhiju, Rizza, xxi
Sarajevo, xix, 5, 16–17, 28, 33, 35, 41,
    54–56, 69, 72, 74–75, 87, 96, 103,
    105–6, 109–12, 148–49, 151, 154,
    172–73
SDA, xiv, xviii, 22–26, 29, 35, 44–46, 49–
    50, 55, 57, 59, 78, 81
SDS (Serbian Democratic Party), 22, 42,
    44, 77–78
Security Council Resolution, 132–33
Selimoski, Jakub, 151
Selimović, Mehmed "Mesha," xxii, 10
Senad, 42
Sendijarević, Vahid, 115, 144, 147, 149, 153,
    158, 165
Serbia, xi, xviii, xx, xxii, 3–6, 9, 19, 26–27,
    31–34, 37, 40, 42, 46, 51, 54, 64–66,
    108–9, 139, 161–63, 167–70
Serbia, Republic of, 104, 126
Serbian, xv–xxii, xxv–xxvii, 3–13, 15–20,
    22–23, 25, 31–32, 34–38, 41–55,
    57–58, 65–69, 71–72, 74–75, 77–83,
    85–90, 98, 100–101, 103–5, 107–12,
    136–39
Serbian Army, xxi, 104
Serbian Orthodox Church, 3, 42
Šešelj, Vojislav, xxii, 16–18
Šiber, Stjepan, 63, 111
Sijerćić, Zlatko, 144, 150, 165
Silajdžić, xxii, 102, 115
SKJ, xiv, xxi

Slovenia, xvi–xvii, xix, xxi, 26–28, 30–33,
    35, 37, 101
Social-Democratic Party of Bosnia-
    Herzegovina, 23
Socialist Federal Republic of Yugoslavia,
    30
Socialistic Federate Republic Yugoslavia,
    36
Solina, 41, 50
Soviet Union, 39, 93
Srbinović, Mladen, 21
Srebrenica, xv, xx, 5, 47, 52, 54, 69, 72,
    74, 92, 98–99, 101, 104–8, 112, 115,
    136–37, 163, 168, 172
Srejović, Dragoslav, 21
Srpska, xx, 122–24, 126, 128
Stonltenberg, Thorvald, xxii
Switzerland, xxii, 142, 144–45

T

Tadić, Ljubomir, 21
Tanković, Šemso, 49, 102
Tito, Josip Broz, xvii, xxii, 28, 37
TO (Territorial Defence Force), xiv, 35, 46,
    48, 51, 90, 117, 146
Tuđman, Franjo, xiii, xviii–xix, xxi–xxii,
    8–9, 11, 20, 36–38, 51–52, 63, 83,
    106–8, 117, 142
Turks, xv, xxi, 6–7, 11, 13, 51
Tuzla, 5, 24, 29, 32–33, 35, 41–55, 57–59,
    62, 72, 74, 105–6, 109, 111, 115
    government of, 44
Tuzla City, 45, 57
Tuzla City Council, 45, 48, 57
Tuzla Corpus, 41, 52–53
Tuzla region, 41, 44, 51, 54

U

UDBA, xiv, 95–96
Ukraine, xxvi
UN (United Nations), xiv–xvi, xxvii, 31,
    34, 39–40, 63–64, 66–68, 70, 74–
    75, 81, 90–91, 94, 100, 102, 104,
    106–8, 110, 138, 144, 162–63
UN Charter, xvi, 30, 67, 119, 121, 138, 163,
    170

United Nations Security Council, 99, 169
University of Tuzla, 32, 44, 49
UNPROFOR (United Nations Protection Force), xiv–xv, 99, 119
USA (United States of America), xvi, xxvi, 39–40, 49, 66, 70, 75, 84–85, 90, 94, 97–101, 115–16, 125, 135–36, 138, 140, 142, 144–46, 162, 172–73
US Administration, 136–37
US Congress, 81, 99–101, 107
Ustaše, xxii, 7, 13

V

Vance, Cyrus, xxii, 62
Vance-Owen Plan, 49, 61, 63, 69, 74, 79
van Thijn, Ed, 145–47
Velić, Besim, 94
Višegrad, 48
Visoko, 44
Vojvodina, xix, 5–6, 27, 30, 37
Vran Mountain, 47

W

war criminals, xviii–xx, xxvii, 57, 68, 136
Warsaw Pact, 39
Washington agreement, 83
World Court, 123, 134, 160–63
World War I, 27
World War II, xiv, xxii, xxvii, 7–8, 27, 77, 93, 95–96, 169

Y

Yugoslav, xiv, xvii–xviii, 4, 9–10, 12, 31–32, 34, 37, 95
Yugoslav Army, 29, 35, 37, 64, 78, 95–96
Yugoslav Constitution, xvi, xxii, 15, 19–20, 30, 37
Yugoslav Federation, xiii–xiv
Yugoslavia, xiii, xvi–xvii, xx, xxii, 3, 6, 8, 12, 15–16, 19–22, 25, 27–28, 30–33, 36–37, 50, 66–67, 95, 101, 118, 132–33
Yugoslav People's Army, xxii, 16, 25, 28, 169
Yugoslav Presidency, xvi–xvii, xix, xxi, 30
Yugoslav republics, xxii, 3, 31, 33, 37
Yugoslav states, 19, 31, 33, 36–38

Z

Zagreb, 49, 51, 74, 81, 151
Zagreb Mosque, 81
Zajednicar, 138
ZAVNOBIH, xiv
Zenica, 5, 24, 52, 54, 105, 109
Žepa, 54, 69, 72, 92, 104, 106, 108
Živinice, 43
Zubak, Krešimir, 102, 156
Zulfikarpašić, Adil, 22, 31, 173
Zvornik, 5, 43, 50–51, 69, 72–73, 80, 95, 111

Printed in the United States
By Bookmasters